YOUR HERITAGE
OF WORDS WILL

- Add thousands of exciting, interesting and powerful words to your vocabulary

- Tell you how many words you now have in your vocabulary and show you how to add many, many more

- Tell you the fascinating and colorful stories behind hundreds of everyday expressions

- Show you how to make the correct and important distinctions between *imply* and *infer, bimonthly* and *semimonthly, uninterested* and *disinterested* and other often misused words

- Introduce you to the fascinating story of how our American language has grown by adding words from all the world's languages

- Delight you with a variety of quick quizzes to sharpen your wits

- Reveal important words and phrases from the worlds of Business, Music and the Fine Arts, Literature, and World Affairs

- Guide you to newly developed techniques for increasing your vocabulary quickly and interestingly at home, in the office—or in the classroom

YOUR HERITAGE OF WORDS

HOW TO INCREASE YOUR VOCABULARY INSTANTLY

William Morris

A DELL BOOK

Published by
Dell Publishing Co., Inc.
750 Third Avenue
New York, New York 10017
Dell (R) TM 681510, Dell Publishing Co., Inc.
Printed in the United States of America
First printing—October 1970

Acknowledgments

To acknowledge my indebtedness to all the people who, directly or indirectly, have influenced my own education in the world of words would require a volume the size of the one you now hold. The most immediate sources of inspiration, of course, are my many fellow workers on *The American Heritage Dictionary of the English Language*. James Parton, formerly president of Heritage, was the person who initiated the project and chose me as its editor in chief. In the early days when many key decisions were made, Joseph Thorndike, editorial vice president of Heritage and one of the most brilliant editors I have ever been privileged to work with, made many acutely perceptive and unfailingly helpful suggestions. Of my scores of editorial associates, many should be named but space permits only the acknowledgment of vital aid and counsel from Norman Hoss, managing editor of the project, Bruce Bohle, usage editor, and Irwin Glusker, art director.

Of my current associates at Dell Publishing Company, two have made signal contributions to this volume, Walter B. J. Mitchell, Jr., who fostered the book from idea to completion, and Nancy E. Gross, whose many constructive editorial suggestions have been most gratefully received and acted upon.

For the original inspiration of materials from the jargons of the stage and soda fountain that figure in the next-to-last chapter, I suppose credit is due to my one-time University Players associates, Henry Fonda, Joshua Logan, Margaret Sullavan and Jimmy Stewart, as well as my nameless fellow slaves at various Liggett's soda counters.

And always, of course, to Mary Morris, collaborator on all my books and newspaper columns and a most valued contributor—though without by-line recognition—to both this volume and to *The American Heritage Dictionary of the English Language*.

YOUR HERITAGE OF WORDS

Contents

1. The Wonderful World
of Words

Greetings! Welcome to the wonderful world of words. As many of you already know, this is an ever-changing, ever-fascinating world. Every day new words are invented and old ones pass out of use. In a single day the word *sputnik* was on the lips of virtually every living human. In a matter of a few days, the expression *lunar module* was known throughout the world and —for the first time in history—spoken in outer space. Other words, having had their day, fade away. Who today cares much or knows much about *boondoggle* or *globalony*—headline words only a few decades ago.

Most of the elements of our language, though, change very little with the passing of the years. Although we have many words that Shakespeare never heard of, most of the ones he used are still active and valuable to us today. What is important for all of us is to learn as many words as we can in order to develop rich, flexible vocabularies and—equally important—learn how to use them effectively. That is what this book is all about.

We shall be investigating the riches of the language we call English—incalculably the richest language mankind has ever known, because it has borrowed words from every other language spoken on the face of the earth.

Mostly we shall be directing our attention to what H. L. Mencken called The American Language, the English spoken not only in North America but increasingly throughout the world as our financial and diplomatic interests have spread to all foreign nations except, at this writing, mainland China. With astonishing swiftness, in the two decades following World War II, American English became the international language of the business community, the lingua franca of virtually all the world's peoples.

And now let's pause for a moment to take a look at that

expression *lingua franca*. It is a term we have borrowed without change from Italian and its literal meaning is "Frankish tongue." How did it come to mean "international language," for that is the sense in which we have just used it? Simply because the first lingua franca was a mixture of French, Spanish, Greek, Turkish and Arabic used by traders in the countries of the Eastern Mediterranean. And here we have a good example of the freedom with which English borrows from the other world languages, often extending the meaning of the original phrase, as has happened here.

But how did English begin? What were its earliest origins? As far as the language spoken in Great Britain at the dawn of the Christian era is concerned, it began with the simple spoken dialects of the natives, the Angles, Jutes and Saxons, and was strongly influenced over the ensuing centuries by the speech of various Viking marauders. Many of the simplest words may be traced to the Vikings, nouns such as *bull, birth, freckle, seat, leg* and *gate*. From them too came adjectives like *ugly, ill* and *rotten* and verbs of action such as *crawl, nag, gasp, scream, call* and *take*.

When William the Conqueror invaded England at the time of the Norman Conquest (1066), the language became incomparably richer. The Normans brought with them many thousands of words from French and from Latin. When, in 1204, the French recaptured the Duchy of Normandy, the invaders began to regard England as their permanent home and grafted on to the native tongue many expressions from Norman French that had their ultimate origin in Latin. From this period of the evolution of English we trace the entrance into English of many words of relative elegance—at least by comparison with the rude simplicity of Anglo-Saxon. Words such as *discipline, sacrifice, traitor, nativity, prayer, parliament, penalty* and *chancellor* added a new ornateness to the native tongue. Even though their path into English was through the Norman French, many of them still clearly show their Latin origin—*discipline* from the Latin "disciplina," knowledge or instruction, which in turn came from "discipulus," disciple or pupil.

The new elegance contributed by the Normans even extended to cookery. Where the earliest inhabitants had been content with simple fare cooked—at its most elaborate—over the yule log, the invaders brought with them a foretaste of the *haute cuisine* of today's Parisian chef in new words such as *pastry*, *feast, roast, receipt* and *recipe*. The two last words, incidentally, are—etymologically at least—identical, since they both derive from the Latin "recipere," meaning to take or receive. Thus a cook's favorite *recipe* or *receipt* is usually something "received" or handed down from some great cook of the past.

The next three or four centuries saw the greatest period in all the annals of English writing. Seizing upon the new richness of the tongue—further enlivened by borrowings from the Dutch, Italian, and Spanish, and from the classic writings of Virgil, Homer and the other ancients—Shakespeare, Marlowe, Jonson, Milton, Spenser, Dryden and many more gave beauty, grace, style and form to their literary creations, enhancing the common tongue in the process. To a very limited degree, their work had been anticipated by Chaucer, who himself had borrowed themes and stories from Boccaccio and other continental masters. But the age of greatest creativity and intellectual ferment undoubtedly began with the reign of Elizabeth and the writings of that incomparable group of towering giants headed by the master dramatists Shakespeare, Marlowe and Jonson.

Then and later, there were centuries of rivalry between the British, the Dutch and, to lesser degrees, the French and the Spanish in the development of international trade and, eventually, in colonizing far-flung parts of the globe. One consequence of this interchange—our sociologists today call it the "cross-fertilization of cultures"—was that English was greatly enriched by borrowings from the languages of the countries with which England traded. From India came words such as *thug, madras, coolie, bungalow* and *dungaree*. The Dutch contributed *schooner, scour, scum* and *freight*. Thanks to the famous assault on England in 1588, the Spanish word *armada* came quickly into the language, and later words such as *potato, tobacco* and *hurricane* were borrowed from the same source. Even France, which had already contributed so greatly through the infusion of Norman French, contributed such words as *bombast, duel, volunteer* and *bizarre* during this era of international mercantile competition.

The next and perhaps the greatest source of new words was, of course, America. Beginning with the earliest days of colonization by English-speaking settlers in the Bay Colony, there was a considerable amount of what today's engineers call "feedback" to the mother country. As Henry L. Mencken rightly noted in his *The American Language,* the first colonists were forced to invent a lot of new words to describe things—costumes, birds, animals and a new variety of their fellow man —that they had never seen before. Some of the results were ludicrous. The *Indian* is, of course, not an *Indian* at all—if the word is interpreted in its truest sense—but a native of India. And the *turkey* that we make such a ceremony of roasting each Thanksgiving in memory of our early American forebears was not at all like the turkey hen or turkey cock of the mother country. That was actually the guinea fowl—much more like a pheasant than the bird the early colonists called *turkey*. Incidentally, the reason the English used *turkey* as a nickname for the guinea hen is that they thought the species had originated in Turkey. Actually it originated in Africa—in Guinea, to be precise—but it reached first Portugal and then England by way of Turkey.

Trade with the Indians led to the translation into English of a very considerable number of native expressions. Names for animals never seen in England included *moose, skunk, raccoon* and *possum*. Unfamiliar vegetables, trees and nuts contributed words like *squash, persimmon, hickory* and *pecan*. It is a borrowing process that, of course, continues even today as we make renewed efforts to work with our Indian fellow citizens. Down through the centuries we have borrowed expressions such as *pipe of peace, bury the hatchet, medicine man,* and words like *toboggan, powwow, succotash* and *moccasin*.

The early colonization of Delaware by Swedes seems to have had relatively little influence on the language of the colonies, but the Dutch, because of their long dominance of one of the two major seaports of the Northeast, contributed many words to American English and thus, eventually, to English English. To them we owe *boss, coleslaw, spook, dope, snoop* and *Santa Claus*. To the Dutch, also, we owe the generic label by which Americans have become known throughout the world—*Yankee*. This was originally a blend of two Dutch words *Jan,* John, and *kees,* cheese. It was a label originally applied, not too flatteringly, to Dutch inhabitants of New Amsterdam (now, of course, New York). In time it came to be used for all New York Staters and New Englanders and in recent times, thanks largely to the discourteous "Yankee, Go Home" slogan, it has been applied to all American nationals.

Although Spain had occupied a number of islands in the West Indies during this colonial period, relations between Spain and

England were, to put it mildly, standoffish, so there was very little linguistic borrowing from the Spanish into American English at this time. However, in later generations the American cowboy borrowed a considerable number of expressions from his Mexican-Spanish counterpart, the *vacquero*. To this source we trace such colorful terms as *desperado, lasso, stampede, hoosegow, barbecue* and, of course, *rodeo*.

With the coming of the American Revolution and its successful conversion of thirteen somewhat competitive colonies into one United States, the new citizens had to decide what language they would make the official tongue of the new nation. In the halls of Congress very serious discussions were held on whether the English language should be abandoned and Hebrew substituted. This, of course, is what actually happened in recent times in Israel where Hebrew—for nearly a millennium a written but not a spoken language—was revived. But there was every logic in support of this effort by the Israelis, while there was none at all behind the proposal that Hebrew become the new language of America, so the idea quickly died. Then another enterprising congressman,—inspired like his predecessor chiefly by an understandable hatred of England, the newly vanquished foe—proposed that the new nation adopt Greek as its official language. This suggestion was similarly speedily sunk by the comment that "it would be more convenient for us to keep the language as it is—and make the English speak Greek."

This resoundingly chauvinistic statement carried the day, and English, at least the characteristically American brand of English, remained our official method of communication. Indeed, as late as 1854, an American Secretary of State, William L. Marcy, found it desirable to remind all diplomatic officers reporting to him to use "only the American language."

Much has been written about the similarities and differences between the American brand of English and English English. Indeed, Henry L. Mencken produced perhaps the most readable linguistic work—and a feat of towering scholarship it is—in his three-volume *The American Language* (A. A. Knopf, N.Y.). And George Bernard Shaw once described England and America as two countries "divided by a single language."

But the influence of the American occupation of Britain in World War II during the long "cold war" period before the Normandy invasion and the very extensive "cross-fertilization" on every level of intellectual, social and business interchange in the years since has effected, at the very least, a mutual understanding of each other's national idiom. If the English seem to be borrowing rather more Americanisms than we do Briticisms, the reason may very simply be that there are more than 200 million of us and less than a third as many of them. Furthermore, what with satellite television and all the other recent advances in communications, not even England can now be, in Donne's phrase "an island, entire of itself."

So the heritage of our American language, whether borrowed directly or through our English cousins, is now entering or has indeed already entered upon a new phase—one in which this wonderfully rich and versatile tool is put to the service of all the world's peoples.

2. Names Make Words

One fascinating aspect of the heritage of our language is the number of men and women who have contributed their names to the language—in the form of words that, as dictionary editors would put it, started out as proper names and, through popular use, became generic terms or common nouns.

Almost anyone over forty will recall the Morris chair, first of the adjustable, reclining-back lounge chairs. It was rather crude by comparison with the elegant overstuffed versions we see today, but in the early years of this century it served admirably to cushion the cares of many a weary man, including William Morris, English poet, social reformer and designer, who invented it and after whom it was named.

Not all proper names become generic or fall into the public domain, of course. Every girl and woman is familiar with *nylon* as the common name of the material used in her stockings or pantyhose. But how many realize that it was once a registered trademark of the Dupont Company, the original creator of the fabric? This is a rather special case, since the Dupont people, with their first completely man-made fabric to merchandise, deliberately made no attempt to protect the word by taking legal action to enforce the trademark. Today the trademark owners of such designations as Dacron, Dynel, Coke (for Coca-Cola) and Kodak are extremely vigilant in prosecuting anyone who fails to spell the name of their product with a capital initial letter or otherwise acts to detract from the value of their registered trade names.

A few years ago, when motion pictures were going through one of their periodic revolutions, many companies began to experiment with various forms of wide-screen projection. Noting that the developers of the early "3-D" (three-dimensional) movies had failed to trademark the name, the devisers of the new techniques were careful to protect such names as Cinerama and Cinemascope. On one occasion your author had an informative, if brief, conversation with the late Mike Todd, whose

7

film *Around the World in Eighty Days* was not only a land-mark of cinema history, but a fine example of the possibilities of the then new Todd-A-O projection method. "I'm planning a newspaper column on the new wide-screen processes, Mr. Todd," said I, "and I plan to lead off with a discussion of the merits of Todd-A-O. Is there anything you would like to say on the matter?" After a grunt and an exhalation of a cloud of cigar smoke, Mike pointed the foot-long Havana straight at my face—just inches away from my nose—and said: "Just be sure you cap 'Todd', cap the 'A', and cap the 'O'. I don't want Todd-A-O to become no blank-blank generic term!" Which proved that Mike, besides being a master showman, had learned well the lessons of trademark law and the dollar-and-cents value of a trademark.

However, most of the names that have come into our language did so many years before such concepts as trademark and copyright existed. When Doctor Guillotin invented the contraption that insured his lasting fame, the thought of apply-ing for a trademark never entered his mind. Similarly, when Rezin Bowie (not his brother Jim) invented the Bowie knife, such niceties as trademark protection were entirely unknown on the American frontier. But now let's look at a few dozen of the names that have become part of the linguistic heritage of all English-speaking peoples—the men and women, both real and fictional, and the places that have found their ways into our dictionaries.

Appropriately enough, we'll begin with the first man, Adam, who has made his way into the popular tongue through at least two phrases.

Adam's ale. This, of course, is simply plain water. It takes its name from the assumption that, in the unspoiled paradise that was Eden before the Fall, there would have been no beverage other than water.

Adam, the Old. As founder of the race, Adam also symbolized original sin and the unregenerate side of human nature. As the Bay Psalm Book put it: "In Adam's fall, we sinneth all." So a person with a "touch of the Old Adam" was likely to be a bit of a hellion.

ampere. Andre Marie Ampere was a noted French physicist and mathematician of the late eighteenth and early nineteenth century. His experiments in electricity resulted in the adoption of *ampere* as the name for the basic unit of electric current.

benedict. The original sense of *benedict,* strangely enough, was a perennial bachelor, a celibate in the tradition of St. Benedict who founded the Benedictine order of monks. But, Shakespeare created a character named Benedick who, though trying to preserve his bachelorhood, found himself entrapped into matrimony. So, thanks to Shakespeare, the meaning changed and today a *benedict* is a married man, especially one recently wed.

blarney. As every Irishman knows, this takes its name from the Blarney Stone located at Blarney Castle a few miles north of Cork. It's a bit hard to reach and the usual maneuver involves hanging by your heels in order to kiss the stone. Anyone brave enough to do this is believed to be henceforth endowed with great gifts of persuasion, eloquence and charm —in short, with the gift of blarney.

bloomers. In a time when pant suits are commonplace on women of nearly every age, it's a bit hard to believe that, only a century or so ago, one woman, Amelia Bloomer, created a major sensation by proposing a costume for the "emancipated" woman that consisted of loose-fitting trousers gathered at the ankle, complete with a knee-length outer tunic. The fashion never actually caught on very widely, but the name *bloomers* was used for decades afterwards to describe the billowing pants, gathered by elastic at the knees, that generations of schoolgirls wore with middy blouses while exercising.

bohemian. In an age when hippies, yippies and other radical splinter groups take center stage as exemplars of youthful radicalism and unrest, one seldom hears the word *bohemian* in comments on them and their conduct. Yet, not so long ago, this was a common label for raffish nonconformists and their behavior. It comes, of course, from the place name Bohemia, which was once part of Austria and was for centuries thought to be the home of wandering gypsies who roamed through Western Europe. And gypsies, then as now, had a reputation for nonconformist behavior.

bowdlerize. The Rev. Thomas Bowdler (pronounced in England with the first syllable rhyming with *how,* but in America with the first syllable rhyming with *beau*) was a man who knew very well what other men and women should be allowed to read—and Gibbons' *Decline and Fall of the Roman Empire* and the works of William Shakespeare did not measure up to his ideas of propriety. So he undertook to prepare expurgated editions of these works, deleting all references to "limbs" and the like, which he deemed improper. In 1818 he issued *The Family Shakespeare*—such a drastic expurgation that his name has gone down in history, in the form of the word *bowdlerize,* to designate excessively prudish censorship of literary works.

bowie knife. Several generations of American youth have been reared in the belief that the second bravest hero of the Battle of the Alamo was Jim Bowie, the bravest being, of course, Davy Crockett. Equally firm is the belief that Jim Bowie invented the *bowie knife,* the foot-long, single-edged hunting knife that was one of the most useful items in a frontiersman's equipment. But alas, this is untrue. Though Col. Jim Bowie's fame doubtless had a lot to do with the knife's popularity, the evidence seems clear that it was actually invented by his brother, the little-known Rezin Bowie.

boycott. As we indicated earlier, there actually was a Captain Boycott, Charles Cunningham Boycott, to give him his full name. A retired British army officer, he had a post in County Mayo, Ireland, as land agent for an absentee owner. In 1880 he insisted upon payment of every penny of rent to which his employer was entitled despite the fact that many of the tenant farmers were desperately poor and the crops far below their normal yield. His tactics so infuriated the farmers of Mayo that they mounted all sorts of reprisals against him, including complete ostracism and efforts to cut off his supply of food. Thus was born the word *boycott,* meaning to protest by refusing to use or purchase goods or services.

bunk. The relatively small and thinly populated county of Buncombe in northwestern North Carolina is responsible for the very useful word *bunk,* meaning anything—especially talk —that is of small value. In 1820 a congressman from this county made a speech that, even by congressional standards, was notable for its windy, meaningless pomposity. But Felix Walker, for that was the legislator's name, had about him a refreshing candor rare among politicians. Noting the nodding heads of some of his fellows and the departure from the

chamber of many others, he interrupted his oratory to remark: "You're not hurting my feelings, gentlemen. I am not
speaking for your ears—I'm only talking for Buncombe."
The phrase struck his colleagues' fancy and for years there-
after any particularly windy and fatuous oration was called
talking for Buncombe. Gradually the expression became
talking buncombe, then *talking bunkum* and finally simply
bunk.

cabal. A *cabal* is a conspiracy of political figures, usually highly
placed and often plotting to control a government either
openly or by clandestine operations. The most famous cabal
in history was one credited with strongly influencing the
conduct of political affairs during the reign of Charles II
of England. His cabinet consisted of Clifford, Arlington,
Buckingham, Ashley and Lauderdale, the initial letters of
whose names spell *cabal*. The story is fairly widespread that
this was the origin of the word—that *cabal* was one of our
very first acronyms (words made up of the initial letters of
other words forming a phrase). Unfortunately, however, there
is evidence that the word existed in English at least fifty
years earlier. Indeed, it can be traced via French and Latin
to the Hebrew "qabbalah," the doctrines received by Moses
and handed down by word of mouth by the elders of the
Jewish faith. Because they were privy to special knowledge,
some people during the Middle Ages thought these men pos-
sessed special occult power—and thus *cabal* came to have
overtones of secret plotting.

Caesarian section (or **operation**). This method of surgical in-
cision to deliver babies gets its name from the legend that
Julius Caesar was delivered in such a fashion. There is an
interesting parallel between Caesar's name and the Latin
word for cut, "caesus" (past participle of "caedere," if there
are any Latin students among you). There is even a theory
that that's how he got his name—from the Latin phrase "a
caeso matris utere," from the incised womb of his mother.

cardigan. The perennially popular sweater that buttons down
the front takes its name from James Thomas Brudenell, the
Seventh Earl of Cardigan. It's perhaps just as well that he is
remembered chiefly for creating this design—or at least having had it named after him—because his military career was
something less than spectacularly successful. In fact it was
Cardigan who led the famous Charge of the Light Brigade

at Balaclava in the Crimean War—a gallant but militarily foolish undertaking.

champagne. This ever popular sparkling white wine gets its name from the former province of northeastern France where it was first made and where the highest quality champagnes are still bottled. Because of failure to police the use of the name, however, it has now become a generic term and is widely used as a description for similar "bubblies" produced far from the shores of France.

chauvinism. This label for intense and often narrow-minded patriotism comes from the name of Nicolas Chauvin, a soldier in Napoleon's army. Though wounded in battle, he was so inspired by his peerless leader that, even with Napoleon in exile, he never ceased to extoll his achievements. Since most of his fellow Frenchmen thought themselves well rid of the Little Corporal, Chauvin found himself the target of considerable mockery. Nonetheless his name lives on as the symbol of blind, unreasoning patriotism.

chesterfield. The fourth Earl of Chesterfield is famous for having written a volume entitled *Letters to his Son,* in which he set forth cynical but sound rules for getting along in the world. This is the Chesterfield, presumably, after whom the brand of cigarettes is named. However, one of his successors, a nineteenth century Earl of Chesterfield, managed the remarkable feat of having two items named after him. The first was the elegant man's velvet-collared, fly-front topcoat which first appeared about 1889. Then, about 1900, the classic overstuffed sofa named chesterfield appeared on the scene.

cicerone. *Cicerone* (pronounced sis–er–OH–nee) is simply a highfalutin name for a sight-seeing guide. The chief characteristic of such guides is their ability to talk on and on endlessly. Hence the term, from the name of Rome's greatest —and longest-winded—orator, Marcus Tullius Cicero.

coach. Would you believe that athletic coaches and railroad coaches both take their name from the same source, a small town in Hungary? It all began many centuries ago when the first coaches, vehicles designed to carry a number of passengers, were made in Kocs, Hungary. The name of the town was applied to the carriages and, as early as the middle of the sixteenth century, the word *coach* was common in England. Then, during the early part of the nineteenth century, pupils in English universities began to call their tutors *coaches,* perhaps from the notion that their guidance "carried" them through their examinations. From there it was a very brief step indeed to designating the teachers of athletics as *coaches.*

cognac. *Cognac* is brandy, but not all brandies are cognacs. Properly used, the word applies only to those brandies produced in the Cognac area of Western France.

crichton, admirable. With the gradual disappearance of domestic servants, the phrase *admirable crichton* has virtually ceased to have much meaning. But, earlier in this century, it was widely used to describe the ideal manservant or butler. James M. Barrie created the phrase with his play *The Admirable Crichton* (1902) in which a British family, complete with servants, is shipwrecked on a desert island. Crichton, the butler, proves the person best qualified to run matters, so he takes command and the group weathers adversity. In time, a rescue party appears and Crichton, ever the correct servant, relinquishes command and reverts to his former role. But that's only half the story. Barrie took the title of his play from the name of an actual Crichton, a child prodigy of the sixteenth century. Called *admirable* because of his unquestioned brilliance, he was a versatile linguist and master of a variety of sciences before he was twenty. The lad also displayed remarkable amatory proclivities, but made the sad mistake of wooing a nobleman's wife. His end was abrupt —he was set upon and murdered by three masked men.

Derby. The twelfth Earl of Derby was directly responsible for the first famous horse-racing Derby, held annually since 1780 at Epson Downs in England. The British pronounce this DAR–bee, while we, when using it as part of the name of our premier race for three-year-olds, the Kentucky Derby, call it DER–bee. At one time it was fashionable for men attending the British Derby to wear the stiff felt hat with a rounded crown which we now call a *derby.* However, just to keep matters complicated, the British usually call the hat not a *derby* but a *bowler.*

derrick. Today's skyscrapers would not be possible without the use of the enormous cranes we call *derricks*—but the first derrick was put to a very different purpose. It was a gallows used at the infamous Tyburn gaol in England and was named after a celebrated hangman of the 1600s, Derrick.

derringer. Time was when ladies who, in the Victorian phrase, were "no better than they should be" often packed *derringers,* short-barreled pistols, in their purses. These modest but lethal weapons got their name from an American nineteenth century gunsmith named Henry Deringer (one "r" please). In recent years youngsters in street play have been heard referring to their mock pistols as *dillingers.* This is probably a corruption of derringer, by the process known to linguists as "folk etymology," which converted it to the name of the noted 1930s gangster, John Dillinger.

donnybrook. This name for a classic knockdown, drag-out brawl comes from the celebrated Donnybrook Fairs, held in the town of that name near Dublin for several centuries. They started in medieval times and became notorious, first for the licentiousness of their entertainment, and secondly, and more lastingly, for the fact that they invariably wound up in mass fisticuffs. By the mid-nineteenth century the authorities decided that things were getting a bit too rough, so they closed down the fair—but the expression *donnybrook* lives on.

draconian. This is a useful adjective meaning harsh, severe or extremely rigorous. It comes from one of the first law-and-order advocates, Draco, an Athenian lawgiver who promulgated the Draconian Code in 621 B.C. Most of the crimes he cited were punishable by death, leading one Greek wit to comment that "The Draconian Code is written in blood."

dukes. The use of *dukes* in the sense of fists is now largely limited to the expression "put up your dukes"—as a challenge to a fist fight. There seems to be little doubt that the duke in question was the great Duke of Wellington, Napoleon's conqueror. The Duke, though a notable favorite of the ladies, was not quite what you would call handsome because his nose was of a prominence to rival that of Cyrano or even Durante. At first large noses came to be called *dukes;* from this it was only a short step to calling fists *dukebusters,* eventually shortened to *dukes.*

dun. When a bill collector *duns* you for payment of overdue charges, he is following in the footsteps of the legendary bailiff of Lincoln, Joe Dun. In the time of Henry II, Joe achieved such an awesome reputation for his diligence in bill collecting that his name became part of the language.

dunce. This noun, meaning simpleton or fool, comes, incredibly enough, from the name of one of the most learned and brilliant men of the Middle Ages, John Duns Scotus. This

notable theologian found himself out of sympathy with some
of the changes effected by the Reformation. His conservative
approach attracted many followers, most of them far less
learned than he, and, in time their beliefs came to be labeled
by their more progressive rivals as evidence of reactionary,
hidebound stupidity. So, ironically, the name of a man of
authentic brilliance came to be used as an epithet for dolts
and fools.

Dutch. *Dutch* in phrases like "Dutch treat," "Dutch courage"
and "doing the Dutch" refers, of course, to an entire people,
not a single person. All terms have derogatory implications
and reflect the period of intense commercial rivalry between
the English and the Dutch during the seventeenth and
eighteenth centuries. One method of demonstrating superiority
over a rival is to resort to "putting him down" with deprecatory remarks. Hence, translated, these expressions mean:
"Dutch treat"—everyone pays for himself; "Dutch courage"
—courage obtained from the bottle; and "do the Dutch"—
commit suicide.

epicure. The first epicure—a person devoted to good food and
the luxuries of fine living—was a Greek philosopher named
Epicurus who lived in the third and second centuries B.C. His
school of philosophy opposed that of the Stoics, who took
the view that life is earnest, grim and, on balance, likely
to be unpleasant. Epicurus did not take so dim a view, feeling that there was pleasure to be found during our mortal
existence and that it was no sin to seek it. Over the centuries, his teachings have been somewhat distorted and made
to seem to proclaim purely hedonistic aims—pleasure for
pleasure's own sake. That's how the idea of the epicure as
a devotee of luxurious living came in.

farad. One of the most remarkable men in the entire history of
science, Michael Faraday, gave his name to two terms common in electricity: the *farad,* a unit of electrical capacitance,
and the *faraday,* the quantity of eletricity required to dissolve
or deposit a certain amount of a substance by means of elec-
trolysis. Faraday made many important discoveries in several
fields of scientific research but his best known achievement
was the demonstration of electromagnetic induction, the basic
principle that led to the development of the dynamo and the
electric motor.

Ferris wheel. We have all seen these marvelous rotating wheels with suspended cars that carry hundreds of amusement park patrons to dizzying heights. They get their name, logically enough, from George Ferris, the American engineer who designed the very first one, which went on display at the great Columbian Exposition of 1893 in Chicago.

Fritz, on the. This expression, meaning that something has gone awry, probably comes from the name of one of the characters in what may well be America's longest-running comic strip, the Katzenjammer Kids. Hans and Fritz, the "kids," are constantly making hash of their elders' carefully laid plans. No matter what the grownups plan, the kids see to it that it ends up *on the Fritz*.

Garrison finish. This is a breathtakingly close finish in any kind of race, but it was first applied to horse racing. Edward H. "Snapper" Garrison was one of the top-ranking jockeys of the late nineteenth century but he caused near heart failure to many an habitué of the tracks. Garrison's technique was to hold back his horse until nearly the final furlong. Then he would pour on the pressure and, almost invariably, his horse would win by a nose.

gasconade. This is a word (pronounced gas–kuh–NAYD) that we have taken over unchanged from the French. It means bragging and reflects the French belief that most inhabitants of Gascony are prone to the practice of talking big—especially when they have little to boast about.

gat. This is thieves' argot for pistol or revolver, very common in gangster movies of the 1930s. It's a shortened form of *gatling gun*, the first machine gun, designed by Richard J. Gatling, an American inventor.

gerrymander. Elbridge Gerry was a distinguished American patriot, signer of the Declaration of Independence, presidential emissary to France during John Adams' term of office, and later Governor of Massachusetts. But he lives in memory as the father of the Gerrymander Bill of 1812 that so redistricted the Commonwealth of Massachusetts that most of the Federalist voters were concentrated in a few oddly shaped districts, sharply limiting their power. A cartoon showed the redistricted area in the form of a salamander. Thus the word *gerrymander* was coined and has served ever since as the generic term to describe reapportioning political areas in order to give one party an unfair advantage over another. Incidentally, Gerry's grandson, Elbridge Thomas Gerry, was

a social reformer of the nineteenth century, very active in
obtaining legislation to limit or eliminate child labor. Because of the so-called "Gerry laws," child actors were banned
from theaters in some cities of the nation, much to the irri-
tation of producers and vaudeville bookers of the period.

Gibson. The *Gibson cocktail,* like the *Gibson girl,* takes its
name from the distinguished popular illustrator of the turn
of the century, Charles Dana Gibson. At New York's theatrical club, The Players, Gibson called one evening for a dry
Martini cocktail. The bartender, Charley Connolly, apolo-
gized for having run out of olives, then considered an indispensable element in the Martini. "Well, why not toss in one
of those pearl onions?" asked Gibson. Connolly did—and the
Gibson was born.

gin. This is a corruption of the original name of the spirits,
geneva. However, this does not mean that the first gin was
distilled in Geneva, Switzerland. Actually this *geneva* was a
bad British translation for the French "genievre" or juniper,
a flavoring element used in the product.

Great Scott! This expression of astonishment was probably inspired by the military exploits of General Winfield Scott,
hero of the Mexican war.

grog. The term is now somewhat loosely used to indicate any
variety of spirits but originally it was the rum and water
combination issued to British sailors at sea. It was in the
eighteenth century that an English admiral, Edward Vernon
by name, first authorized the issue. He was known affectionately—or at least as affectionately as any commanding officer
can be known by enlisted men—as "Old Grog," from his
invariable habit of wearing a coat of grogram (grosgrain),
a coarse, stiffened fabric.

guillotine. This famous French instrument of execution was
named for its inventor, Dr. J. I. Guillotin. A medical doctor,
Guillotin was passionately interested in humanitarian pursuits, especially in the reduction of pain whenever possible.
Thus his invention of the guillotine was inspired by his desire
to inflict less pain on the victim than did the hitherto standard
practice of hanging or the protracted tortures that had been
used.

Heaviside layer. This is the lower region of the ionosphere,
some sixty miles above the earth's surface. Its main importance is that it reflects back to earth radio waves of rela-

tively low frequency, thereby enabling reception of radio broadcasts at much greater distances from the point of origin than would otherwise be possible. Although one could very well assume that the name derives from the belief that this layer of the ionosphere constitutes its "heavy side," in fact the designation comes from the name of its discoverer, English physicist Oliver Heaviside.

henry. This is the unit of electrical inductance, named after the American physicist Joseph Henry who made many studies of electromagnetic phenomena in the nineteenth century.

Hobson's choice. This, of course, is no choice at all. You accept what is offered you with as much grace as you can summon, because you have no alternative. The original Hobson was a stablekeeper in Cambridge, England, during the sixteenth century who ran his stable with the proverbial whim of iron. Insisting that all his horses be exercised in regular rotation, he saw to it that every person coming to hire a horse was required to take the horse nearest the stable door—with no ifs, ands, or buts about it.

hooliganism. This synonym for roughhousing and petty gangsterism is derived from a family named Hooligan, obviously of Irish descent, who made quite a reputation for themselves in late nineteenth century London. One commentator noted that they "enlivened the drab monotony of life in the Southwark district," and this seems to have been a very considerable understatement. The impact of the word on the American language was greatly strengthened by the appearance in one of our early comic strips of a character named "Happy Hooligan," a somewhat dimwitted but harmless chap who was forever flirting with disaster in a rather slaphappy fashion.

Hoyle. "Play the cards according to Hoyle" has been a standard expression among gamesmen since the sixteenth century when Edmund Hoyle, a prominent clubman of the period, undertook to codify the rules for whist. His book *A Short Treatise on the Game of Whist* was immediately accepted as authoritative and, with many revisions and the addition of dozens of other sets of game rules, it is still the basic authority. So the expression "according to Hoyle" has been extended beyond mere cardplaying to cover any activity that must be conducted according to well-established rules.

inverness cape. This is a combination outercoat and cape of the sort affected by Sherlock Holmes. Its name comes from Inverness, a county seat in Scotland, whose inhabitants doubtless need and appreciate the double-layer of outer clothing.

Jacob's ladder. This is the rope or chain ladder, usually with wooden or metal rungs, used by harbor pilots when climbing aboard ocean liners. It gets its name from an incident in the Book of Genesis (28:12). Jacob falls into a deep sleep: "And he dreamed, and behold a ladder set up on the earth, and the top of it reached to heaven; and behold the angels of God ascending and descending on it." That's rather an elegant, not to say celestial, origin for the name of anything as homely and utilitarian as a pilot's ladder. There is also a plant called *Jacob's ladder*. It's of the genus *Polemonium,* has blue flowers and leaves that grow in pairs, somewhat resembling the rungs of a ladder. And, just to round out the uses of this phrase, it was formerly used in England to describe what American women call *runs* in their nylons. Now they are simply called *ladders*.

jodhpurs. These are the wide-hipped riding breeches, closely fitted at knee and ankle, first popularized by polo players and now standard costume at horse shows. The name comes from Jodhpur, a former princely state in northwestern India where this item of native dress was adapted by British colonial officers to their own purposes.

Joe Miller. This term for a tired, worn-out joke comes from an actual Joe Miller, a comedian in England in the early eighteenth century. Joe was a sort of legend in his time, so in his memory, a man named John Mottley put together a collection of Joe's japeries which he entitled "Joe Miller's Jests." It became a valuable "swipe file" for comedians and was updated from time to time. Eventually, of course, the humor in the gags disappeared from overuse and a *Joe Miller* acquired its present meaning.

joey. To this day circus clowns are called *joeys* in tribute to one of the greatest of the genre, Joseph Grimaldi, who plied his trade to the delight of children and adults alike in eighteenth century England.

knickerbockers. These are the baggy men's pants, tightly gathered below the knee, that were standard garb for golfers during the 1920s. The name seems to have originated with Diedrick Knickerbocker, who was the protagonist of Washington Irving's book *A History of New York*. Knickerbocker was supposed to be a typical Dutch settler in the early days of New Amsterdam. When a British edition of the History appeared, it was illustrated by Cruikshank, who also illustrated some of Dickens' works, and it was he who garbed Irving's hero in the trousers that were to become so stylish a century later.

Levis. These reinforced blue jean pants take their name from Levi Strauss, a San Francisco clothier of the Gold Rush period. He was the first to strengthen the construction of the pants by putting rivets at the corners of the pockets, thus enabling prospectors to put gold nuggets into their pockets without tearing them. Incidentally, the fabric *jean* in *blue jeans* is derived from Genoa, Italy, where it was first woven, and *denim* is a corruption of the phrase "serge de Nimes" from the city of Nimes, France, where it was first made.

Listerine. This is, of course, the trademarked name of a popular mouthwash. It gets its name from Joseph Lister, a distinguished British surgeon and the founder of antiseptic surgery. In his *The American Language,* H. L. Mencken reports that Lister was not very happy about this use of his name but his protests fell on deaf ears.

Lucy Stoner. Lucy Stone anticipated the Women's Liberation movement by more than a century. Though married to Henry Brown Blackwell, she flatly refused to change her name and insisted on being addressed by her maiden name. Nor was she alone. In this century *Lucy Stoners* included people like Ruth Hale, first wife of Heywood Broun and mother of sportscaster Heywood Hale Broun.

macadam. This technique of paving highways was the invention of John L. McAdam, a Scottish engineer who came to America after the Revolution and developed methods of paving roads with crushed stone.

Mach. The speed of aircraft, especially those traveling at transsonic or supersonic speeds, is measured in *Machs.* A *Mach* is the ratio of air speed to the speed of sound. Thus an aircraft traveling at the speed of sound is said to be traveling at a speed of Mach 1. The word comes from the name of a noted Austrian physicist and philosopher, Ernst Mach.

mackintosh. A Scottish chemist named Charles Mackintosh, of the late eighteenth and early nineteenth centuries, was the first person to develop a truly waterproof fabric. As a result his name, often shortened to *mac,* became a generic term, especially in England, for raincoat. Incidentally, the McIntosh apple, a variety very popular in the United States, was originally developed in Ontario in 1796 by John McIntosh.

madras. This cotton cloth derives its name from the Indian city of Madras where it is thought to have. originated. One point to note, however, is that the American pronunciation of the fabric MAD–ras differs from that of the Indian city, which is properly either muh–DRAHS or muh–DRAS.

malaprop or **malapropism.** This term for the misuse, through ignorance, of fancy-sounding words, comes from Richard Brinsley Sheridan's famous comedy *The Rivals* and the character Mrs. Malaprop. Sheridan in turn took it from the French "mal à propos," meaning inappropriate, out of place or unsuitable.

Manhattan. This cocktail, made of whiskey and vermouth, obviously derives its name from the Borough of Manhattan, New York. In similar fashion the Bronx cocktail (gin and orange juice) takes its name from the only mainland borough of New York. For reasons unknown, there has never been a Queens, Brooklyn or Staten Island cocktail, and for the sake of our national sobriety, perhaps that's just as well.

martini. This cocktail derives its name from Martini & Rossi, one of the makers of an important ingredient, vermouth.

masochism. The Austrian novelist Leopold Sacher-Masoch gave his name to the practice of subjecting oneself to physical abuse to obtain sexual gratification. The word has since become extended in meaning to cover any sort of physical or psychic self-torment.

maverick. A *maverick* is a loner, one who doesn't want to be categorized and who refuses to conform to the dictates of any one group, especially if that group is a political party. The first Maverick was a Texas rancher named Sam Maverick who earned the dislike of his fellow cattlemen by refusing to brand his steers.

McCoy, the real. This is the real article, the genuine thing, not an imitation. The expression was popularized and perhaps even invented by a prizefighter of the 1890s named "Kid" McCoy. The story goes that he was once challenged by a heckler who was trying to goad him into a fight. At length the heckler said, "If you were the real McCoy, you'd not be afraid to fight." At that the Kid dusted the heckler off with a single punch, remarking, as he stepped over the prostrate body, "That's the real McCoy!"

Melba toast and **peach Melba.** The first is, of course, a thin dry toast that is a staple with calorie-counting dieters. The second, a rich peaches and ice cream dessert, is death to any diet. Both were named after the fabulous Australian diva, Dame Nellie Melba, who was in her day—if you'll forgive the expression—the operatic toast of three continents.

mesmerize. When you have been completely brainwashed, entirely persuaded of the truth of a proposition, you may be said to have been mesmerized. The first mesmerist, Prof. Frans Anton Mesmer, was a very successful hypnotist who claimed all sorts of cures as a result of his command of animal magnetism. In the late eighteenth century the French government appointed a committee to investigate him. The committee reported that he was a quack, but his name lives on in the language in a word that is a synonym for hypnotize.

mho and **ohm.** The *mho* is the unit of electrical conductance, while the *ohm* is the unit of electrical resistance. These diametrically opposed concepts were both named for their discoverer, Georg Simon Ohm, a nineteenth century German physicist.

Molotov cocktail. This is a crude bomb consisting of a breakable container, usually a glass bottle, filled with gasoline and plugged with a rag that, when ignited, acts as a fuse. The first such devices were created by the Finns and used against invading Russian tanks during the brief Russo-Finnish War of 1940. Needless to say, the Finns did not intend the reference to Russian Foreign Minister V. M. Molotov to be flattering.

morris dances. These British country dances, miming themes from the Robin Hood legend, actually were imported from Spain during the fourteenth century. Originally called *Moorish dances,* because they had been adapted from Moorish military dances, the name eventually was assimilated in English as the more familiar form *morris.*

Munchausen. A congenital fabricator of tall tales is often called a *Munchausen* after Baron Münchhausen, an eighteenth century German soldier who was widely credited as having been the most prodigious liar of all time. In recent years doctors have employed the phrase "Munchausen syndrome" to describe the state of mind of certain hypochondriacs who invent symptoms in order to get increased attention from their doctors or even, in extreme situations, to obtain admission to hospitals.

nicotine. This essential and pernicious element in tobacco gets its name from Jean Nicot, French ambassador at Lisbon who, in 1560, was given some tobacco seeds by Portuguese sailors newly returned from America. He planted them and thus became the person responsible for the debatable honor of introducing tobacco to Europe.

ohm. (See **mho,** above.)

oxford cloth. This famous shirting material was named, pretty obviously, for Oxford University in England. What is not so well known is that at one time there were also cambridge cloth, harvard cloth and even yale cloth—all three now long forgotten.

panic. When you go into a *panic,* either figuratively or literally, you are reacting as the ancients did when they heard the pipes of Pan. A favorite figure in Greek mythology, Pan was given to light-hearted frolicking through field and glen, playing on his shrill pipes. He also was wont to burst suddenly into view, so startling the unwary passerby that he was thrown into a panic. Nor is this surprising, since Pan had a human torso, and a goat's legs, head and ears—a combination calculated to panic almost anyone at a glance.

peeler. The *peelers* were, and are, London policemen, although they are more commonly known as *Bobbies.* Both names come from the same man, Sir Robert Peel, who reorganized the London police force in 1828.

peeping Tom. A *peeping Tom* is, of course, a voyeur, one who secretly spies on another, usually out of prurient interest. The first such was Tom of Coventry, the one resident of the town who violated the communal pledge not to look when Lady Godiva took her celebrated ride in the buff. She was, as you may recall, fulfilling her part of a challenge she had laid down to her husband: if he would reduce the oppressive taxes on the townspeople, she would ride naked through the town. Never thinking she would go through with her part of it, he accepted the challenge—and the rest is legend.

plimsoll mark. The safety of ocean-going vessels depends very greatly on some rather unobtrusive marks on the sides of every ship's hull. Also called the *load lines,* they indicate the maximum depth to which a ship may be loaded under varying conditions. They are named after Samuel Plimsoll, a British Member of Parliament, who pressed the legislation through in 1876. During a century or more before this time, trans-Atlantic ships were often criminally overloaded because of the cupidity of shipowners and the eagerness of so many poor and desperate people to reach the New World. So many ships foundered in heavy gales that they came to be known as *coffin ships.* But Plimsoll's marks put an end to this.

poinsettia. This traditional evergreen plant of Christmas was named for Joel Poinsett of South Carolina, onetime U.S. Ambassador to Mexico. He discovered the plant there and brought it to this country. Other flowers and plants named for their discoverers or developers include: Begonia (Michel Begon, French botanist); Magnolia (Pierre Magnol, ditto); Gardenia (Alexander Garden, an American); Dahlia (A. Dahl, Swedish botanist), Camellia (George Joseph Kamel, a Moravian Jesuit who brought the shrub from the Orient); Fuschia (Leonhard Fuchs, German botanist); and Wisteria (Caspar Wistar—that's right, Wistar, not Wister—American botanist).

Pullman. The *Pullman sleeping car* has virtually disappeared from the railroad tracks of America and with its departure go just about the last recollections of a man who was once one of America's most powerful magnates, George M. Pullman. He invented what was first called the *Pullman Palace car,* made a fortune from it, built a town named for himself and fought one of the most bitterly contested strikes in American labor history. Eugene V. Debs gained fame from his role in the strike, as did the Pinkertons and Gov. John P. Altgeld, Governor of Illinois at the time. Of all the glory, fame and money, only the town still remains—and that has now been absorbed into Chicago.

raglan coat. A *raglan coat* or jacket is one that has slanted shoulder seams and sleeves that extend all the way to the neckline. It is named after Field Marshal Lord Raglan who, like Cardigan, was one of the non-heroes of the British war in the Crimea. Indeed, Raglan was the supreme commander in that ill-fated venture. Although Queen Victoria praised

Raglan for the operation, less prejudiced military experts found it easy to contain their enthusiasm for his prowess.

raising cain. A person who *raises cain* creates a tumult or noisy disturbance. The expression comes from the fact that Cain, brother of Abel and the world's first criminal, was often invoked by religious folk who feared to use the word *devil.* So instead of *raising the devil,* they *raised cain.*

Rube Goldberg. An extremely and unnecessarily intricate plan for effecting a fairly simple end is often called a *Rube Goldberg,* after the American cartoonist and sculptor of that name, who used to draw a phenomenally successful cartoon panel featuring such madcap "inventions."

sadism. This term for sexual gratification based upon the subjection of other persons to cruelty or brutality comes from the writings of Compte Donatien de Sade, a French writer whose works extolled such sex-motivated violence.

Sam Browne belt. This is the belt with a diagonal shoulder strap once worn by U.S. army officers to help support sidearms. Though virtually abandoned by the army except for rare wear on ceremonial occasions, it is very much a part of the garb of the children who serve as school-crossing guards and whose white *Sam Browne belts* make them quickly identifiable by motorists. The original Sam Browne was a Sir Samuel Browne, a general in the British army under Victoria. According to one report, Browne lost his left arm and, unable to support his sword without it, devised the belt to serve that purpose.

sandwich. Perhaps the best-known tale of a word originating from a proper name is the story about John Montague, the Fourth Earl of Sandwich, an inveterate gambler during the reign of George III. Unwilling to interrupt his demoniacal addiction to dice, he ordered his servant to bring him a slice of meat between slices of bread, so that he could eat while still gambling. And so the *sandwich* was born. Less well known is the fact that the gambling Earl was even better known by the nickname "Jemmy Twitcher." Just think of having to order a "ham-and-cheese Twitcher on toasted rye."

schlemiel. A *schlemiel* is a dolt, a habitual bungler, the chap who never seems to get things right. The origin of this Yiddish slang term may be found in the Bible, in the Book of Numbers, Chapter 2. Shelumiel was the son of the leader of the tribe of Simeon. All the other leaders were victorious in battle, but Shelumiel lost every one he fought. So the name, in slightly altered form, has come down through the centuries as the perfect name for the born loser.

serendipity. An ancient name for Ceylon was Serendip. Horace Walpole used it as the locale of a fable, "Three Princes of Serendip," about three men who were, he wrote "always making discoveries of things they were not in quest of." So *serendipity* has come into the language as the happy faculty for making fortunate discoveries completely by accident.

shanghai. To capture a person and bundle him off against his wishes for compulsory service, especially aboard a ship, is to *shanghai* him. The practice has long been abandoned, at least among civilized nations, but in the nineteenth century and earlier, it was common to impress captured men into service on sailing ships bound for Shanghai.

shillelah. This is a formidable stick, often of oak or blackthorn, used by Irishmen either as a club or a cane. It gets its name from the town of the same name in County Wicklow, and it's pronounced shih–LAY–lee.

sideburns. These elegant mutton-chop whiskers were named for General Ambrose Everett Burnside, a Northern general during the American Civil War. Like other generals whose names have come down to us in association with some item of fashion (see **cardigan** and **raglan,** above), Burnside wasn't any great shakes as a general. Indeed, he officiated at the disastrous defeat of the Union forces at Petersburg and came close to being drummed out of the army after a court of inquiry looked into his conduct of the battle. However, he eventually became Governor of Rhode Island and achieved a lasting fame, though in a slightly backward fashion, by having his name, reversed to *sideburns,* used as the generic label for that kind of hirsute adornment. Incidentally, a somewhat silkier version of sideburns is known as a *dundreary*. This style gets its name from a Lord Dundreary, who was just as dull as his name sounds. He would long have been forgotten except for the fact that he was a character in the play *Our American Cousin* and, in case you have forgotten, that's the show that played Ford's Theatre in Washington the night President Lincoln was assassinated.

simon pure. With amateur athletics virtually at the vanishing point, it may be well to recall when such athletes were almost invariably referred to on the sports pages as *simon pures.*

The first such was a character in *A Bold Stroke for a Wife,* an eighteenth century drama in which Simon Pure, obviously the hero, was pitted against a villain with the equally unsubtle name of Colonel Feignwell.

solon. This is a favorite of headline writers because it says *senator* at a saving of two type characters. The first *solon* was an Athenian statesman and poet of the sixth century B.C.

spoonerism. This is the tongue-twister of the sort dreaded by all radio and TV performers. The classic was uttered by a White House correspondent many years ago when he portentously proclaimed: "And now, Ladies and Gentlemen, the President of the United States, Mr. Hoobert Heever." The first and most famous creator of spoonerisms was the man who gave them their name, William A. Spooner, a clergyman at Oxford. He is reported to have completed a marriage ceremony with this advice to the groom: "Son, it is now kisstomary to cuss the bride."

Stetson. The wide-brimmed sombrero-like felt hat affected by America's cowboys gets its name from its first maker, the John B. Stetson Co., of Philadelphia. Cowboys also sometimes called it the *John B.* and often referred to it as the *ten-gallon hat.*

volt. The unit of electrical potential and electromotive force gets its name from Count Alessandro Volta, an Italian research pioneer in electricity.

watt. This unit of power, especially of electrical power, gets its name from James Watt, noted Scottish engineer and inventor.

welsh. This word meaning to cheat on a bet or debt is another of the items (see **Dutch**) of calculatedly derogatory reference which somehow made its way into the language. Naturally, no self-respecting Welshman would use it, although he might be willing to admit that, like our own Yankee traders or the legendary Scotsman, the Welsh have a well-merited reputation for sharp trading.

wimpy. Here's a word that most Americans under thirty have never seen, one which is nearly forgotten by those over that age, and yet, it's one which all England thinks is a staple part of American slang. It all goes back to the name of a character in E. C. Segar's comic strip "Popeye" who always seemed to have a hamburger in his hand or to be in quest of one. During the American occupation of the British Isles before the Normandy invasion of World War II, the English learned about our American hamburger sandwiches for the first time and liked them mightily. After the first wave of postwar austerity, hamburger stands began to crop up in London and elsewhere and, naturally enough, they were labeled Wimpy stands. Although poor Wimpy has been virtually forgotten in the land of his birth, he's still a household word back in blighty.

zany. Any eccentric or foolish chap may be labeled a *zany* as may be any eccentric or foolish behavior. The word comes, not from slang as you might expect, but from the language of the Italian commedia dell'arte, a traditional, highly stylized theatrical entertainment not unlike American burlesque of a few decades ago. In the commedia dell'arte, one of the stock characters was *zanni*, who usually mimicked the clown. The British changed the spelling to "*zany*" and gave it the meaning it has now. Incidentally, since *zanni* was a nickname for "Giovanni," the Italian word for John, you might say that the first *zany* was John.

3. Foreign Words and Phrases

As we have already seen, English has borrowed many thousands of words from the other languages of the world. Usually these borrowings become, so to speak, domesticated in a few generations. A word like *martinet*, which was originally the name of a French army officer noted for his strict discipline, has been so long a part of English that most people have forgotten its French origin. Other words and phrases, though, seem to resist domestication. Borrowings from the language of French cookery, such as *hors d'oeuvre* and *à la carte*, appear in every cookbook and on many restaurant menus and still retain their essentially French aspect.

Now we're going to look at fifty such borrowings from other languages—words we may very well meet in everyday reading or conversation but which still retain enough of the characteristics of their mother tongues to require some special explanation and, often, careful attention to pronunciation. You will find that you are already familiar with some of these expressions but, even so, you're likely to learn something about each of them that you didn't know before. If you're still skeptical, try an *hors d'oeuvre*. Look ahead to that item and see if it doesn't tell you something you never knew about how these appetizers got their name.

And, at chapter's end, a brief brush-up quiz that will serve the dual purpose of showing you how much you have learned and of reinforcing your knowledge of these colorful additions to English.

ad infinitum (ad–in–fin–EYE–tem). This term is borrowed from Latin and its literal meaning is "to infinity." Usually it's used figuratively, as when we say that the speaker droned on and on *ad infinitum*. There's a bit of doggerel that sums it up neatly: "Great fleas have little fleas upon their backs to bite 'em. And little fleas have lesser fleas and so ad infinitum."

aficionado (uh–fee–see–uh–NAH–do). This term, borrowed from Spanish, means a devoted follower, especially of a sport or art form. The true *aficionado* steeps himself in the lore of the subject of his enthusiasm. If his topic is baseball, he'll know Harry Heilmann's lifetime batting average as well as Tom Seaver's won-lost record the year the Mets won the championship. In other words, your true *aficionado* is a dedicated enthusiast, even though he may not have the slightest personal ability in the field of his mania. Incidentally, the pure Castillian Spanish pronunciation is ah–fee–thee–uh–NAH–do.

à la carte (ah lah kart). This is a term familiar to all restaurant-goers. In French it means "by the card," and card, of course, means menu. When you order *à la carte,* you are charged separately for each item ordered, in contrast to a meal ordered *prix fixe* (at fixed price) or *table d'hôte* (table of the host) in which one price covers everything from appetizer to dessert.

al fresco (ahl FRES–koh). With backyard barbecues commonplace throughout our country, lots of people are dining *al fresco* without even knowing it. This phrase, from Italian, literally means "in the fresh or cool," but it's nöt inappropriate even on a sweltering summer day.

apéritif (ah–pay–ree–teef). A light libation before eating, such as a dry sherry, is properly called an *apéritif.* It's a French word meaning "an opener," and that's just what it does. It opens the meal suitably by stimulating your appetite.

au courant (oh koo–rahn). If you are completely up-to-date with current happenings, you're *au courant.* It's a French phrase literally meaning "in the current." So if you are well-posted on events in the world, you may consider yourself in the mainstream.

blasé (blah–zay). Here's a word which had a great vogue in the 1930s. It means sophisticated, world-weary. It also connotes a person consumed with his own importance—all puffed up with ego. This is appropriate since the word, which we borrowed from French, actually began as the Dutch word "blasen," meaning to blow up or swell.

bon vivant (bon vee–vahn). This chap might well be *blasé,* but he needn't be, since a *bon vivant* is merely a person who likes fine living—"high on the hog," as the homely American phrase puts it. The original French phrase simply means "good living" and that's what your true *bon vivant* (always a male by the way; the phrase "bonne vivante"—which would be a woman—couldn't even exist) seeks.

carte blanche (kart blahnch). The original *carte blanche* was simply a white card bearing nothing but the signature of a person in authority. The bearer of the card could fill it in to suit his own whim, with assurance that whatever he requested would be granted. So today we use the term, a French phrase, to mean the power to take whatever action one pleases.

caveat emptor (KAV–ee–ut EMP–tor). This warning, posted in the market places of ancient Rome, stands today as excellent advice: "Let the buyer beware!"

chef d'oeuvre (sheh der–vreh). A person's masterpiece, the crowning achievement of his career may be labeled *chef d'oeuvre,* a French phrase literally meaning the "chief work."

cherchez la femme (shair–shay lah fam). This phrase from the French, literally "look for the woman," used to be the tip-off to the solution of most whodunits. Nowadays, mystery writers are a bit more sophisticated and a trifle less obvious in their plotting, but it's still a good idea to keep close track of the females. They may lead the way to the solution.

comme il faut (kom eel foh). This is a useful expression meaning, in free translation from the French, "as it is fitting and proper that it should be." If her teen-age daughter should wander into a formal reception clad in her bikini, her mother might well suggest that her costume is not *comme il faut.*

coup de grâce (koo deh grahs). In the original French this means "blow of mercy." Just the same, it means the finishing blow—the stroke that marks the end of the matter. So, when an enterprising young executive presents a program for the complete reorganization of his company, he must not be surprised if the chairman of the board administers the *coup de grâce.*

déjà vu (day–zhah voo). All of us have had the experience of feeling that an experience we are now going through has happened to us before, with precisely the same people involved and the same words being spoken. The occurrence is so common that psychologists have adopted this French phrase to describe it. And it's completely appropriate, since *déjà vu* means "already seen."

dernier cri (dair–nee–ay kree). This means literally "the last cry," but the cry is anything but a howl of anguish. Indeed, it means the very latest thing, especially in fashion.

de trop (der troh). When youngsters say "That's simply too much," they are unwittingly echoing this French phrase. When something is *de trop,* it is literally too much, or superfluous.

Doppelgänger (DOP–el–gang–er). This word which, in the original German, means "double-goer" appears in the fairly widely believed Theory of *Doppelgängers.* And what is this theory? Simply that each of us has, somewhere in the world, an exact duplicate, a person who looks and speaks enough like us to be taken for our twin. Mention of the theory in my newspaper column some years ago brought dozens of letters reporting instances of this phenomenon.

double entendre (doo–b'l on–ton–dreh). This is a statement which can be understood in two ways, and the second meaning is usually sly and improper. It's a French term meaning "double understanding," but we usually use it simply to indicate a phrase with two meanings.

du jour (doo zhoor). We have all seen this on restaurant menus. It's the French phrase meaning "of the day," and it's usually used as the label for whatever soup the chef prepared for that particular day.

ennui (on–wee). Another borrowing from the French, this is a rather elegant synonym for weariness. It also has an implication of boredom and dissatisfaction with routine matters.

entourage (on–toor–AHZH). Again, this is a rather elegant expression from the French for a fairly commonplace situation. One's *entourage* is simply his companions, especially those who regularly accompany him. So you might say that a movie star attended the premiere of her latest film with her customary *entourage* of press agents and photographers.

entrée (ON–tray). Here is a bit of an oddity. In French cuisine an *entrée,* literally "entrance" was a dish served before the main course or one served between two principal courses. In America now, it simply means the main course of a meal. *Entree* also has the meaning of admittance or right of entry, especially to some select group.

flambé (flahm–BAY). Flaming is as realistic a translation as we can make of this French word, although it literally means "that which has been flamed or singed." In any event, some restaurants make a specialty of serving main and dessert courses wreathed in flames. The technique does create a spectacle, though some gourmets question its merits.

forte (fort—NOT for–TAY). Again we go to French for this word which literally means "strong" but in our use means strong point or special skill.

gardez la foi (gar–day lah fwah). This expression, usually used jokingly in farewell, means "Keep the faith!"

Gesundheit (geh–SOONT–hite). This is the German word for health, often used in Germany as a toast, just as we say "To your good health." In America, though, it is almost invariably used as a gesture of sympathy when a companion sneezes. The custom of offering such sympathy goes back to the Middle Ages, when sneezing was considered an indication that the sneezer must have contracted the dreaded plague. From this belief also comes the origin of the common expression "not to be sneezed at."

grande passion (grahn pah–syon). This means precisely what it seems to mean and it's an expression, taken from the French, used nowadays more in jest than in seriousness. But in grandfather's day stars of the silver screen like Pola Negri and Rudolph Valentino were often depicted in the throes of what could only be called *grande passion*.

habitué (huh–bit–choo–ay). Again from the French, here is an elegant term for a commonplace occurrence, hanging around. One who can be found in the same club or restaurant every day at the same time is an *habitué* of the place.

hacienda (hah–see–EN–duh). In Spain this term means an entire estate, often a ranch of some size. In its adaptation to life in the Southwestern United States, though, it can simply mean a ranch house.

hoi polloi (hoy puh–LOY). This is Greek for "the masses." It's generally used condescendingly, as "I seldom mingle with the hoi polloi." It is worth noting that "the hoi polloi" is redundant, since *hoi* means "the." However, this may be filed in the Lost Causes Department, for we have yet to hear or to see in print "the polloi."

hors d'oeuvre (or derv). An easy bet to win at a cocktail party is that nobody will know how *hors d'oeuvres* got their name.

Someone may well come up with the literal translation, which is "outside the work," but how did that come to be applied to tid-bit appetizers served with cocktails? Answer: the first *hors d'oeuvres* were intended to precede a formal dinner and the dinner was the *chef d'oeuvre* (see **chef d'oeuvre,** above) or simply the *oeuvre.* So the appetizers were literally "outside the work."

in loco parentis (in LOH–koh puh–REN–tis). This is practically a historical item by now, but, at least until the second half of the twentieth century, many colleges and schools regarded themselves as acting *in loco parentis,* in the place of the parent, and exercised disciplinary procedures in dormitories and classrooms that parallelled those presumably observed in the pupil's home.

in toto (in TOH–toh). From Latin we borrow this phrase which means "in sum" or "as a whole."

in vino veritas (in–VEE–noh VAIR–ih–tahs). "In wine is the truth" says this Latin phrase, and we all know of occasions when, thanks to overindulgence in warming spirits, things are said that could better have been left unsaid.

joie de vivre (zwah duh VEE–vruh). This French phrase, literally meaning "the joy of living," knows no limitations of age or sex. Anyone glad to be alive is displaying *joie de vivre.*

mañana (mun–YAH–nah). This Spanish word literally means simply "tomorrow," but in actuality it evokes a whole philosophy of life. By leaving serious matters to tomorrow one shows a carefree attitude reminiscent at times of the Italian phrase *dolce far niente* (DOL–chay far nee–EN–tay) "the sweetness of doing nothing."

mazel tov (MAH–z'l tof). This is the Hebrew way of saying "Congratulations!"

ménage (may–nahzh). In the original French *ménage* simply means "household" or "household management." The word has become increasingly common as part of the phrase *ménage à trois,* meaning a household with three adults living together, with all-too-predictable complications.

mot juste (moh zhoost). French for "the right word." Careful writers search long and painstakingly for *le mot juste.* They well know Mark Twain's admonition: "the difference between the right word and the almost right word is the difference between lightning and the lightning bug."

noblesse oblige (noh–bless uh–BLEEJ). "Nobility obliges" or, more freely translated, "the obligations of royalty or high position" is the meaning of this French phrase. We all know that there are certain things that a man or woman of good reputation simply does not do. A failure to observe these responsibilities subjects one to the allegation of being, in Heywood Hale Broun's felicitous term, "N.Q.O.S."–Not Quite Our Sort.

nolo contendere (NOH–loh kon–TEN–deh–reh). This is legal Latin meaning "I do not wish to contend" and it's used by the lawyer for a defendant in a criminal action to indicate that his client, while not admitting guilt, does not wish to contest the charge. Lawyers usually contract the phrase by saying that their client "pleads nolo."

non sequitur (non SEK–wih–toor). "It does not follow" is the English version of this Latin phrase, but it's a term usually used to indicate a conclusion that simply doesn't follow from the evidence established. "The day dawned bright and clear, so Yale won the ball game" is, lacking further details, a *non sequitur*.

persona non grata (pair–SOH–nuh non GRAH–tuh). In the technical language of diplomacy an "unwelcome person," for that is what this Latin phrase means, is one who is denied permission to enter a country. Specifically, the term is applied to a person named to serve in a foreign embassy but regarded as unwelcome by the country to which he is sent. The term is sometimes used in reference to an applicant for membership in a private club who is N.Q.O.S. (See **noblesse oblige,** above.)

raison d'être (ray–zon det'r). Literally "reason for being," this French expression is used in such expressions as "Caring for her child has become Ethel's sole raison d'être."

sang-froid (sahn–frwah). While this French phrase literally means "cold blood," it is most commonly used to refer to a person who has retained his composure under trying circumstances, who has, in the popular expression, not "lost his cool."

savoir faire (sav–wahr fair). "To know how to do" is the French equivalent of the American "know-how"—with a little polish added. It indicates skill and tact in getting things accomplished.

soigné (swah–nyay). Well turned-out, in the British phrase. Well-groomed in ours. That's the meaning of this French adjective which literally means "cared-for."

sotto voce (SOT–oh VOH–cheh). This Italian phrase literally means "under the voice," but it's used to mean "in a very hushed or quiet voice."

sui generis (SOO–ee JEN–er–iss). From Latin comes this phrase meaning, literally, "of his own kind" or "of its own kind." We use it to mean unique.

vaya con dios (VAH–yuh con DEE–ohs). This charming Spanish farewell says, literally, "May you go with God."

QUIZ ON FOREIGN WORDS
AND PHRASES

Down below you will find ten of the words and phrases you have just been reading about. Each is followed by three English words or phrases. Try to choose the one closest in meaning. If (b) means the same thing or nearly the same thing as 3, your answer should be 3b. You will find the answers on page 182.

1. **Caveat emptor:** (a) Let the king rule!;
   (b) Talk shows rule the airwaves!;
   (c) Let the buyer beware!
2. **Flambé:** (a) fractured; (b) burning;
   (c) sprinkled with wine.
3. **Habitué:** (a) drug addict; (b) regular attendant;
   (c) cloistered nun.
4. **Al fresco:** (a) out-of-doors; (b) Italian boxer;
   wall-painting.
5. **Mazel tov:** (a) Israeli guerrilla; (b) Congratulations;
   (c) lox with bagel.
6. **Mañana:** (a) money: (b) tomorrow; (c) country house.
7. **Mot juste:** (a) presiding justice; (b) right word;
   (c) beneath contempt.
8. **Double entendre:** (a) double-thick chop;
   (b) double meaning; (c) sick joke.
9. **Nolo contendere:** (a) I won't contend;
   (b) I won't marry the woman; (c) Let me out of here.
10. **Blasé:** (a) flaming; (b) notch in tree back; (c) nonchalant.

4. Words and Phrases from the Worlds of Business and Industry

Every trade and profession has its own special jargon or shop talk. Some of it is deliberately designed to prevent outsiders from knowing what the insiders would like to keep to themselves. Other expressions are simply colorful and often evocative phrases that serve no other purpose than the healthy one of brightening the day for those who know and use them. So a used car dealer will privately describe his stock as ranging from *cream puffs* to *klunks,* although he would not admit to a prospective customer that any of the latter could be found on his lot. And a furniture salesman touting a bedroom suite would never confess—except to a brother salesman—that the suite (pronounced "suit" not "sweet," by the way) was really *borax,* or even *schlock.*

The stock market has its special jargon too, not quite as colorful but still metaphorically ingenious, with *bulls* and *bears* selling *short* and *long,* and not always *blue chips,* either. And all businesses, sad to say, have occasion to use unhappy words like *default, defalcate, kite* and *kickback.*

So now let's look at approximately forty such expressions from the world of business. Some you will know already. Others will be new and, we trust, fascinating. Then, at chapter's end, another quick brush-up quiz so that you can display your new-found knowledge.

amortization (AM–or–tih–ZAY–shun). The average person encounters the process of amortization either in connection with a house mortgage or a bank loan. It is simply a method of accounting, by which payments of both interest and principal are calculated over a given period with the result that all payments are equal. A breakdown of such *amortization* would show most of the earlier payments credited to interest and most of the later ones to principal. The term is also used for a similar method of writing off an expenditure over a period of time.

arbitration (ahr–bih–TRAY–shun) and **mediation** (meed–ee–AY–shun). The two words are given together because each represents a form of settling a dispute or controversy. In *arbitration,* the disputing parties agree—or are forced by law—to submit their difference to a disinterested party (or panel) whose judgment they are bound to accept. In *mediation,* the third party has only the power of persuasion to bring about a settlement.

bears and **bulls.** *Bears* and *bulls,* in stock market terminology, are speculators who employ widely different tactics. When the prices of stocks and bonds are on the decline, the *bear* is one who places an order to sell a given number of shares (which he may not even own at the time). When the price of the stock declines further, he buys an equivalent number of shares to replace the ones he "sold" at a higher price. When the market is on the upswing and prices are steadily rising, the *bull* buys stock shares in anticipation of further rise, planning to sell when the market is at its peak. Thus we get the terms *bear market* and *bull market.*

binder. This is a term that is used most frequently with regard to the purchase of insurance or real estate. It is a written statement of the agreement which makes it legally binding while the full contract is being drawn up. Fire and auto insurance companies issue *binders* as soon as a request for coverage is made.

Life and health insurance companies seldom issue their *binders* until medical history and present health are reviewed but they will insist that your *binder* (money) is submitted with the application.

In real estate, the written statement is called a *contract of sale* and the term *binder* is reserved for the down payment made at that time.

blue chip. In poker, the *blue chip* has the highest value of all the chips used. In the stock market, a *blue chip stock* is one of good value, not only because of its selling price but because of its history of stability in earnings.

borax and **schlock.** Each of these is a name for shoddy and inferior goods. *Borax* is a term of the furniture trade which means cheap, flimsy furniture. *Schlock* is a Yiddish term for any merchandise of inferior quality.

cartel (kahr–TEL). A *cartel* is a group of independent business enterprises organized for the purpose of controlling price, production and distribution of a product or an entire industry. Its objective is the limitation of competition. It is illegal in this country. (In another sense, *cartel* means an official agreement between governments, particularly regarding exchange of prisoners of war.)

collateral (kuh–LAT–er–ul). *Collateral* is the security, such as securities or property, that is offered to assure repayment of a loan. If the loan is not paid on schedule, the *collateral* can be seized or sold by the lender to reimburse him.

cream puff and **klunk.** In the jargon of the used car dealer, a *cream puff* is a car which is in over-all excellent condition. A *klunk,* on the other hand, is a worthless piece of junk, even though it may not look it. *Klunks* are also known in the trade as *dogs, loads* or *orphans.*

default and **defalcate** (deh–FAL–kayt). To *default* is to fail to make a payment, either loan or installment, when it is due. To *defalcate* is to embezzle that for which one is responsible. An example of defalcation would be the theft of money or property by a trustee.

demurrage (deh–MER–ij). *Demurrage* is the detention of a freight car, trailer or other cargo carrier beyond the agreed upon schedule, usually caused by delay in loading or unloading. Also, the fee charged by the transportation company as compensation for such delay.

earnest money. When a price for a property has been agreed upon, the buyer gives the seller *earnest money,* both as a down payment and as a *binder* (see **binder,** above). If the buyer fails to complete the purchase, the *earnest money* is forfeited to the seller to compensate him for the time the property was off the market.

easement. If a person wishes a right of way over a piece of real property, he must obtain an easement from the property owner. This is a legal document that is filed in the same manner as a deed or incorporated in a deed.

eminent domain. The right of *eminent domain* is the right of a government to take over private property if it is essential to the public good. Government appraisers usually determine the amount to be paid for the property, although the matter sometimes goes to the courts. This right is exercised many times in the building of thruways.

escrow. Money held in *escrow* is money held by a third party for a specific purpose and until a specific time. If your mortgage bank pays your taxes, it will place part of each mortgage payment in *escrow* until the taxes are due. Also, a deed, bond or piece of property can be held in *escrow* by a third party until certain conditions are met.

factoring. Factoring is the practice of using accounts receivable as a means of obtaining immediate cash. A company may either sell its accounts receivable to a *factoring agent* for less than the face value of the accounts or it may put them up as security for a short-term loan.

fiscal. *Fiscal* means pertaining to the finances of a government, company or individual. It is most often used in *fiscal year*, any twelve consecutive months that are the basis of financial operation. The *fiscal year* is not necessarily the same as the calendar year.

franchise. This is a legal authorization by a government or company for someone else to function on its behalf. Governments grant *franchises* to public utilities such as bus lines, gas and electric companies and radio stations. Manufacturers grant *franchises* to local dealers to sell or distribute their products.

gross national product. This is the sum of the value of all products and services of a nation over the period of one year. Often abbreviated GNP, it is used as a basis for comparison of a nation's current prosperity with its prosperity in previous years or with the prosperity of another country.

increment. This can mean any increase, addition or gain in quantity or value. A growth in population may cause a piece of property to increase in value, thus acquiring an *unearned increment*. However, if the increase results from improvements by the property owner it amounts to an *earned increment*. The distinction is sometimes made by tax officials.

infringement. *Infringement* in the legal sense consists of trespassing on the rights of others. Any right protected by law —such as copyright, patent or trademark—is jealously guarded by the owner and any *infringement* of that right may lead to legal action.

kickback. A *kickback* is a sum paid, through confidential arrangement, by a seller to a purchasing agent or someone else capable of influencing a purchase. It is a form of extortion in that the person handling the buying is threatening to withhold the purchase unless he gets a *kickback*.

kiting. There are two ways of *kiting* a check. One is by taking another person's check and raising the amount for which it is written without the knowledge or consent of the check writer. The other is by writing a check against insufficient bank funds in order to obtain temporary cash or credit.

lien. A *lien* is a claim on a piece of property which must be satisfied before the property can be transferred or sold. In extreme cases, property can be sold to satisfy the *lien*. Most contracts for sale specify that all *liens* be met before any sale can be completed. The most usual are mechanics', plumbers', electricians' and carpenters' *liens*.

liquidation. *Liquidation* is the settlement of all claims against a company or a person's estate through the use of available cash or sale of assets. Just as such a settlement occurs at the death of a person, so it occurs at the closing down of a business or enterprise.

loss leader. Many of the "one-day specials" advertised by retail outlets can be classified as *loss leaders*. The designation comes from the fact that, while the store may make no profit, and even take a loss by selling at that price, the purpose is to lead customers into the store in the hope that they will also purchase other more profitable items.

margin. The *margin* on the stock market, as established by the Securities Exchange Commission, is the difference between the cost of a stock and the amount of credit that a stock broker is allowed to extend for its purchase. In other words, it amounts to partial payment which allows the customer to obtain title to more stocks than he can pay for. However, under SEC regulations the *margin* (stated in terms of percentage) is kept fairly high and represents the greater part of the cost of a stock.

odd-lot sale. In many industries, products are sold only in lots or units consisting of a set number of items. A partial unit is an *odd-lot*. An *odd-lot* sale of shoes would mean the sale of odds and ends of styles or sizes. Whether on the wholesale or retail level, such a sale is in effect a clearance at a lower price. In the stock market the usual *lot* is one hundred shares and a sale involving fewer than that is an *odd-lot* sale.

portal-to-portal pay. Under the conditions of *portal-to-portal pay,* a worker is paid from the time he passes through the entrance (*portal*) of his employer's property until he leaves the property at the end of the work day. This means he is not docked for the time needed to don his uniform or reach his work station.

prospectus (pros–PEK–tuss). This is a formal written description of a proposed enterprise or venture, compiled for the information of those who may invest or participate in it. A *prospectus* for a reference book should contain a statement of the scope of a book, its potential market, suggestions for a title, an outline and a sample chapter. A *prospectus* for a company which is planning a new stock issue must give a complete picture of the company's financial history and present condition, as well as the prospects for future profits.

proxy. A *proxy* is formal authorization for another person to exercise one's voting rights. In the business world, *proxies* are important at the time of a stockholders' meeting, since many holders of small amounts of stock do not bother to attend the meetings and are willing to give their *proxies* either to those who control the company or to others who are trying to achieve control.

push merchandise. In the retail trade, *push merchandise* (or PM as it is known) is merchandise that is not selling well which salesmen are told to urge on their customers. Sometimes it merely represents an overstock and sometimes it consists of inferior goods.

quality control. To avoid variation in the quality of their products, manufacturers use a system called *quality control.* It consists of careful, regular inspection—as, for example, of every tenth or every fiftieth finished item.

retainer. The fee paid a lawyer or other professional to assure that he or she will be available when needed. As opposed to salary, it does not usually call for full-time activity on behalf of the client, but is based on an agreement that, for a specified amount, the professional's services will be available for broadly defined duties. In the case of an attorney, the *retainer* may be only the advance payment, with further fees to be based on the amount of time and work involved.

royalty. A *royalty* may be a percentage of the selling price or a fixed sum for the item produced. An author's contract may call for a graduated *royalty* on the sale of his book, with the percentage increasing with increased sales. Composers receive *royalties* on the sale or performance of their work; inventors' *royalties* are based on the number of items sold; land owners' *royalties* may be based on the amount of natural resources taken from land which they have leased on a *royalty* basis.

stock split. When a company announces a *stock split,* it means that each shareholder then holds twice or triple the number of shares he held before, depending on whether the *split* was two-for-one or three-for-one. However, the total face value of all his shares remains unchanged. The *stock split* is a device to lower the market price of the individual share of stock in order to encourage further sales and, in some cases, wider participation by stockholders in the affairs of the company.

taxpayer. In this instance, a *taxpayer* is a building, not a person. Rather than let a piece of land remain vacant while taxes build up, the owner may erect a temporary building, the income from which he knows will be only sufficient to meet the taxes. This building is known as a *taxpayer.* Usually the owner has plans for more profitable use of the land sometime in the future.

test marketing. Before putting a new product on the market nationally, it has become the practice of manufacturers, particularly those making household products such as detergents, to select an area or several areas of the country for *test marketing.* Sales and promotion of the item in these areas are watched very carefully. If changes need to be made in the packaging or in the advertising, they can then be made more simply than if nationwide distribution had taken place at once. When the manufacturer is satisfied he has the best approach worked out, he proceeds with general distribution. This is why the new laundry detergent or auto wax which you may encounter when traveling may not yet be available in your area.

time and motion study. This invention of efficiency experts is designed to increase profits as well as efficiency. The time it takes a worker to complete each step of his job is measured by a stop watch and then compared with the time taken by another worker on an identical job. Motions of various workers are filmed and compared. The result may be a change in method, a change in equipment, or a change in workers.

underwriter. In the insurance field, the *underwriter* is the company which guarantees the payment of a fixed sum in case of death or accident in return for payment of premiums, the amount of which is fixed in a contract signed by an officer of the company. Having signed the contract, he has "underwritten" the agreement. In the stock market, an *underwriter* is a broker who agrees to handle the sale of all stock in a new venture, guaranteeing that he will purchase all shares which are not sold to the general public.

venture capital. Money invested in an enterprise which is highly risky is known as *venture capital.*

write-off. This is an accounting term, much used by big business. It can mean elimination from "accounts receivable" of bad debts or uncollectable accounts. It can mean figuring the depreciation of a valuable asset over a period of years. All this, of course, is considered in light of, and reflected in, tax returns. Hence the phrase *tax write-off* as applied to such things as planes for company executives, since the costs are deducted as business expenses.

QUIZ ON TERMS FROM THE WORLDS OF BUSINESS AND INDUSTRY

Let's see how well you can cope with the language of the business world. As in the previous quiz, try to determine which lettered word or phrase most nearly matches the meaning of each numbered word. You will find the answers on page 182.

1. **Cartel:** (a) high-stakes stock market plunger;
   (b) combination in restraint of trade;
   (c) disposal place for discarded Edsels.
2. **Borax:** (a) fodder for mule teams; (b) flashy furniture;
   (c) artificial support for sagging stock prices.
3. **Eminent domain:** (a) right to condemn property;
   (b) right of Crown Prince to rule Wales;
   (c) failure to secure proper copyright.

4. **GNP:** (a) Great National Productions;
 (b) Gross National Performance;
 (c) Gross National Product.
5. **Liquidation:** (a) unexpected downpour;
 (b) emergency sell-off;
 (c) abrupt change in top management personnel.
6. **Proxy:** (a) former N.Y. theater magnate; (b) stand-in;
 (c) resident manager.
7. **Schlock:** (a) devalued stock; (b) used car dealer;
 (c) inferior merchandise.
8. **Klunk:** (a) sharp blow in the market;
 (b) fiscal irresponsibility; (c) poor used car.
9. **Stock split:** (a) dissension among stockbrokers;
 (b) devaluation of value of stock;
 (c) precarious theatrical venture.
10. **Blue chip:** (a) saddened stock analyst;
 (b) top-flight stock;
 (c) insider's hot tip on speculative stock.

5. Words and Phrases from the Worlds of Art, Literature and Music

Art, literature and music all have their own special vocabularies and all borrow from the general storehouse of language. Phrases like *coloratura soprano,* and *basso profundo,* for example, belong uniquely to the world of music and, more precisely, to the operatic and concert stages. Other words, primarily musical, have considerable value and wide application in general speech and writing. *Pianissimo,* strictly interpreted, is a musical instruction meaning "play very softly." But it also may be used in ordinary conversation, especially when a companion is discussing events or details of a business transaction in tones loud enough to be overheard. A quiet but firm "Pianissimo, please" should have the desired effect.

Strictly speaking an *epitaph* is an inscription on a gravestone or, as it has been facetiously defined, "a memorial that usually lies above about the one that lies below." But it can also be used figuratively in such a sentence as "Eisenhower's farewell address was the epitaph for an era." So it is with many another term, primarily literary in meaning, but capable of much wider general application. *Lampoon, irony* and *satire,* are examples.

The same of course is also true of many words borrowed from the arts. A word like *choreograph* would seem very strictly limited in application to the creating of dance patterns for ballet, opera or musical comedy. Yet even such an apparently limited word as this can add an extra dimension to such a sentence as: "From the first question of the press conference to the final 'Thank you, Mr. President,' it was a carefully choreographed performance."

Here, then, are some seventy-five words from the arts, literature and music—each with a precise meaning in its original field but often having extended senses which will add color, subtlety and strength to your conversation and writing. As usual, we'll have a quick brush-up quiz at the end of the chapter.

abstruse (ab–STROOS). A word we have borrowed directly from Latin, *abstruse* had the meaning of "hidden." It's used, chiefly in literary criticism, to indicate writing that is difficult to understand, obscure, complicated and unnecessarily hard to fathom. The writings of many scientists seem hopelessly *abstruse* to the layman, though there are a few notable exceptions such as the works of Isaac Asimov and George Gamow.

aesthete (es–THEET). This term has been used since the times of the ancient Greeks to indicate a person notable in his devotion to beauty, art and other aspects of culture. He is one who "has the love of the beautiful," as Bouchard once put it. Unfortunately there have been many poseurs over the centuries, many who have affected this devotion to beauty without truly feeling it. So *aesthete* and its adjectival form *aesthetic* (es–THET–ik) may also be applied to persons whose artistic protestations seem overdone and pretentious. Such a person, in the view of some critics, was the man whose name at the turn of the century was virtually synonymous with *aesthete*, Oscar Wilde.

allegory (AL–eh–gor–ee). This is a work, usually literary, that tells a relatively simple story intended as a parable, to refer to a deeper but parallel story of great significance. Thus the story of the quest for the Holy Grail can also be considered to be an *allegory* for man's everlasting search for spiritual truth. Many of the New Testament parables may be thought of as *allegorical* (al–eh–GOR–ih–k'l) devices for teaching deeper truths.

alliteration (uh–lit–er–AY–shun). This is a literary device involving the repetition of the same sound, often for humorous effect. "Weary Willie walked warily from Waukegan to Waukesha without once wetting his windbreaker." Note in this case that "once," while not commencing with the letter "w" does begin with the sound of "w."

andante (ahn–DAHN–tay). This is a musical instruction suggesting a moderate tempo. A conductor might well tell the orchestra: "We'll take this *andante*."

anticlimax. This can be either deliberate or accidental but, in any event, it involves the abrupt descent from a rather high plane to one ridiculously low or trivial. The late Monty Wooley, onetime drama coach at Yale, is reported to have described "For God, for Country and for Yale" as the most consummate *anticlimax* in the English language.

arabesque (ar–uh–BESK). An *arabesque* is an elaborate ornamentation, often a design containing intertwined floral and foliate figures. The term is also used to describe a ballet pose in which the dancer stands on one foot while the other leg is extended backward with the arms in any of a variety of standard positions. The word originally meant "of or in the Arabic fashion."

archive. This is a storage place, especially one designed to preserve rare and valuable documents. One of the most interesting buildings in our nation's capital is the National Archives Building where many of the country's most precious documents are stored.

aria (AH–ree–uh). Literally "air," this is an Italian word used in opera to mean a song for solo voice accompanied by orchestra.

arpeggio (ar–PEJ–ee–oh). This musical expression means that the notes of a chord are to be played in rapid succession, rather than simultaneously. The expression originally meant "played as on a harp" and, if you recall the sounds a harp makes, you will find the meaning of *arpeggio* easy to remember.

bibliophile (BIB–lee–oh–file). This is a person who truly loves books. The word itself, indeed, comes from two Greek words "biblion," meaning book, and "philos," meaning love. However, while every *bibliophile* is a book collector, it does not follow that every book collector is a *bibliophile*. The true *bibliophile* concerns himself with many features of each individual volume: the date of its printing, the quality of paper, the name of its designer, the condition of the binding and so on.

bilingual, multilingual. A person who converses and writes easily in two languages is *bilingual,* while one who is knowledgeable in three or more tongues is *multilingual.* One famous linguist, Charles Berlitz, is truly multilingual—he is fluent in thirty-two different languages and can "get around" in a few more.

brochure (broh–SHOOR). A pamphlet, especially a fairly elaborate pamphlet such as a company's Annual Report is often called a *brochure*. The word is borrowed from the French and means, literally, "stitching," from the fact that the leaves of early *brochures* were lightly stitched together.

cadenza (kuh–DEN–zuh). When a soloist adds elaborate ornamental flourishes to an aria or concerto he is embellishing it with *cadenzas*.

calligraphy (kuh–LIG–ruh–fee). An art that has been close to extinction but now seems to be experiencing a slight revival is *calligraphy*, beautiful handwriting or penmanship.

cavort (kuh–VORT). Bounding about in a gay, carefree manner is *cavorting*. One would not expect to find dancers cavorting in the classic ballet, but they well might in a madcap musical comedy.

chiaroscuro (kee–ar–uh–SKOOR–oh). In art, especially in painting, the distribution of light and shade is described as *chiaroscuro*. The word, which we take directly from Italian is a blend of "chiaro," meaning light or clear, and "oscuro," dark. Our word *obscure* is, of course, related to "oscuro."

choreography (kor–ee–OG–ruh–fee). Today's programs for musical plays invariably carry the notation "Choreography by So-and-so," meaning that So-and-so designed and directed the dances for the show. Until the late 1930s such program notations simply read "Dances by So-and-so." But then the great ballet master Balanchine was prevailed upon to do the dances for the musical "On Your Toes" and Richard Maney, the show's press agent, felt that a more elegant label was required. And so *choreography* was borrowed from the ballet, made the Broadway scene, and has been there ever since.

coloratura. Ornamental trills and runs in vocal music, especially when they are of a florid, showy nature, are referred to as *coloratura*. A soprano who specializes in this type of performance is known as a *coloratura soprano*. A trumpet soloist may perform a *cadenza* (see **cadenza** above) but not *coloratura*.

consonant (KON–suh–n'nt). A *consonant*, as every schoolboy knows, is anything in the alphabet that is not a vowel. However, *consonant* has another meaning commonly used in critical writing: in line with or in accordance with. So you might say: "Hemingway's posthumously published novel is completely *consonant* with his earlier work."

conundrum (kuh–NUN–drum). This may be any kind of a riddle, but it is usually one best answered with a pun. Here's a sample: "Why is a heavy snowfall easily understood? Because everyone can see the drift."

curator (KYOOR–ay–tor). The person who administers a museum or a particular collection within a museum is usually called the *curator*. The word comes from the Latin verb "curare," meaning to care for something.

definitive (deh–FIN–ih–tiv). When you want to say that a book, for example, is the last word on a subject, the most complete and authoritative treatment of a topic, say that it is the *definitive* work.

discordant (dis–KOR–d'nt). A harsh, unpleasant, inharmonious sound, as when one fiddle is badly out of tune or the lead trumpet fluffs a high note, is *discordant*. The term is also used in criticism. One might say, "The author's penchant for petty punning struck a *discordant* note in an otherwise entirely serious and commendable work."

disquisition (dis–kwih–ZISH–un). This is a rather elegant word that should be reserved for use in describing only the most formal discussions or learned essays. But a *disquisition* need not be dull. Bertrand Russell, Kenneth Clark and Robert Graves have all written *disquisitions* that managed to reflect their great erudition while remaining immensely readable.

doggerel (DOG–er–el). This is light, trivial verse, usually of little merit. Thus the work of versifiers like Ogden Nash, David McCord and Frank Sullivan, while light and humorous, is certainly not *doggerel*. For an example of *doggerel*, contemplate this:

> Fortyish girls who think that they
> With miniskirts can get away
> Shouldn't.

dulcet (DUL–set). Sweet-sounding, gentle to the ears. The word comes from the Latin word for sweet and Milton used it, for example, in writing of "*dulcet* symphonies and voices sweet."

dysphemism (DIS–phem–ism). Here's a rare word that just might come in handy. It's the opposite of *euphemism* which is, of course, a nice word for an unpleasant subject. When sociologists talk about the "inner city" and really mean slums, they are using a *euphemism*. But when the patron of a diner calls for some more "ink" when he means coffee, he is using a *dysphemism*.

elegy, eulogy. These two words are often confused with each other. An *elegy*, properly speaking, is a poem written in memory of or in tribute to a person who has died. It usually —as is to be expected—records the admirable deeds of the late departed, in accordance with the old Latin motto "De mortuis nil nisi bonum," Say nothing but good of the dead. A *eulogy*, on the other hand, is a tribute, not necessarily or even very often in verse, to a person who may still be very much alive. "The remarks of the Board Chairman at the retirement dinner constituted a warm, if somewhat sugary, eulogy of the departing Sales Manager."

enigma (eh–NIG–muh). This is a puzzle, usually of an intellectual nature. It may also be used to refer to a person or nation that baffles onlookers. Sir Winston Churchill once said: "I cannot forecast to you the action of Russia. It is a riddle wrapped in a mystery inside an enigma."

epigram (EP–ih–gram). This is a concise and often witty statement, usually with a satiric twist. Originally *epigrams* were short poems, though nowadays prose is more common. One verse *epigram* that has held up well over three and a half centuries is the following by Sir John Harington (1618):

Treason doth never prosper; what's the reason?
For if it prosper, none dare call it treason.

epigraph (EP–ih–graf). This should not be confused with *epigram*, though both come from the same Greek word "epigraphein," to write on. An *epigraph* is an inscription, usually engraved on a statue or building, though it may also be simply a dedication in a book. The most famous *epigraph* in America is probably the one on the Main Post Office building in New York City. Freely adapted from the Greek historian Herodotus, it reads: "Neither snow, nor rain, nor heat, not gloom of night stays these couriers from the swift completion of their appointed rounds."

epitaph (EP–ih–taf). As we have already seen, an *epitaph*, literally, is an inscription on a gravestone. Usually these are very serious indeed, but occasionally wit comes into play. Here's one that appeared on a dentist's gravestone: "Stranger, tread this ground with gravity; Dentist Brown is filling his last cavity." Occasionally, an epitaph will have a jaunty tone: "If there is a future world, my lot will not be bliss; but if there is no other, I've made the most of this." And then there is the rueful note sounded by comedian W. C. Fields who asked that his *epitaph* read: "On the whole I'd rather be in Philadelphia."

epitome (eh–PIT–uh–mee). An *epitome* may be a concise summary of a book or play, an abridgement faithful to the spirit and style of the original. It may also be the symbolic essence of an entire class or the embodiment of a whole way of life: "Sinatra seems the epitome of the successful swinger."

eponym (EP–uh–nym). In an earlier chapter of this book (Names Make Words), you will find many examples of *eponyms,* names of real or legendary people that have become common words. Caesar, for instance, lives on in the phrase *"Caesarian section,"* just as the Twelfth Earl of Derby was the *eponymous* ancestor of both the Epsom Downs Derby and the Kentucky Derby.

exhortation (ex–hor–TAY–shun). This is a rallying call, a speech designed to stir the listeners to action. There have been many stirring *exhortations* in our history, most of them for important causes, some pleading for nothing more than victory in a sports contest. Perhaps the most famous of the latter was the legendary half-time *exhortation* given by Notre Dame's football coach, Knute Rockne, when he "exhorted" his losing team to "Go out and win this one for the Gipper." The "Gipper" was George Gipp, a Notre Dame football hero who had recently died.

extempore (ex–TEM–puh–ree). This is a direct borrowing from Latin where it meant, literally, "out of time." We use it to mean without advance preparation, as in an *extempore* speech. It also appears in an adjective form as *extemporaneous* and verbally as *extemporize.* In show business *extemporizing* is usually called *ad libbing.*

falsetto (fol–SET–oh). This is a male voice pitched artificially high, well above its normal range. It's a word we take from the Italian word for "false."

florid (FLOR–id). This can mean either ruddy or flushed—as one might have a *florid* face. In the literary sense, it means exaggerated, fussy, ornate, flowery: "In writing company memoranda, you do well to avoid florid language."

forté (FOR–tay). In music this is a direction meaning "play, it loudly and powerfully."

grotesque (groh–TESK). Ugly, misshapen, ludicrously distorted, bizarre, these are the common senses in which this word is most often used. In Fine Arts it refers specifically to a style of art developed in sixteenth century Italy and characterized by groupings of monstrous or unnatural forms.

idyll (EYE–dil). Originally an *idyll* was a short poem, usually devoted to the simple pleasures of rural life. Now it can mean any episode characterized by refreshing naturalness and simplicity.

impresario (im–preh–SAR–ee–oh). In the worlds of opera, ballet and concert, the man who is ultimately responsible for organizing and producing the show is the *impresario*. It's a word we take unchanged from Italian, where it means "manager." The legendary *impresario* of this century is, of course, Sol Hurok who has brought the greatest talents from all the world to our country and has taken our greatest talents to the rest of the world.

irony (EYE–ruh–nee). This is wit more gentle than satire and much less broad than lampoon. It is usually touched with subtle humor and it always gently deflates any pomposity in its subject. Its technique is to employ words—just as satire often does—in precisely the opposite of their customary meanings. The famous speech in Shakespeare's *Julius Caesar* in which Marc Antony repeatedly refers to Caesar as "an honorable man" is considered a masterpiece of *irony*.

lampoon (lam–POON). This is broad, almost clownishly slapstick satire. It was a literary term often reserved for satire and mockery so sharp as to be abusive and intended to make its subject seem utterly contemptible. In modern usage, *lampoons* may be a bit more light-hearted, but they are still far less subtle than either *irony* or *satire*.

largo (LAR–goh). A musical instruction, meaning to proceed at a slow, stately pace. Like many musical terms, it comes from Italian where it meant slow or broad. Handel's *Largo* is one of the most justly popular items in the classical repertory. Not that it really matters, but the correct name for this piece is "Ombra mai fu" ("Shade never was") and it is an aria in his opera *Xerxes*. But the tempo indication was *Largo*

—and so the work has always been known in the public mind.

libretto (lih–BRET–oh). Literally "little book," this term is used to refer to the text of an opera or light opera. In musical comedy it's usually simply called the book, as in "Book by Morrie Ryskind, Lyrics by Ira Gershwin, Music by George Gershwin."

lucubration (loo–koo–BRAY–shun). When you ponder something long and carefully, you are "lucubrating" and the result of all your *lucubration* may well be a stuffy, pretentious and pedantic bore.

maestro (MY–stroh or mah–ES–troh). Again a word from Italian, where it means simply "master." A *maestro* may be a conductor, first-rank performer or respected music teacher.

mellifluous (mel–IF–loo–us). "Smooth and sweet as honey" is a common expression, and that's exactly what *mellifluous* means. It comes from two Latin words "mel," meaning honey, and "fluere," to flow. You might speak of the *mellifluous* tones of a well-played cello.

obbligato (ob–lih–GAH–toh). This means musical accompaniment, but it means something more than just that. It is an essential element in the performance of a piece of music: *obbligato,* in Italian, means "obligatory," "indispensable."

omnibus (OM–nih–bus). We all know that the motor bus gets its name from *omnibus,* the Latin word meaning "for everyone." But in its literary application an *omnibus* is usually a collection of various writings of a single author, for example, *The Faulkner Omnibus.*

oratorio (or–uh–TOR–ee–oh). This is a formal musical composition for chorus and orchestra, usually treating a sacred subject. The word comes from the Latin word "orare," to pray. From this came the word *oratory,* meaning a place for prayer. In the sixteenth century the Oratory of St. Philip Neri in Rome was famous for the quality of the musical services held there, and that's where *oratorio* comes from.

ornate (or–NATE). Elaborately ornamented, flashy, showy or flowery. As a term of literary criticism, it is not very flattering. "The style is ornate and many of the opinions outrageous."

paean (PEE–an). The original *paeans* in Greece were hymns of praise to Apollo. Then the word came to mean any exultant shout or song of joy.

panegyric (pan–eh–JY–rik or pan–eh–JIR–ik). This, in Greek, was any formal speech intended to be delivered at a great public occasion. Since such speeches had a way of ending up full of praise for the leader of the day, *panegyric* gradually came to mean a speech highly praising a particular person. Now it has extended its meaning to cover any sort of excessive eulogy or elaborate praise.

parody (PAIR–uh–dee). This is a mocking imitation or burlesque, especially of a work of literature or of the style of a particular author or publication. One of the most notable *parodies* of recent years was Wolcott Gibbs' New Yorker magazine *parody* of the style then characteristic of Time magazine. One specialty of Timestyle, as it was called, was the backward-running sentence, with the subject at the end rather than at the beginning. The final sentence of Gibbs' article summed it up neatly: "Where this all will end knows God."

pastiche (pas–TEESH). In Italian this word means pretty much the same as our hodgepodge or miscellany. It's usually used to describe a work, literary, dramatic or musical, made up of a variety of odds and ends which satirize elements of previous compositions.

peroration (per–or–AY–shun). This is the formal windup of a speech. In some instances, to the lasting pain of the listeners, the *peroration* lasts almost as long as the oration itself and the speaker's "one last word" seems never-ending.

persiflage (PER–sih–flahzh). This is light-hearted, humorous banter, the kind of airy interchange characteristic of the early Cary Grant and Fred Astaire films.

perusal (per–OOZ–ul). Examining and reading a book or document, especially with critical intent, is *perusal*.

pianissimo (pee–uh–NISS–ih–moh). As we have already seen, this musical term from Italian literally means "play very softly" and may be used in non-musical contexts as an admonition to a companion to talk more quietly. We tend to think of *piano* only as the name of a musical instrument, yet it originally was the Italian word for "soft." The original name for the instrument, incidentally, was *pianoforte,* a blend of the Italian phrase "piano e forte," soft and loud, which is certainly what a *piano* can be when in skilled hands.

picaresque (pik–uh–RESK). The epitome of the *picaresque* rogue is unquestionably Fielding's Tom Jones. This devil-may-care rapscallion has had many imitators but few equals. The *picaresque* novel originated in Spain and takes its name from the Spanish word "pícaro," rogue.

pleasantry (PLEZ–un–tree). This is simply a light-hearted, jesting remark or comment.

preciosity (presh–ee–OSS–ih–tee). This term means over-fastidiousness in style of writing, affected refinement, indeed over-refinement in language. This quality is seldom encountered in today's literature but it was fairly common in the works of nineteenth century writers.

satire (SAT–ire). George S. Kaufman, the playwright, once defined satire thus: "Satire is what closes Saturday night." What he meant, of course, is that the subtleties of true *satire*, the use of wit to expose human folly or wickedness, are lost on Broadway audiences accustomed to broad comedy of a slapstick or pratfall variety.

sibilant (SIB–ih–l'nt). If you have trouble with your "S's" and people think you're hissing when you really aren't, you had better begin to worry about your *sibilants*. The word, logically enough, comes from the Latin "sibilare," to hiss or whistle.

solecism (SOL–eh–sizm). An improper grammatical construction, especially one that flagrantly violates the proprieties of speech or writing is a *solecism*. The word comes from Greek and it originally referred to a dialect spoken by Athenian colonists at Soloi in Cilicia, an ancient country in Asia Minor. Apparently what they did to Athenian Greek struck as harshly on the ears of the proper Athenians as, shall we say, a South Boston accent strikes a proper Bostonian. Anyhow, *solecism* became the name for any grammatical or linguistic impropriety. If you hear someone saying "irregardless" or using "flout" when he means "flaunt," you may justly accuse him of committing a solecism. But you had better be ready to duck.

synopsis (sin–OP–sis). This is a brief digest version of a story or novel, the highlights, as it were, of a longer narrative.

tautology (taw–TOL–uh–jee). This is a sin we have all been guilty of at one time or another—needlessly repeating the same idea in different words. It comes from two Greek words "tautos," same or identical, and "logos," word.

timbre (TIM–ber or TAM–ber). The distinctive peculiarity of a musical sound that distinguishes it from other sounds of the same pitch and volume is its *timbre*. It may also refer to the human voice. One can say that he recognizes a friend's voice on the phone because of its distinctive *timbre*.

travesty (TRAV–ess–tee). A grotesque burlesque, especially one broadly ridiculing a well-known work. "Some shocked auditors regarded the rock version of the 'Star Spangled Banner' as nothing short of an obscene travesty."

trivia (TRIV–ee–uh). The term literally means "trifling things." The word comes from the Latin word "trivium," meaning "three roads" or the place where they meet. In a public place nothing of consequence would be talked about.

QUIZ ON TERMS FROM THE WORLDS OF ART, LITERATURE AND MUSIC

Here are ten of the words you have just been reading about. After each you will find a choice of three words or phrases, one of which means the same or nearly the same as the numbered word. Choose the one you think is closest in meaning. If you think that (b) is closest in meaning to 2, your answer is obviously 2b. When you have checked all ten, look at the answers on page 182. If you answered wrong, the thing for you to do is to review the word and make it yours for keeps.

1. **Abstruse:** (a) concise; (b) hard to fathom; (c) complicated.
2. **Bibliophile:** (a) librarian; (b) writer of books;
   (c) book collector.
3. **Calligraphy:** (a) wall-writing; (b) penmanship;
   (c) soprano's trills.
4. **Epigraph:** (a) pithy saying; (b) digest version;
   (c) wall-writing.
5. **Eponym:** (a) word from name; (b) plagiarism;
   (c) operatic song.
6. **Lucubration:** (a) deep thought; (b) grease job;
   (c) careful speech.
7. **Pastiche:** (a) hodgepodge; (b) clown makeup;
   (c) brisk tune.
8. **Perusal:** (a) dress rehearsal; (b) reading;
   (c) dedication to patron.
9. **Sibilant:** (a) close relative; (b) hissing; (c) counterpoint.
10. **Solecism:** (a) lonely poet; (b) gross error;
    (c) broad mockery.

6. Words and Phrases from the Language of World Affairs

For the first three centuries of its existence, America was a remarkably isolated continent. Until the revolution, our country was simply one of many colonial concerns of the major world powers—England, Holland, France and Spain. Even after the colonies declared their independence from the mother land and became the United States of America, most Americans not directly involved in international trade or diplomacy lived lives of—in retrospect—amazing isolation. Though we shared, as has been noted earlier in this volume, a common language with England, we had little of Great Britain's worldly outlook. Perhaps because we had our hands full extending what historian Walter Prescott Webb called "The Great Frontier," we paid little attention to matters outside our borders.

Even when, toward the end of the nineteenth century, we became involved in warfare with Spain over Cuba and the Philippines, our national involvement was relatively trifling. The war itself was of such insignificance that Secretary of State John Hay could label it "a splendid little war" and Theodore Roosevelt could dismiss the war which brought him to "rough-rider" fame as "not much of a war, but the best we had."

World War I seemed to change all this. For the first time many hundreds of thousands of our young men saw Europe, through the courtesy of the armed forces. But the centuries-old spirit of isolationism was still strong, the attempt to involve us in world affairs through membership in the League of Nations was rebuffed, and, during the 1920s and early 1930s, most Americans acted as though the rest of the world didn't exist. The words of Washington's Farewell Address, "steer clear of permanent alliances, with any portion of the foreign world," were piously quoted in newspaper editorials times without number.

But World War II and its aftermath changed all that, and the day is long past when any one of us can afford to ignore the language of world affairs, the special words and phrases peculiar to diplomats and envoys, peacemakers and warriors alike. We ignore at our peril terms like *junta, insurgent, sabotage, protocol* and *reprisal.*

All these words and many more of immediate interest and concern to all of us in globally conscious America are discussed in the next few pages. As usual, there will be a brisk brush-up quiz at the chapter's end.

aggrandizement (uh–GRAN–diz–m'nt). Aggrandizement is an increase in influence, power, stature or wealth. It may be personal or national but is usually the latter.

ambassador (am–BAS–uh–dor). While we tend to think of the term *ambassador* as applying only to the highest ranking diplomatic official representing his country in another nation, there are several types of *ambassador.*

An *ambassador-at-large* is one who is not assigned to any one country but who may be called upon to represent his nation anywhere and at any time the President requests. An *ambassador extraordinary* is one who is assigned to accomplish a specific mission. An *ambassador plenipotentiary* is one who is authorized to negotiate treaties.

The man whom we usually think of just as *ambassador* is really *ambassador extraordinary and plenipotentiary,* the highest ranking diplomatic official representing his country in another nation, assigned specific duties and empowered to negotiate treaties. Since he resides in a foreign nation, this type of ambassador is not "at large."

attaché (at–ash–AY). Included in an ambassador's diplomatic corps are the various *attachés,* such as *military attaché* and *cultural attaché,* men attached to and advising the ambassador. Each is an expert in the field on which he advises. His badge of office is his *attaché case,* a small, stiff brief case which has now become the hallmark of the big city business executive.

bloc (BLOK). This was originally a French word which literally meant "block." In international affairs, a *bloc* is an informal grouping of nations which can be expected to act in unison, such as the Soviet *bloc.*

brush fire war. Recent years have seen a number of brush fire wars within nations or between smaller nations, particularly in Africa. A *brush fire war* is one that quickly ignites as from a spark, flares and spreads rapidly. It can also end as abruptly as it started.

communiqué (kuh–myoo–nih–KAY). A French word meaning communication, this term has a more specific meaning in English. It is used to designate an *official* communication concerning an important event or situation. A military *communiqué* is meant to inform officially what actions have been taken or will be taken.

concordat (kon–KOR–dat). This is a formal agreement between a pope of the Roman Catholic Church and the head of government of a nation regarding the administration of church affairs. In general use, it can also mean any formal agreement.

consul (KON–s'l). While a *consul* is appointed by his government to reside in a foreign city, his duties are not really of a diplomatic nature. He represents the commercial interests of his country. In addition, he is able to give advice and assistance to his fellow citizens residing or visiting in that city. For major cities in which a country has extensive commercial interests, a *consul general* is appointed. In addition to his duties within that particular city, the *consul general* supervises the other *consuls* in his area.

de facto, de jure (dee–FAK–toh, dee–JOOR–ee). Here are two Latin phrases. The first, *de facto,* means "in fact" or actual. The second means "according to law." Thus a *de facto* government is the one which is actually in power. It is not necessarily the *de jure* government, the one which has the legal right to govern.

deputation (dep–yoo–TAY–sh'n). A person or group authorized to act as a delegation.

détente (day–TAUNT). We have taken this word from the French to describe an easing or lessening of tensions between nations.

embargo (em–BAR–goh). An *embargo* is the suspension, by government order, of foreign trade. It may be total or it may affect a specific commodity. The term may also mean a government order prohibiting the movement of merchant ships in and out of its ports. In a narrower sense, it means an injunction prohibiting any common carrier from accepting certain items for shipment.

embassy (EM–buh–see). The word *embassy* may mean either the building that serves as the official headquarters of an ambassador or it may refer to the ambassador and his staff.

emissary (EM–ih–sehr–ee). An *emissary* is a person sent on a special mission, particularly a secret or delicate one.

enclave (ON–klayv). Derived from an Old French word "enclaver," to enclose. An *enclave* is a territory which is completely surrounded by a foreign country and has no access to the rest of the world except via foreign land. Vatican City and San Marino are *enclaves* in Italy.

entente (on–TAUNT). Here is another word which the French have contributed to the language of diplomacy. Taken from the Old French "entendre," which means to understand, *entente* is an understanding between or among nations. It is not a formal treaty but an agreement, arrived at through diplomatic conversation, which leads to common action and policy. Such an agreement, known as the *Entente Cordiale* existed between France and England prior to World War I. When Russia joined with them it became the *Triple Entente*.

envoy (EN–voy). A diplomatic representative sent on a special mission is known as an *envoy*. This is another word of French derivation, being taken from the word "envoyer," to send.

ex cathedra (ex kuh–THEE–dra). The literal translation of this Latin phrase is "from the chair." It is used as an adjective to describe a pronouncement or statement from the seat of authority, as from a high-ranking official. Originally it was used only for papal pronouncements but its use has extended into the field of diplomacy.

fifth column. This phrase was coined during the Spanish Civil War by one of Franco's generals, Emilio Mola, who boasted that he had four columns of soldiers to lead against Madrid and a fifth column of sympathizers within the city. It has come to mean any secret and subversive organization aiding an enemy of a country.

geopolitics (jee–oh–POL–ih–tix). *Geopolitics* is the study of the effect of geography on the politics and foreign policy of a nation. It was the basis of a Nazi doctrine of expansion which called for the reallocation of the world's geographic and political boundaries.

ideology (eye–dee–OL–uh–jee). The political and social philosophy of an individual, group or class.

imperialism (im–PEER–ee–ul–izm). The United States has been accused on a number of occasions of being an *imperialistic* nation as have other great powers since the days of Rome. *Imperialism* is a national policy of extending political authority over other nations either by direct acquisition of territory or by achieving indirect economic control.

in camera. In these days of world-wide television coverage, *in camera* may seem an odd phrase to find in a list of words on world affairs. However, it is pertinent because it is Latin for "in chamber" and applies to a conference which is private and closed to the public, if not entirely secret.

insurgent (in–SER–junt). One who rebels against constituted authority is an *insurgent*. The term is also applied to a member of a political party who does not conform to the policies of his party.

jingo. This word has its origin in a chauvinistic refrain sung by Britishers who wanted to fight Russia in the 1870s. A *jingo* is an extremely nationalistic person, especially one who favors a belligerent foreign policy.

junta (HOON–tuh or JUN–tuh). The word *junta* was originally reserved for a small legislative body or council in Latin American countries. In the course of history, it has come to mean any small group, especially one of military officers, who control a country after a seizure of power.

lobbyist. Being a *lobbyist* is a legitimate profession, although a few dishonest ones have given the term a bad connotation. A *lobbyist* is one who has been hired by a group, organization or government to work for or against the passage of legislation. *Lobbyists* working in Washington for foreign governments must be registered with Congress.

mercenary (MER–s'n–ehr–ee). Once known as a soldier of fortune, a *mercenary* is one who is hired to fight for a foreign country.

moratorium. In 1969, the word *moratorium* acquired a new meaning, that of a mass gathering of people for a political purpose, when people across the nation suspended their usual schedules to gather in demonstrations for peace. The original meaning of the word was the legal authorization for a delay or a suspension of payment of debts, especially those of a nation. By extension, it came to mean a delay of any action.

peaceful coexistence. When two nations of widely different ideologies live at peace with one another, you have peaceful coexistence. Senator J. William Fulbright may not have coined the phrase but he used it thus in a Senate speech on March 27, 1964: "The character of the cold war has been profoundly altered . . . by the implicit repudiation by both sides of a policy of total victory. . . . The effect has been to commit us to a policy that can be accurately, though perhaps not prudently, defined as one of 'peaceful co-existence.' "

plebiscite (PLEB–ih–syte). This word comes from the Latin "plebiscitum" which means people's decree and it is precisely that. A *plebiscite* is a nation-wide vote, which gives all the people a chance to help determine their form of government or choice of ruler.

plenary (PLEE–nuh–ree or PLEN–uh–ree). A *plenary* session of the United Nations is one at which all members are present. The term can be applied to any fully attended meeting.

political asylum (uh–SY–lum). In general use, an *asylum* is a place of safety. The meaning goes back to ancient times when criminals or debtors could find *asylum* in a temple or church where they would be protected from arrest. The basic meaning is retained in the phrase *political asylum*. One way of seeking political asylum is by going to a foreign embassy in one's own country and asking for protection and transportation to another country. The other is to escape to another country and ask to be allowed to stay permanently. Good political reasons are necessary in either case.

portfolio (port–FOH–lee–oh). Actually, a *portfolio* is simply a case for carrying documents. Because diplomats and cabinet members use such cases to carry official documents, the word has come to mean the office and duties of such an official. A *minister without portfolio* is a member of a cabinet who is not in charge of any department of state.

propaganda (prop–uh–GAN–duh). Derived from the Latin word meaning "to spread or extend," *propaganda* is anything —true or untrue—publicized for the purpose of promoting a doctrine or form of government. In light of this objective, the material is carefully selected to present the matter in its most effective form.

protocol (PROH–tuh–kol). The most common use of the word *protocol* is to designate the rules of diplomatic etiquette governing the relationships of heads of state, ministers and members of the diplomatic corps. In addition, it means a first draft of a diplomatic document or a summation of the details of diplomatic negotiations on which a formal treaty will be based.

reparations (rep–er–AY–shuns). At the close of hostilities, a victorious nation may demand *reparations* from the defeated country, meaning that it is demanding compensation for damage it has suffered during the war. *Reparations* may be in the form of money and/or materials and may include indemnity for expenditures for the war. The word comes from the Latin word "reparare" which translates to prepare anew.

reprisal (reh–PRYZE–'l). Under International Law, an act of *reprisal* is the use of military force, short of war, in revenge for an injury suffered.

sabotage (SAB–uh–tahzh). To *sabotage* is to deliberately delay or disrupt. Derived from the French "saboter," to clatter wooden shoes (sabots), hence to work clumsily. The word first appeared in English around 1910 and was used to refer to acts by workers rebelling against their employers. During World War I, it acquired the additional meaning of hindering a nation's war efforts by blowing up bridges, machinery and railroads.

sanction (SANK–sh'n). While *sanction* generally means formal approval, *government sanctions* are quite the opposite. When a nation violates international law, several other nations may join together to invoke *government sanctions* to force that nation to cease its violations. The *sanctions* may take the form of withholding loans or payments, limiting trade relations or blockading its ports.

subversive (sub–VER–siv). A *subversive* program or a *subversive* person is one whose purpose is to destroy or overthrow an established government. It comes from the Latin "subvertere" meaning to turn upside down.

totalitarianism. The complete centralization of all government controls, exercised by coercive measures and resulting in the subordination of the individual to the state.

ukase (yoo–KAYSS or YOO–kayss). In imperial Russia, a *ukase* was a proclamation of the czar which had the force of law. Present-day usage permits its application to any authoritative proclamation, edict or decree.

ultimate weapon. The term *ultimate weapon* is a product of the international arms race in which various nations are seeking a weapon against which there is no defense. The term could be considered a euphemism **for the** device that could bring the end of the world.

vanguard. The soldiers in the front of an army constitute the *vanguard*. Hence, those leading a political or social movement are in the *vanguard* of that movement.

QUIZ ON TERMS FROM
THE LANGUAGE OF WORLD AFFAIRS

Now let's see how well you have mastered the language of the world's diplomats. As in previous quizzes, try to find the lettered word closest in meaning to each numbered word. The answers are on page 182.

1. **Attaché:** (a) person deeply devoted to his native land;
   (b) Madison Avenue advertising salesman;
   (c) ambassador's aide.
2. **Communiqué:** (a) famous French female counterspy;
   (b) official communication;
   (c) satellite transmission of news.
3. **Embargo:** (a) lessening of tensions;
   (b) suspension of trade;
   (c) shipment of arms to guerillas.
4. **De jure:** (a) actual; (b) fictional; (c) legal.
5. **Ex cathedra:** (a) government by intuition;
   (b) pronouncement from on high;
   (c) church-state treaty.
6. **Jingo:** (a) merry melody; (b) chauvinist; (c) subversive.
7. **Junta:** (a) invasion barge; (b) papal principality;
   (c) ruling military clique.
8. **Mercenary:** (a) soldier for hire; (b) undercover agent;
   (c) military paymaster.
9. **Plenary:** (a) annual; (b) ambassadorial; (c) fully attended.
10. **Protocol:** (a) symbol of authority; (b) diplomatic etiquette;
   (c) payments from defeated nation.

7. Colorful Stories behind
Common Expressions

One of the most painless and rewarding ways to increase your interest in words is to discover the often surprising stories behind some of our commonplace expressions. One distinguished linguist of my acquaintance calls such oddities as the origins of *booby hatch, baker's dozen* and *slogan* items for the "Old Curiosity Shop of Etymology." He's right, of course, but he is also slighting one of the truly interesting aspects of our language.

In an earlier chapter (Names Make Words) we traced the history of scores of everyday words like *raglan* and *macadam* that were originally names of people. Here you will find the stories behind expressions you may well use almost any day of your life. Most of them, we'll wager, have entered your vocabulary without your ever having been aware of or even very curious about where they came from. If this chapter serves to pique your curiosity about the stories behind everyday expressions, you may want to explore still further; this material is merely a sampling of the riches available in such books as Brewer's *Dictionary of Phrase and Fable,* Charles Earle Funk's *Thereby Hangs a Tale,* Wilfred Funk's *Word Origins and their Romantic Stories* and, of course, the various volumes of *Dictionary of Word and Phrase Origins* by William and Mary Morris.

Most general dictionaries devote considerable space to tracing the history or etymology of words. However, because of limitations of space, their accounts are necessarily skeletonized, so it remains for such books as those mentioned in the preceding paragraph—and others which your local librarian will be happy to recommend to you—to flush out the full, always interesting and often surprising stories behind everyday expressions. And now, appropriately enough for a book written by an unabashed triskaidekaphile, we'll start with *baker's dozen*. What's that, you don't know what a *triskaidekaphile* is? Well, it's a person who loves the number 13 and it's made up of two Greek words "triskaideka," thirteen, and "philos," love. Your author comes naturally by his affection for the number because he was born on the thirteenth day of April, and, if you count carefully, you'll find that he has thirteen letters in his name.

baker's dozen. A *baker's dozen* consists, of course, of thirteen rather than the conventional twelve. In these days of pre-packaged baked goods, the reality of a *baker's dozen* of doughnuts, for instance, is rare indeed. Still the expression persists. Indeed, it has had a very long life, going all the way back to the fifteenth century when bakers had reputations even worse than today's used car dealers. To put it mildly, bakers were notorious cheaters and short-weighting a customer was close to standard practice. When the laity got its back up and demanded reform, the fifteenth century equivalent of today's Consultant on Consumer Concerns suggested a remedy that would restore bakers to good repute: simply put a thirteenth doughnut, roll or whatever in with every dozen purchased.

At about the same time in history it was a common folk belief that whenever the devil called a meeting of witches, the number that appeared was invariably thirteen. Thus the *devil's dozen* was also thirteen, and, for as long as the bakers were in such disrepute that they had to toss in the thirteenth roll, the word *baker* was regarded as practically synonymous with *devil*. And that's where the oarsman's expression "Pull devil, pull baker" came from.

There was also a theory that the practice of the *baker's dozen* came from the book publishing industry where there was once such an item as a *printer's dozen*. That's right—thirteen again. In those days, the book dealer sold each book at the price he had paid the printer for it so the thirteenth book represented his margin of profit. Interestingly enough, although book retailers nowadays work on a fairly substantial markup between the wholesale and retail prices, the custom of "one free with ten" as a special prepublication promotion offer is still commonplace.

battle royal. A battle in which many persons take part and which is fought to the finish is a *battle royal*. Originally, the term was used for an elimination tournament in the so-called "sport" of cock-fighting in which sixteen cocks fight it out to see who will be the sole survivor.

beer and skittles. In medieval England, a favorite pastime was indulging in *beer and skittles*. Skittles was a game in which a large elliptical wooden "cheese" was hurled at ninepins arranged in the form of a diamond. The hurling was done in much the same fashion as the discus throw in track and field games. So, if some project is "not all beer and skittles," there's little pleasure in it.

behind the eight ball. This is no place to be if you can avoid it. It means you may be, and probably are, in serious trouble. The phrase comes from a game of pool in which the balls are numbered from one to fifteen. The *eight ball* is black. The object of the game is to pocket the balls in numerical succession, with the exception of the *eight ball*, which is last. In the meantime, if another ball strikes the *eight ball*, the player is penalized.

best man. The original *best man* had far more strenuous duties than getting the groom to church on time and handing him the wedding ring at the right moment. Centuries ago in Scotland, the method of acquiring a mate was more of the caveman variety—simply kidnap the girl. To do this the groom needed help and he selected his "groomsmen" from the strongest and bravest of his friends, the strongest and bravest of them all being called the *best man*.

bilk. To *bilk* today means to cheat or defraud. As a variant form of *to balk*, it comes to us from the game of cribbage where it meant to prevent an opponent from scoring.

booby hatch. In nautical terms, a *booby hatch* is the covering over a hatch leading to quarters below deck. The *booby* is a kind of sea bird and this hatch was its favorite resting place. However, *booby* also means a "dunce" and *booby hatch* has long been a slang term for an insane asylum. One theory combining the two meanings is that it was common practice to force a deranged sailor into the *booby hatch*, making it possible to confine him until port was reached.

brand new. If you take the word *brand* in the sense of a piece of burning wood, you have a clue to the origin of this phrase, which dates back to the Middle Ages. In those days when open fires were used to mold metal objects, the finished product when taken from the flames was called *brand new*.

caboose. The last car of a freight train, where the trainmen can work and ride, is known as the *caboose*. It was not always so. The word comes from two Dutch words, "kaban huis," which later melted into one word, "kabuys," and which meant ship's galley. It was used in this sense for many years before it became the name for a railroad car.

corduroy. The ribbed cotton corduroy of today is a far cry from the original "corde du roi," a silk fabric used by French kings for their hunting habits.

curfew. Although a curfew these days is a deadline for being abroad at night, the word is derived from the French "couvre feu," to cover the fire. The first curfews were literally that, a warning to put out all fires. In the Middle Ages the danger of fire spreading through a village was so great that it became the custom to ring a loud bell at the same time each evening as a signal to extinguish all fires.

fascism. This word, which today means dictatorship by the extreme right, goes back to the Latin word "fasces," a bundle of sticks used in ancient Rome as a symbol of authority. One of Aesop's fables had shown that, while sticks could be broken individually, it was impossible to break a bound bundle of sticks. Therefore, the men who accompanied the Roman magistrates carried fasces to command respect for the magistrates. Mussolini took the bundle as a symbol when he marched on Rome in 1922 and his ideology and that of his followers became known as *fascism*.

foolscap. A kind of writing or printing paper approximately 13 x 16 inches, which when folded becomes the size of legal paper, 13 x 8, *foolscap* takes its name from the watermark of the first stationery of this kind. The original *foolscap*, which bore the watermark of a fool's cap and bells, was made in England before the time of Shakespeare.

honeymoon. A modern *honeymoon* can consist of a weekend or a world cruise, depending on the finances of the groom. The *honeymoon* in ancient times, however, consisted of exactly thirty days—or a moon. The custom was for the bride and groom to drink a potion of honey each day for thirty days after their marriage.

jeep. Anyone familiar with the many purposes for which a jeep can be used will not be surprised to learn that its name comes from GP, the Army's code for "general purpose."

left-wing. When we speak of persons or groups as being politically *left-wing* or *right-wing,* we are reflecting the seating arrangements of most legislatures in Europe, where it is the custom to seat the conservative members of the legislature to the right of the chair, and the more radical members to the left.

mace. In the Middle Ages, a *mace* was a heavy club, often with spikes in it, that was used as a weapon. The word has recently been incorporated into the trademarked name, Chemical Mace, a chemical mixture packaged in aerosol containers and used to disable by inflicting intense pain on the eyes, the throat and the lungs. *Mace* is also political slang for the method by which political bosses force public employees to make political contributions. The element of force is common to all three uses.

pants. Pants have become such a routine part of our dress that it seems strange to realize that men, the first to wear pants, once preferred breeches to trousers. When trousers were introduced in England around 1790, most men scoffed and dubbed them *pantaloons.* Only the military were quick to adopt them as more practical. Soon others began to see it their way and the rest is history.

rostrum. When a person takes the *rostrum,* he ascends a raised platform or stand for the purpose of making a public speech. The original *rostrum* was the beak or prow of a ship of Roman times. When an enemy ship was captured, its *rostrum,* which was usually elaborately carved, was taken back to the Forum to be used as decoration. Since speakers in the Forum used it as a platform, a new meaning was added that has by now replaced the original one.

Satan. Derived from a Hebrew word of the same spelling that means "adversary," *Satan* is the name given Lucifer, the fallen archangel who became the Devil.

scot-free. If one goes *scot-free* he escapes all penalty or punishment. But the expression has nothing to do with Scotland. Rather, it dates back to Elizabethan England, when a *scot* was a municipal tax collected, for the most part, by sheriffs. Those who managed to avoid paying the tax were *scot-free.*

shebang, shebeen. "The whole shebang" is the most common way this informal term is used, meaning "the whole situation" or "the whole affair." In Ireland, a *shebeen* was an unlicensed drinking place where drinks were sold illegally. It wasn't much of a place and, as such, wasn't worth much. "I wouldn't give a farthing for the whole shebeen" became "whole shebang" as time went by.

sinecure. Often obtained through political influence, a *sinecure* is a post or position that pays well enough but requires little or no work. Derived from the Latin "sine cura," without care, it was first used to refer to a church position that carried a salary but no responsibility for the care of souls.

slogan. The slogans of today are vital ingredients of politics and advertising but to the early Scottish chieftains a "slaughgairm," from which *slogan* came, was a real battle cry. It was a blend of two Gaelic words, "slaugh," army, and "gairm," a shout, and indicated even in those days that the persons using it meant business.

toast. Simultaneously raising glasses and quaffing a drink in honor of a person, organization or sentiment is the contemporary meaning of *toast*. However, in seventeenth century Europe, the custom took the form that gave the practice its name. Then an actual piece of toast was placed in the bottom of a large ale or wine vessel. The vessel was passed from drinker to drinker with the guest of honor receiving it last. He then consumed not only the last of the drink but the piece of toast also.

whipping boy. A person who is made a scapegoat and forced to take blame or punishment not rightfully his is a *whipping boy,* and it has long been thus. Today the phrase is used in a figurative sense but the practice of four or five centuries ago was a very literal one. A lad of common birth was educated along with every son of royal birth. But it was the commoner who took the lashings when the prince misbehaved.

There have been a number of fairly celebrated *whipping boys* in centuries past, though none, of course, so celebrated as the princelings whose stand-ins they were. There's a tale told about a French king who used not one but two grown men as expiators of his sins. He was Henry IV of France and the occasion was his renunciation of Protestantism in favor of Roman Catholicism in 1595. In atonement for his earlier "errors," he sent two ambassadors to the Vatican.

They knelt in St. Peter's basilica, intoning the *Miserere*. As they concluded each verse, they received a lash across the shoulders. So, although it's small consolation to today's office *whipping boy* when he stands mute before the boss's tongue-lashing, at least he can reflect that his punishment is figurative, not literal, as it would have been four or five centuries earlier.

8. Your Instant Vocabulary Builder

In the next few pages we will discuss some five hundred words specially chosen to add power, variety and color to your speaking and writing vocabulary. Some of them may already be familiar to you. Even when this is true, though, you will find it useful to read the word and its definitions, since you may very well learn that a word you thought you knew well has other meanings and other uses that you didn't already know.

Each word is given with its pronunciation and an example of how it may be used in a sentence. Some of these examples have been taken from the works of famous writers. Others were specially written for this book. Occasionally, when a word has a particularly interesting or meaningful history, an account of its origin will be included. For example, we all know what a *candidate* is, but it's interesting to realize that *candidate* and "*candid*" are very closely related, although *candid* today is precisely what many political candidates are not. And both words can be traced ultimately to "candidus," a Latin word for white, since the candidates for public office in ancient Rome clad themselves in white togas, symbolic of the purity of their motives in seeking office.

The purpose of this chapter is, of course, to help you to enrich your vocabulary. The best way to go about this is to jot down each day a few—say ten or twelve—of these words on a slip of paper or a small file card. The back of an envelope will do in a pinch. Then, as you ride to work—or walk to work, if you're that fortunate—run through the list two or three times. Whenever possible during the day, try to use these words in conversation or letter writing. Do not try to force them artificially into your speech, but do make every effort to use them when they fit naturally into what you are saying or writing. Remember the magic "Rule of Three," a word used three times is yours forever. And bear in mind also that the people you'll be trying your new words on will be friends and family, so there will be no reason for hesitation or embarrassment.

And now let's get started on the road to a richer, more powerful vocabulary. At the end of this chapter, you will find a word game using many of the words you will be learning here. When you check your score on this game, you will know how well you have succeeded in making these words part of your working vocabulary.

abdicate, *verb* (AB–dih–kayt). To renounce, leave, or abandon a claim to something. EXAMPLE: After King Edward VIII abdicated the throne of England, he became the Duke of Windsor. RELATED WORDS: **abdication,** *noun* (ab–dih–KAY–shun) and **abdicative,** *adjective* (ab–DIK–uh–tiv).

aberration, *noun* (ab–er–AY–shun). A wandering from the normal course or operation. EXAMPLE: "Originality is never to be sought for its own sake, otherwise it will be mere aberration." (John Ruskin) RELATED WORDS: **aberrant,** *adjective* (ab–ER–ent) and **aberrational,** *adjective* (ab–er–AY–shun'l).

abeyance, *noun* (uh–BAY–uns). A state of suspension or of being put aside temporarily. EXAMPLE: The settlement of the estate was held in abeyance until all debts were paid. RELATED WORD: **abeyant,** *adjective* (uh–BAY–'nt).

abjure, *verb* (ab–JOOR). To renounce or recant, especially in a formal manner. EXAMPLE: "The heavens rejoice in motion, why should I abjure my so much lov'd variety?" (John Donne). RELATED WORDS: **abjuration,** *noun* (ab–joor–AY–shun) and **abjurer** (ab–JOOR–er).

ablution, *noun* (ab–LOO–sh'n). A washing or cleansing of any part or all of the body, especially with water. EXAMPLE: A leisurely ablution had become part of her daily routine. RELATED WORD: **ablutionary,** *adjective* (ab–LOO–sh'n–er–ee).

abrogate, *verb* (AB–ruh–gayt). To cancel, repeal or call off, especially by official or authoritative action. EXAMPLE: In 1933 the nation abrogated the prohibition of the manufacture and sale of alcoholic beverages by repealing the Eighteenth Amendment. RELATED WORDS: **abrogation,** *noun* (ab–ruh–GAY–shun), **abrogative,** *adjective* (ab–ruh–GAY–tiv) and **abrogator,** *noun* (ab–ruh–GAY–tor).

abstemious, *adjective* (ab–STEE–mee–us). Avoiding excesses, sparing, especially in diet and drink; doing without; moderate. EXAMPLE: A sharp reduction in his income forced him into a more abstemious way of life. RELATED WORDS: **abstemiously,** *adverb* (ab–STEE–mee–us–lee) and **abstemiousness,** *noun* (ab–STEE–mee–us–nus).

accouterments, *plural noun* (uh–KOO–ter–m'nts). Trappings, equipment, furnishings or accessories, especially those of a soldier. By extension, the usual accompaniments of a position. EXAMPLE: He refused the services of a valet and a chauffeur, although these accouterments had been highly prized by his predecessor. RELATED WORD: **accouter,** *verb* (uh–KOOT–er).

acrimonious, *adjective* (ak–rih–MOH–nee–us). Caustic, bitter, biting, especially in speech. EXAMPLE: The critic's acrimonious review of the show distressed the artist and his admirers. RELATED WORDS: **acrid,** *adjective* (AK–rid), **acrimoniously,** *adverb* (ak–rih–MOH–nee–us–lee) and **acrimon'ousness,** *noun* (ak–rih–MOH–nee–us–nus).

acumen, *noun* (uh–KYOO–m'n). Mental acuteness, keenness of intellect or insight, ability for fine discrimination or judgment. EXAMPLE: Although he was less than forty years old, his business acumen had earned him the presidency of the company.

adamant, *adjective* (AD–uh–m'nt). Unyielding, impenetrable, inflexible, firm in position. EXAMPLE: Her father was adamant in his refusal to permit her to use his car for the trip. RELATED WORDS: **adamantly,** *adverb* (AD–uh–m'nt–lee), **adamantean,** *adjective* (ad–uh–man–TEE–un) and **adamantine,** *adjective* (ad–uh–MAN–tin).

adduce, *verb* (uh–DYOOS). To offer as proof or evidence in analysis or discussion; to present facts or reasons on which a decision or conclusion may be based. EXAMPLE: "Let me adduce more pleasing evidence." (Sir Arthur Quiller-Couch) RELATED WORDS: **adducer,** *noun* (uh–DYOOS–er), **adduceable** and **adducible,** *adjectives* (uh–DYOOS–uh–b'l).

adipose, *adjective* (AD–ih–pohs). Fat, fatty. EXAMPLE: The doctor warned him that his adipose condition was the cause of his high blood pressure and that strict adherence to a diet was essential to his health. RELATED WORDS: **adiposeness,** *noun* (AD–ih–pohs–ness) and **adiposity,** *noun* (ad–ih–POSS–uh–tee).

adjudicate, *verb* (uh–joo–dih–KAYT). To hear and decide in a court of law; to settle by judicial process. EXAMPLE: The matter of the disputed bill will be adjudicated in the Small Claims Court on May 20th at 3 P.M. RELATED WORDS: **adjudication,** *noun* (uh–joo–dih–KAY–shun), **adjudicative,** *adjective* (uh–JOO–dih–kuh–tiv) and **adjudicator,** *noun* (uh–JOO–dih–kay–tor).

adroit, *adjective* (uh–DROYT). Skillful, adept, dexterous, ingenious, expert. EXAMPLE: Henry's adroit handling of the various personalities involved solved what had seemed an impossible problem. RELATED WORDS: **adroitly,** *adverb* (uh–DROYT–lee) and **adroitness,** *noun* (uh–DROYT–ness).

aggrandizement, *noun* (uh–GRAN–diz–m'nt). Increase in position, power, importance or influence, honor or wealth. EXAMPLE: "Their countries seek no aggrandizement, territorial or other." (Franklin D. Roosevelt and Winston Churchill) RELATED WORDS: **aggrandize,** *verb* (uh–GRAN–dize) and **aggrandizer,** *noun* (uh–GRAN–dize–er).

allusion, *noun* (uh–LOO–zh'n). Indirect mention of or reference to, but with a definite purpose; suggestion or hint. EXAMPLE: The candidate's allusion to the beauties of the state made it clear that he intended to make conservation a campaign issue. RELATED WORD: **allude,** *verb* (uh–LOOD).

ambiguous, *adjective* (am–BIG–yoo–us). Subject to more than one interpretation in meaning; lacking clarity. EXAMPLE: He made an ambiguous reply to my question. RELATED WORDS: **ambiguity,** *noun* (am–bih–GYOO–ih–tee), **ambiguously,** *adverb* (am–BIG–yoo–us–lee) and **ambiguousness,** *noun* (am–BIG–yoo–us–ness).

ambivalent, *adjective* (am–BIV–uh–lent). Having conflicting feelings, such as simultaneous attraction and repulsion, toward a person, idea or situation. EXAMPLE: Because of her ambivalent reactions to him, she found herself in a quandary as to whether or not to accept his invitation. RELATED WORDS: **ambivalence,** *noun* (am–BIV–uh–lunss) and **ambivalently,** *adverb* (am–BIV–uh–lent–lee).

ameliorate, *verb* (uh–MEEL–yuh–rayt). To improve; to make better. EXAMPLE: "Methods of discipline neither can be nor should be ameliorated." (Herbert Spencer) RELATED WORDS: **amelioration,** *noun* (uh–meel–yuh–RAY–shun), **ameliorative,** *adjective* (uh–meel–yuh–RAY–tiv) and **ameliorator,** *noun* (uh–meel–yuh–RAY–tor).

amenities, *plural noun* (uh–MEN–ih–tees). (Plural) Social conventions or courtesies, pleasantries; (singular) the quality of being pleasant or agreeable. EXAMPLE: The welcome guest is one who is conscious of the amenities of every situation.

amorphous, *adjective* (uh–MOR–fus). Shapeless, formless, undeveloped; indefinite; lacking organization or unity. EXAMPLE: The crowd seemed to him an amorphous mass. RELATED WORDS: **amorphism,** *noun* (uh–MOR–fizm), **amorphousness,** *noun* (uh–MOR–fus–nus) and **amorphously,** *adverb* (uh–MOR–fus–lee).

anathema, *noun* (un–NATH–uh–muh). The subject of repugnance and loathing; a person or thing repelled, reviled or shunned; a curse, formal ban or excommunication. EXAMPLE: The sight of a woman in pants is still anathema to some older persons. RELATED WORDS: **anathematize,** *verb* (uh–NATH–uh–muh–tyz), **anathematization,** *noun* (uh–nath–uh–muh–tuh–ZAY–sh'n) and **anathematizer,** *noun* (uh–NATH–uh–muh–tyz–er).

animadversion, *noun* (an–ih–mad–VER–zhun). Adverse criticism, reproving remarks; blame. EXAMPLE: He faced the meeting calmly although he knew he was due for considerable animadversion. RELATED WORDS: **animadvert,** *noun* (an–ih–mad–VERT), **animadverter,** *noun* (an–ih–mad–VERT–er) and **animadversive,** *adjective* (an–ih–mad–VER–siv).

animus, *noun* (AN–ih–mus). Antagonism, hostility, ill-will. Also, intention or purpose; spirit. EXAMPLE: I was shocked to discover the extent of her animus toward her mother. RELATED WORD: **animosity,** *noun* (an–ih–MOS–ih–tee).

anodyne, *noun* and *adjective* (AN–oh–dyn). As a noun, it means a pain-deadening drug; anything that soothes or lessens pain. As an adjective, it means having pain-lessening qualities. EXAMPLES: The makers of aspirin claim it to be one of the oldest and most effective of the anodynes. The quiet music had an anodyne effect on the patient.

antipathy, *noun* (an–TIP–uh–thee). Aversion, dislike, distaste. EXAMPLE: Her antipathy for dogs was apparently based primarily on fear. RELATED WORDS: **antipathetic,** *adjective* (an–tip–uh–THET–ik), **antipathetical,** *adjective* (an–tip–uh–THET–ih–kul) and **antipathetically,** *adverb* (an–tip–uh–THET–ih–kul–lee).

antonym, *noun* (ANT–uh–nim). A word whose meaning is directly opposite to that of another. EXAMPLE: "Good" and 'bad" are antonyms of each other. RELATED WORDS: **antonymous,** *adjective* (an–TON–ee–mus) and **antonymy,** *noun* (an–TON–ee–mee).

apathetic, *adjective* (ap–uh–THET–ik). Indifferent, lacking interest or feeling. EXAMPLE: "The long mechanic pacings to and fro,/The set gray life and apathetic end." (Alfred, Lord Tennyson) RELATED WORDS: **apathetical,** *adjective* (ap–uh–THET–ih–kul), **apathetically,** *adverb* (ap–uh–THET–ih–kul-lee) and **apathy,** *noun* (AP–uh–thee).

aphorism, *noun* (AF–uh–rizm). A brief statement of truth; a precept. EXAMPLE: The headmaster of the school made it a practice to include at least one aphorism in each of his talks to the students. RELATED WORDS: **aphorist,** *noun* (AF–uh–rist), **aphoristic,** *adjective* (af–uh–RIS–tik) and **aphoristically,** *adverb* (af–uh–RIS–tik–uh–lee).

apocryphal, *adjective* (uh–POK–rih–f'l). False, spurious; of uncertain authority or origin. The Apocrypha (capitalized) refers to fourteen books of the Bible which are rejected by most Protestant churches. EXAMPLE: "In a higher than literal sense, the most apocryphal incidents of this most splendid and imaginative of gossips are full of truth." (George L. Craik) RELATED WORD: **apocrypha,** *noun* (uh–POK–rih–fuh).

apostate, *noun* (uh–POS–tayt). One who abandons his principles or beliefs. EXAMPLE: The labor leader was accused of being an apostate for taking the job of personnel manager. RELATED WORDS: **apostasy,** *noun* (uh–POS–tuh–see), **apostatize,** *verb* (uh–POS–tuh–tize) and **apostate,** *adjective*.

appurtenance, *noun* (uh–PER–tuh–n'ns). An accessory or adjunct. In law, a right, such as right of way, or minor property considered incidental to the principal real estate. EXAMPLE: He is the sort of chap who would insist on all the appurtenances of his position including a corner office, a rug on the floor and at least two secretaries.

archaic, *adjective* (ahr–KAY–ik). Ancient, antiquated; no longer commonly used. EXAMPLE: Many older persons have expressed unhappiness over recent attempts by the churches to eliminate archaic words from the rituals. RELATED WORDS: **archaism,** *noun* (AHR–kay–izm), **archaist,** *noun* (AHR–kay–ist) and **archaistic,** *adjective* (ahr–kay–IST–ik).

artifact, *noun* (AR–tih–fact). Also **artefact.** An article of early human handicraft of special interest to archaeologists or historians. EXAMPLE: One of the most effective ways to promote a child's understanding of past eras is the study of artifacts.

asceticism, *noun* (uh–SET–uh–sizm). The doctrine or practice of self-denial for spiritual reasons; austere existence for the purpose of religious exaltation. EXAMPLE: Many changes are taking place in the Roman Catholic Church because a number of the clergy no longer believe that asceticism is essential.

aspersion, *noun* (uh–SPER–zhun). Defamatory remark, slander, calumny. Usually used in the plural. EXAMPLE: "Who by aspersions, throw a stone/At the head of others, hit their own." (George Herbert) RELATED WORD: **asperse,** *verb* (uh–SPERS).

assiduous, *adjective* (uh–SID–yoo–us). Diligent, unremittingly industrious, steadily persevering. EXAMPLE: Only by assiduous research was he able to establish his client's right to the property. RELATED WORDS: **assiduously,** *adverb* (uh–SID–yoo–us–lee) and **assiduousness,** *noun* (uh–SID–yoo–us–ness).

assuage, *verb* (uh–SWAYJ). To alleviate, lessen, pacify or quench. EXAMPLE: The calm reassurances of her doctor assuaged her fear of entering the hospital. RELATED WORDS: **assuagement,** *noun* (uh–SWAYJ–m'nt) and **assuasive,** *adjective* (uh–SWAY–siv).

attrition, *noun* (uh–TRISH–un). Wearing down; abrasion; weakening under constant stress or harassment. EXAMPLE: The price-cutting campaign initiated by the discount house constituted a war of attrition against smaller stores. RELATED WORDS: **attritional,** *adjective* (uh–TRISH–uh–n'l) and **attritive,** *adjective* (uh–TRY–tiv).

avarice, *noun* (AV–er–iss). Excessive or insatiable greed for money or other personal profit. EXAMPLE: Avarice is an intolerable trait in a public official. RELATED WORDS: **avaricious,** *adjective* (av–er–ISH–us), **avariciously,** *adverb* (av–er–ISH–us–lee) and **avariciousness,** *noun* (av–er–ISH–us–nus).

averse, *adjective* (uh–VERSS). Reluctant to accept, unfavorably disposed; hostile or opposed to. EXAMPLE: She was averse to signing any kind of document until she had read and understood it. RELATED WORDS: **aversely,** *adverb* (uh–VERSS–lee) and **averseness,** *noun* (uh–VERSS–niss).

badinage, *noun* (bad–ih–NAHZH). Banter, playful repartee. EXAMPLE: The interchange had "risen from the level of badinage to that of real grandiloquence." (Frederic Prokosch)

bagatelle, *noun* (bag–uh–TEL). A trifle, a thing of little or no importance. EXAMPLE: Though it was obvious that his gift was fairly expensive, he pretended it was a mere bagatelle.

bailiwick, *noun* (BAIL–ih–wik). A person's own province, especially an area in which he has particular skill, knowledge or authority. EXAMPLE: Although he was a writer, he did not feel that sales promotion was entirely outside his bailiwick.

balderdash, *noun* (BOL–der–dash). Trash, nonsense. EXAMPLE: Of today's poetry one may well say that some is excellent but most is balderdash.

baleful, *adjective* (BAYL–ful). Ominous, menacing, sinister. EXAMPLE: The fortune-teller mouthed baleful prophecies of doom and gloom. RELATED WORDS: **balefully,** *adverb* (BAYL–ful–ee); and **balefulness,** *noun* (BAYL–ful–nes).

banal, *adjective* (buh–NAHL or BAY–nul). Trite, commonplace, hackneyed. EXAMPLE: ". . . a towering structure, sound in plan but banal in construction." (Lewis Mumford) RELATED WORD: **banality,** *noun* (buh–NAL–ih–tee).

baroque, *adjective* (buh–ROHK). Elaborate, ornate, lavishly ornamented. EXAMPLE: ". . . addiction to a baroque luxuriance of language." (Orville Prescott)

bas-relief, *noun* (bah–rih–LEEF). A style of sculpture in which the figures are raised only slightly above their background. EXAMPLE: The committee decided that the memorial should be in the form of bas-relief rather than a statue.

bastion, *noun* (BASS–chun). Originally an outjutting from a rampart that allowed protection of the rampart walls; hence, a well-fortified position or stronghold. EXAMPLE: The state was considered to be a bastion of the Democratic party and the opposition had little hope of winning there.

bathos, *noun* (BAY–thos). An anticlimax; a ludicrous descent from nobility to the commonplace. EXAMPLE: Although the first two acts of the play showed some promise, the final scene was nothing but bathos. RELATED WORDS: **bathetic,** *adjective* (buh–THET–ik) and **bathetically,** *adverb* (buh–THET–ih–kul–lee).

bauble, *noun* (BAW–b'l). A trinket; worthless finery. EXAMPLE: The grandmother kept a collection of baubles for her small granddaughter to enjoy on their visits.

beaux-arts, *noun* (boh–ZAHR). The arts of design, poetry, music, the dance and drama. EXAMPLE: Her background had given her practically no knowledge of the beaux-arts.

behemoth, *noun* (bee–HEE–muth). A huge beast, possibly the hippopotamus, mentioned by Job in the Old Testament, hence something of enormous size or power. EXAMPLE: The director anticipated some difficulty in casting the leading role because the script called for a behemoth of a man.

belles-lettres, *noun* (bel–LET–reh). Fine literature as distinguished from practical or technical writings. EXAMPLE: The chronicles of his adventures abroad were interesting and amusing but certainly not to be ranked with the belles-lettres of the decade.

bellicose, *adjective* (BEL–ih–kohs). Quarrelsome; pugnacious. EXAMPLE: It was obvious from his bellicose manner that it would be difficult to persuade him to change his mind. RELATED WORDS: **bellicosely,** *adverb* (BEL–ih–kohs–lee), **bellicosity,** *noun* (bel–ih–KOS–uh–tee) and **bellicoseness,** *noun* (BEL–ih–kohs–nes).

bellwether, *noun* (BEL–weth–er). A male sheep wearing a bell that is the leader of the flock; hence, one who takes the lead or initiative; leader. EXAMPLE: You can count on Frank Thomas to be the bellwether of any conservation movement in the county.

benighted, *adjective* (bih–NITE–ed). Unenlightened; ignorant. EXAMPLE: It seemed incredible to him that, in these days of mass media, she could remain so benighted about political issues. RELATED WORDS: **benightedly,** *adverb* (bih–NITE–ed–lee) and **benightedness,** *noun* (bih–NITE–ed–nes).

benign, *adjective* (bih–NINE). Gracious, kindly, gentle. In medicine, mild; not malignant. EXAMPLE: Behind his benign manner lay a fierce determination to expose any corruption in the city government. RELATED WORDS: **benignly,** *adverb* (bih–NINE–lee), **benignancy,** *noun* (bih–NIG–nun–see), **benignant,** *adjective* (bih–NIG–n't), **benignantly,** *adverb* (bih–NIG–n't–lee), and **benignity,** *noun* (bih–NIG–nih–tee).

berserk, *adjective* (ber–SERK). Frenzied; insanely violent. EXAMPLE: His wife complained to the police that he had gone completely berserk when she told him she was filing suit for divorce.

billet-doux, *noun* (BILL–ay–DOO). A love letter. EXAMPLE:

Instead of study for his examinations, he spent the evening composing a billet-doux to Marie.

blandishment, *noun* (BLAN–dish–ment). Coaxing through flattery. EXAMPLE: ". . . in the midst of love's fair blandishments." (Thomas Kyd) RELATED WORDS: **blandisher,** *noun* (BLAN–dish–er) and **blandish,** *verb* (BLAN–dish).

blatant, *adjective* (BLAY–t'nt). Crudely and offensively obvious, conspicuous or loud. EXAMPLE: The boy's explanation of the accident was a blatant lie. RELATED WORDS: **blatancy,** *noun* (BLAY–t'n–see) and **blatantly,** *adverb* (BLAY–t'nt–lee).

bombastic, *adjective* (bom–BAS–tik). Flowery and extravagant in language; pompous. EXAMPLE: "Kingly superiority sustains itself in bombastic titles and hollow liturgies of court etiquette." (J. R. Seeley) RELATED WORD: **bombastically,** *adverb* (bom–BAS–tih–kuh–lee).

bourgeois, *adjective* (boor–ZHWAH). Of or relating to the middle class; concerned with material or capitalistic interests; tending toward mediocrity. EXAMPLE: The boy accused his father of leading a bourgeois life and of not being interested in the finer things. RELATED WORD: **bourgeoisie,** *noun* (boor–zhwah–ZEE).

braggadocio, *noun* (brag–uh–DOH–shee–oh). Empty boasting or bragging; cockiness of manner. EXAMPLE: Although his braggadocio offended most of the people in the room, a few were amused by it.

calumny, *noun* (KAL–um–nee). Slander; false accusations deliberately made to damage another's reputation. EXAMPLE: The calumny directed at the governor in the last days of the campaign cost him the election. RELATED WORDS: **calumniate,** *verb* (kuh–LUM–nee–ayt), **calumniation,** *noun* (kal–lum–nee–AY–sh'n), **calumniator,** *noun* (kal–LUM–nee–ay–tor), **calumnious,** *adjective* (kuh–LUM–nee–us) and **calumniously,** *adverb* (kuh–LUM–nee–us–lee).

canard, *noun* (kuh–NARD). A lie; a false or fabricated story or report. EXAMPLE: Further investigation proved that the claim of ore deposits on the land was an absolute canard.

capricious, *adjective* (kuh–PRIH–shus or kuh–PREE–shus). Fickle; subject to sudden whim or notion; unpredictable. EXAMPLE: His client's capricious behavior made it difficult for the lawyer to prepare a proper defense. RELATED WORDS: **capriciously,** *adverb* (kuh–PRIH–shus–lee) and **capriciousness,** *noun* (kuh–PRIH–shus–nus).

captious, *adjective* (KAP–shus). Fault-finding; overly critical and inclined to entrap or confuse through argument. EXAMPLE: The student felt that the professor had been captious in his comments on the paper, particularly since it was intended only as a first draft. RELATED WORDS: **captiously,** *adverb* (KAP–shus–lee) and **captiousness,** *noun* (KAP–shus–nus).

carnage, *noun* (KAHR–nij). Extensive slaughter, especially in war; the many dead bodies resulting from a massacre. EXAMPLE: The nation was shocked by the belated reports of carnage at My Lai.

carouse, *verb* (kuh–ROWZ). To engage in excessive drinking as a means of revelry. EXAMPLE: The landlord sought to evict them because of their tendency to carouse almost every weekend. RELATED WORDS: **carousal,** *noun* (kuh–ROWZ–ul) and **carouser,** *noun* (kuh–ROWZ–er).

castigate, *verb* (KAS–tih–gayt). To criticize or punish severely; to chastise; to reprove sternly. EXAMPLE: "He came, the gentle satirist [Addison] who hit no unfair blow; the kind judge who castigated only in smiling." (W. M. Thackeray) RELATED WORDS: **castigation,** *noun* (kas–tih–GAY–sh'n) and **castigator,** *noun* (kas–tih–GAY–tor).

cataclysmic, *adjective* (kat–uh–KLIZ–mik). Creating a violent upheaval or drastic change; resulting in a momentous event. EXAMPLE: The merger of the two companies had a cataclysmic effect on the morale of the staff. RELATED WORDS: **cataclysm,** *noun* (KAT–uh–klizm) and **cataclysmal,** *adjective* (kat–uh–KLIZ–mul).

caustic, *adjective* (KAWS–tik). Sharp, cutting; severe; bitter. Also, capable of destroying by chemical action. EXAMPLE: Her brother's caustic remarks about her appearance hurt doubly because they were at least partly true. RELATED WORDS: **caustical,** *adjective* (KAWS–tih–kul), **caustically,** *adverb* (KAWS–tih–kul–lee) and **causticity,** *noun* (kaws–TISS–ih–tee).

celerity, *noun* (suh–LEHR–ih–tee). Speed, swiftness, rapidity. EXAMPLE: The celerity with which his invitation was accepted made him wonder why he had ever hesitated to extend it.

chicanery, *noun* (chih–KAYN–er–ee). Trickery; deception through subterfuge or conniving stratagem. EXAMPLE: "Charges of political chicanery were brought against Van Buren but he invariably extricated himself by artifice." (B. P. Poore) RELATED WORDS: **chicane,** *verb* and *noun* (chih–KAYN) and **chicaner,** *noun* (chih–KAYN–er).

choleric, *adjective* (KOL–uh–rik or kuh–LEHR–ik). Easily angered, irascible; short-tempered. EXAMPLE: She found it impossible to work for him because of his choleric disposition. RELATED WORDS: **cholerically,** *adverb* (KOL–uh–rik–uh–lee or kuh–LEHR–ik–lee) and **cholericly,** *adverb* (KOL–uh–rik–lee).

circumlocution, *noun* (ser–kum–loh–KYOO–shun). A roundabout and excessively wordy way of talking; evasion through an indirect and wordy manner of speaking or writing. EXAMPLE: Circumlocution can be most annoying when a prompt decision is needed. RELATED WORD: **circumlocutory,** *adjective* (ser–kum–LOK–yoo–tor–ee).

circumvent, *verb* (ser–kum–VENT). To thwart or defeat, especially by cunning or ingenuity. EXAMPLE: He managed to circumvent their efforts to collect the bill by moving to a distant state. RELATED WORDS: **circumventer,** *noun* (ser–kum–VENT–er), **circumvention,** *noun* (ser–kum–VEN–shun) and **circumventive,** *adjective* (ser–kum–VENT–iv).

cognizant, *adjective* (KOG–nih–z'nt). Being aware of; having knowledge about; fully conscious of. EXAMPLE: Although he was fully cognizant of the danger involved, he deliberately broke the law as a way of bringing a test case in the courts. RELATED WORDS: **cognition,** *noun* (kog–NISH–un), **cognizable,** *adjective* (KOG–niz–uh–b'l) and **cognizance,** *noun* (KOG–nih–z'ns).

comatose, *adjective* (KOM–uh–tohs). Being or appearing to be in a state of coma; affected by deep or prolonged unconsciousness; excessively lethargic. EXAMPLE: The stock market drifted into a prolonged, comatose slump. RELATED WORDS: **coma,** *noun* (KOH–ma) and **comatosely,** *adverb* (KOM–uh–tohs–lee).

compendium, *noun* (kum–PEN–dee–um). An abridgement; a brief but complete summary. EXAMPLE: For the convenience of the staff members, the personnel manager compiled for each of them a compendium of the provisions of all the insurance policies each one held. RELATED WORDS: **compendious,**

adjective (kum–PEN–dee–us) and **compendiously,** *adverb* (kum–PEN–dee–us–lee).

complicity, *noun* (k'm–PLIS–ih–tee). Participation, especially in a wrong-doing or crime. EXAMPLE: The boy was not arrested at the time, but he was later accused of complicity in the theft of the auto.

consummate, *adjective* (kun–SUM–it), *verb* (KON–suh–mayt). *Adjective*—complete; utter; perfect; supreme; *verb*—to bring to a successful conclusion or fulfillment. EXAMPLE: He performed the piano concerto with consummate skill. RELATED WORDS: **consummately,** *adverb* (kun–SUM–it–lee), **consummative,** *adjective* (KON–suh–may–tiv) and **consummation** *noun* (kon–suh–MAY–shun).

contention, *noun* (kun–TEN–shun). Argument; controversy; discord; struggle. Also, a point or statement used in an argument. EXAMPLE: The use of a car is the source of contention in many families, especially those with teen-age children. It is our contention that parents have first claim.

context, *noun* (KON–tekst). The parts of a written or spoken statement that include (or precede and follow) a given word, phrase or sentence; surrounding text which specifies meaning. Also, a situation which affects significance or meaning. EXAMPLE: Many motion picture advertisements contain statements by critics that have been taken out of context to make them seem more enthusiastic than they actually are. RELATED WORDS: **contextual,** *adjective* (kon–TEKST–yoo–ul) and **contextually,** *adverb* (kon–TEKST–yoo–ul–lee).

contingent, *adjective* (kun–TIN–j'nt). Possible but not certain; conditional; dependent on something which has not yet happened. EXAMPLE: "The continuance of the latter is wholly contingent on the presence of the former." (C. H. Grandgent) RELATED WORDS: **contingence,** *noun* (kun–TIN–juns), **contingency,** *noun* (kun–TIN–jun–see) and **contingently,** *adverb* (kun–TIN–j'nt–lee).

contumacy, *noun* (KON–tyoo–muh–see). Contempt for lawful authority; rebelliousness; disobedience; insubordination. EXAMPLE: There was a small group within the senior class whose contumacy presented a real problem to the school administration. RELATED WORDS: **contumacious,** *adjective* (kon–tyoo–MAY–shus); **contumaciously,** *adverb* (kon–tyoo–MAY–shus–lee) and **contumaciousness** (kon–tyoo–MAY–shus–nus).

cortege, *noun* (kor–TEZH). A retinue or a number of attend-
ants. Also, a funeral train or any ceremonial procession.
EXAMPLE: Although his is one of the smaller nations of the
world, he brings with him a cortege equal to that of any head
of state.

covenant, *noun* (KUV–uh–nunt). A solemn and binding agreement or pact. In theology, God's promises to man as recorded
in the Old and New Testaments. EXAMPLE: The court ap-
pointee was embarrassed when it was discovered that he and
his neighbors had signed a restrictive covenant governing the
sale of their properties. RELATED WORDS: **covenantee,** *noun*
(KUV–uh–nun–tee), **convenanter,** *noun* (KUV–uh–nun–ter)
and **convenantor,** *noun* (KUV–uh–nun–tohr).

covert, *adjective* (KUH–vert). Hidden, concealed, disguised.
Also, protected or sheltered. EXAMPLE: He viewed the mis-
fortunes of his former associate with covert malice. RELATED
WORDS: **covertly,** *adverb* (KUH–vert–lee) and **coverture,**
noun (KUV–er–choor).

cozen, *verb* (KUZ–'n). To cheat, defraud or deceive, especially
in a petty fashion. To trick. EXAMPLE: Some used car dealers
cozen unsuspecting buyers by turning back the speedometers
of the cars. RELATED WORDS: **cosenage,** *noun* (KUZ–'n–ij)
and **cozener,** *noun* (KUZ–'n–er).

crass, *adjective* (KRAS). Crude or coarse, insensitive; stupid or
dense. EXAMPLE: The widow resented his crass questions
about the size of her husband's estate. RELATED WORDS:
crassly, *adverb* (KRAS–lee) and **crassness,** *noun* (KRAS–
nus).

craven, *adjective* (KRAY–v'n). Cowardly; excessively afraid.
EXAMPLE: It was craven of him to refuse to testify in defense
of his friend. RELATED WORDS: **cravenly,** *adverb* (KRAY–'n–
lee) and **cravenness,** *noun* (KRAY–'v–nus).

criterion, *noun* (kry–TEER–ee–un). A standard or rule by
which something can be measured or judged. EXAMPLE: A
basic criterion for the selection of a federal judge should be
absolute integrity.

critique, *noun* (krih–TEEK). A critical estimate or analysis of
a literary or artistic work. EXAMPLE: The author was painfully
aware that the sale of his book would be affected by the
critique in the Sunday newspaper. RELATED WORDS: **critic,**
noun (KRIT–ik), **critical,** *adjective* (KRIT–ih–k'l), **criticism,**
noun (KRIT–uh–sizm) and **criticize,** *verb* (KRIT–uh–syze).

cul-de-sac, *noun* (KUL–duh–SAK). A blind alley; one-way street; impasse. EXAMPLE: Every line of investigation the detectives tried led them into a cul-de-sac.

culpable, *adjective* (KUL–puh–b'l). Deserving blame; guilty. EXAMPLE: It was obvious that he was culpable of negligence. RELATED WORDS: **culpability,** *noun* (kul-puh–BIL–ih-tee), **culpableness,** *noun* (KUL–puh–b'l–nus) and **culpably,** *adverb* (KUL–puh–b'l–lee).

curmudgeon, *noun* (ker–MUJ–un). A mean or disagreeable person;. a miser. EXAMPLE: Harold Ickes, the Secretary of the Interior under Franklin D. Roosevelt, often called himself "the Old Curmudgeon." RELATED WORD: **curmudgeonly,** *adverb* (ker–MUJ–un–lee).

cursory, *adjective* (KER–suh-ree). Superficial;. hastily done. EXAMPLE: The customs official gave his luggage only a cursory examination before allowing him to leave the docks. RELATED WORDS: **cursorily,** *adverb* (KER–suh–rih–lee) and **cursoriness,** *noun* (KER–suh–rih–nus).

dally, *verb* (DAL–ee). To waste time in idle play; to loiter, linger. EXAMPLE: She dallied so long on her way from school that she missed her club meeting. RELATED WORDS: **dalliance,** *noun* (DAL–ee-unss) and **dallier,** *noun* (DAL–ee–er).

debase, *verb* (dih–BAYSS). To reduce in quality, status, dignity; to degrade. EXAMPLE: The actions of the student rebels served, in the eyes of the faculty, to debase the college's ethical standards. RELATED WORDS: **debasement,** *noun* (dih–BAYSS–ment) and **debaser,** *noun* (dih–BAYSS–er).

decelerate, *verb* (dee–SEL–er–ayt). To retard, slow down, reduce in speed. EXAMPLE: The President said his actions would decelerate the war. RELATED WORDS: **deceleration,** *noun* (dee–sel–er–AY–shun) and **decelerator,** *noun* (dee–sel–er–AY–tor).

deft, *adjective* (DEFT). Skillful, adroit, dexterous. EXAMPLE: The magician made his tricks especially convincing by deft manipulation of the objects he used. RELATED WORDS: **deftly,** *adverb* (DEFT–lee) and **deftness,** *noun* (DEFT–ness).

demure, *adjective* (dih–MYOOR). Prim, proper, shy, affecting modesty. EXAMPLE: When it served her purpose, Scarlett O'Hara was able to assume a very demure expression. RE-

LATED WORDS: **demurely,** *adverb* (dih–MYOOR–lee) and
demureness, *noun* (dih–MYOOR–ness).

deprecate, *verb* (DEP–reh–kayt). To belittle, demean, show dis-
approval of through unfavorable comment. EXAMPLE: He insisted that his feat was modest and he deprecated the honors
showered upon him. RELATED WORDS: **deprecating,** *adjective*
(DEP–reh–kay–ting) and **deprecatory,** *adjective* (DEP–rih–
kuh–tor–ee).

depredation, *noun* (dep–reh–DAY–shun). Plundering, preying
upon, laying waste. EXAMPLE: Seldom has an army committed
such depredations upon a helpless foe as did Sherman's on
his march to the sea. RELATED WORDS: **depredate,** *verb* (DEP–
reh–dayt), **depredator,** *noun* (dep–ruh–DAY–to) and **depred-
atory,** *adjective* (deh–PRED–uh–tor–ee).

derisive, *adjective* (deh–RY–siv). Mocking, scornful, ridiculing,
scoffing. EXAMPLE: The dean's pleas for restoration of order
brought only derisive hoots from the student rebels. RELATED
WORDS: **derision,** *noun* (deh–RIZH–un), **derisively,** *adverb*
deh–RY–siv–lee) and **derisiveness,** *noun* (deh–RY–siv–ness).

derogatory, *adjective* (deh–ROG–uh–tor–ee). Disparaging, belittling, disdaining, detracting. EXAMPLE: The network insisted that the broadcasters refrain from using derogatory
racial labels. RELATED WORDS: **derogate,** *verb* (DEH–roh–
gayt), **derogation,** *noun* (deh–roh–GAY–shun) and **deroga-
torily,** *adverb* (deh–rog–uh–TOR–ih–lee).

despoil, *verb* (des–POIL). To deprive of property or belong-
ings; to strip, plunder, rob. EXAMPLE: The marauding invaders
fell upon the towns and despoiled them. RELATED WORDS:
despoiler, *noun* (des–POIL–er), **despoilment,** *noun* (des–
POIL–ment) and **despoliation,** *noun* (des–poh–lee–AY–
shun).

desultory, *adjective* (DES–ul–tor–ee). Intermittent, haphazard,
erratic, disorganized, random, rambling. EXAMPLE: They carried on a desultory conversation, jumping from topic to topic
by fits and starts. RELATED WORDS: **desultorily,** *adverb* (des–
ul–TOR–ih–lee) and **desultoriness,** *noun* (des–ul–TOR–ih–
ness).

devotee, *noun* (deh–voh–TEE). An ardent partisan; one devoted to a particular sport, pursuit or religion. EXAMPLE:
Forest Hills was crowded with tennis devotees who had come
to watch the national championships. RELATED WORDS: **de-**

vote, *verb* (dih–VOHT), **devoted,** *adjective* (dih–VOH–ted) and **devout,** *adjective* (dih–VOUT).

dexterous, *adjective* (DEX–strus). Skilled, adroit, clever, especially in the use of one's hands. EXAMPLE: One could not help admiring the dealer's dexterous manipulation of the cards. NOTE: All these words are derived from the Latin adjective "dexter," meaning right. For many centuries, probably simply because more people are born right-handed than left-handed, words from this Latin base have connoted cleverness and skill, while words derived from the Latin word for left, "sinister," have the evil and unpleasant connotations obvious in that word. RELATED WORDS: **dexterously,** *adverb* (DEK–strus–ly), **dexterousness,** *noun* (DEK–strus–ness) and **dexterity,** *noun* (dex–TER–ih–tee).

diatribe, *noun* (DY–uh–tribe). Invective, verbal abuse, especially in the form of carefully prepared speech or writing. EXAMPLE: When the senator rose to his feet, observers knew that a diatribe against the proposed legislation was coming.

diffident, *adjective* (DIF–ih–dent). Shy, lacking in self-confidence, timid. EXAMPLE: The salesman who approaches a prospective customer in a diffident manner is doomed before he opens his mouth. RELATED WORD: **diffidently,** *adverb* (DIF–ih–dent–lee).

dilapidation, *noun* (dih–lap–ih–DAY–shun). Condition of decay, neglect, ruin or disrepair. EXAMPLE: The tenements in the ghetto areas were in a shocking state of dilapidation. RELATED WORDS:**dilapidate,** *verb* (dih–LAP–ih–dayt) and **dilapidated,** *adjective* (dih–LAP–ih–day–ted).

dilatory, *adjective* (DIL–uh–tor–ee). Slow, procrastinating, delaying. EXAMPLE: The umpire threatened to throw the pitcher out of the game because his dilatory tactics were prolonging the contest beyond reason. RELATED WORDS: **dilatorily,** *adverb* (dil–uh–TOR–ih–lee) and **dilatoriness,** *noun* (dil–uh–TOR–ih–ness).

discernment, *noun* (dih–SERN–ment). Acuteness of vision, keen perception, precision in judgment, clear-sightedness. EXAMPLE: The chairman of the board showed keen discernment in finding the flaws in the company's annual report. RELATED WORDS: **discern,** *verb* (dih–SERN) and **discerning,** *adjective* (dih–SERN–ing).

disdainful, *adjective* (dis–DAYN–ful). Contemptuous, overbearing, scornful, haughty. EXAMPLE: The mayor was utterly disdainful of his critics, although they later proved to be right. RELATED WORDS: **disdain**, *verb* (dis–DAYN) and **disdainfully**, *adverb* (dis–DAYN–ful–ee).

disheveled, *adjective* (dih–SHEV–eld). Mussed, untidy, disarranged, rumpled. EXAMPLE: When Professor Higgins first saw Eliza Doolittle, the cockney flower girl looked extremely disheveled. RELATED WORDS: **dishevel**, *verb* (dih–SHEV–el) and **dishevelment**, *noun* (dih–SHEV–el–ment).

disparaging, *adjective* (dis–PAR–uh–jing). Belittling, reducing in importance, derogatory, slighting. EXAMPLE: "We'll overlook that critic's disparaging remarks," said the author. "Nobody takes him seriously—except himself." RELATED WORDS: **disparage**, *verb* (dis–PAR–ij), **disparagement**, *noun* (dis–PAR–ij–ment) and **disparagingly**, *adverb* (dis–PAR–ij–ing–lee).

dissident, *noun* and *adjective* (DIS–ih–dent). As a noun, it means one who dissents or disagrees. As an adjective, it means differing, dissenting, disagreeing, especially in regard to a religious or political belief. EXAMPLES: The faculty meeting was interrupted by cries from student dissidents. Many changes have been effected in the church because dissident voices were finally listened to. RELATED WORD: **dissidence**, *noun* (DIS–ih–denss).

dogmatic, *adjective* (dog–MAT–ik). Dictatorial, opinionated, arrogantly positive. EXAMPLE: The mayor was so dogmatic in his claim of police innocence in the riot that there was little point in trying to argue with him. RELATED WORDS: **dogma**, *noun* (DOG–muh), **dogmatism**, *noun* (DOG–muh–tism) and **dogmatist**, *noun* (DOG–muh–tist).

doleful, *adjective* (DOHL–ful). Suffering, grieving, sorrowful, mournful, melancholy. EXAMPLE: The wistful waif turned a doleful gaze on the lady from whom she begged alms. RELATED WORDS: **dolefully**, *adverb* (DOHL–ful–lee) and **dolefulness**, *noun* (DOHL–ful–ness).

dossier, *noun* (DOSS–ee–ay). File of papers and documents pertaining to a single person or project. EXAMPLE: "Give me the dossier on T. Patrick Zinss," ordered the FBI chief. NOTE: This is a word we have taken unchanged from the French, where it means simply a bundle of papers with a label on the back.

dotage, *noun* (DOH–tij). Senility, old age, especially regarded as involving foolish or feeble-minded behavior. EXAMPLE: Some Florida cities, havens for retired people, have more than their fair share of people in their dotage. NOTE: Because elderly people often like to tell stories about events of the past, a useful word has been coined to describe this characteristic: *anecdotage.* It's a blend, of course, of *anecdote* and *dotage.*

dour, *adjective* (DEWR or DOW'R). Stern, forbidding, harsh, gloomy. EXAMPLE: When he went down to defeat at the final hole, the unhappy golfer strode from the course with a dour expression on his face.

drivel, *noun* (DRIV–'l). Silly babbling, nonsensical prattle; childish talk; twaddle. EXAMPLE: To many parents the chatter of teenagers is just so much drivel. RELATED WORDS: **drivel,** *verb* (DRIV–'l); **driveler,** *noun* (DRIV–ul–er).

drollery, *noun* (DROHL–er–ee). Amusing behavior, especially quaintly comic acts; quietly amusing activity. EXAMPLE: The antics of pratfall comics are not to be compared to the subtle drolleries of polished farceurs. RELATED WORD: **droll,** *adjective* (DROHL).

dulcet, *adjective* (DUL–set). Sweet-sounding; harmonious. EXAMPLE: "The dulcet sound . . . of that melting flutelike quality." (W. H. Hudson)

eclat, *noun* (ay–KLAH). Stunning brillance, especially in performance. Also, acclamation, approbation or renown resulting from such. EXAMPLE: The critics all agreed that she had played the role with eclat.

efface, *verb* (eh–FAYSS). To obliterate, wipe out. Also, to make one's self deliberately inconspicuous. EXAMPLE: As a result of all the publicity about her trial, she found it difficult to efface herself in any crowd. RELATED WORDS: **effaceable,** *adjective* (eh–FAYSS–uh–b'l), **effacement,** *noun* (eh–FAYSS–m'nt) and **effacer,** *noun* (eh–FAYSS–er).

effete, *adjective* (eh–FEET). Barren; exhausted; no longer productive; lacking in vigor. EXAMPLE: The news media gave great prominence to his statement about "effete snobs."

efficacious, *adjective* (ef–ih–KAY–shus). Powerful; capable of producing the desired effect or result. EXAMPLE: Few household cleansers are as efficacious as the advertisements imply. RELATED WORDS: **efficaciously,** *adverb* (ef–ih–KAY–shus–lee) and **efficaciousness,** *noun* (ef–ih–KAY–shus–nus).

effusion, *noun* (eh–FYOO–zhun). Unrestrained expression of feeling in speech or writing; gushing speech. EXAMPLE: The effusion with which our hostess greeted us made us very uncomfortable. RELATED WORDS: **effuse,** *verb* (eh–FYOOZ); **effusive,** *adjective* (eh–FYOO–siv), **effusively,** *adverb* (eh–FYOO–siv–lee) and **effusiveness,** *noun* (eh–FYOO–siv–ness).

eleemosynary, *adjective* (el–eh–MOS–uh–nehr–ee). Of or pertaining to charity; dependent on charity or provided by charity. EXAMPLE: She spent most of her time in eleemosynary activities, although she herself had little money to give.

elicit, *verb* (eh–LIS–it). To draw out or bring forth; to evoke. EXAMPLE: Because of her nearly hysterical condition, it was not possible to elicit much information from her about how the accident had happened. RELATED WORDS: **elicitation,** *noun* (eh–lis–ih–TAY–shun) and **elicitor,** *noun* (eh–LIS–ih–tor).

emanate, *verb* (EM–ih–nayt). To originate (from); to flow out or come forth; to issue. EXAMPLE: Investigation proved that the gossip about his home life emanated from the office of a business rival. RELATED WORDS: **emanation,** *noun* (em–ih–NAY–shun) and **emanative,** *adjective* (em–ih–NAY–tiv).

embellish, *verb* (em–BEL–ish). To enhance by adding to, as by decoration or ornamentation. Also, to add imaginary details to a story or statement. EXAMPLE: By the time he had related the story of the burglary three or four times he had embellished it so that it bore little relation to the truth. RELATED WORD: **embellishment,** *noun* (em–BEL–ish–m'nt).

empathy, *noun* (EM–puh–thee). Capacity for understanding the feelings, ideas and motives of another. EXAMPLE: It is unusual to see such a degree of empathy between two men of such widely different ages.

encomium, *noun* (en–KOH–mee–um). Elaborate or formal expression of high praise; eulogy. EXAMPLE: My father was flattered by the encomiums at the dedication of the new dormitory named for him. RELATED WORDS: **encomiast,** *noun* (en–KOH–mee–ast) and **encomiastic,** *adjective* (en–koh–mee–AST–ik).

endemic, *adjective* (en–DEM–ik). Also **endemical,** *adjective* (en–DEM–ih–kul). Peculiar to a particular people, region or nation. EXAMPLE: ". . . the many shades of radicalism endemic in Spain." (Harper's Magazine) RELATED WORDS: **endemically,** *adverb* (en–DEM–ih–kul–lee) and **endemism,** *noun* (en–DEM–izm).

enervate, *verb* (EN–er–vayt). To lessen the strength or vigor of; to weaken; to debilitate. EXAMPLE: The shock of a sudden death in the family can seriously enervate one. RELATED WORDS: **enervation,** *noun* (en–er–VAY–shun) and **enervator,** *noun* (EN–er–VAY–tor).

ensconce, *verb* (en–SKONSS). To settle comfortably. Also, to protect or hide. EXAMPLE: She was angry because her brother-in-law had ensconced himself in the guest room and showed no inclination to leave.

ephemeral, *adjective* (eh–FEM–er–'l). Existing only temporarily; transitory; living only a short time. EXAMPLE: Because she thought her happiness only ephemeral, Cinderella did not leave the ball until it was almost too late. RELATED WORDS: **ephemerality,** *noun* (eh–fem–er–AL–ih–tee) and **ephemerally,** *adverb* (eh–FEM–er–uh–lee).

erudite, *adjective* (EHR–uh–dite). Profoundly learned; extremely scholarly and well-read. EXAMPLE: We are fortunate to have such an erudite man as head of our philosophy department. RELATED WORDS: **eruditely,** *adverb* (EHR–uh–dite–lee) and **erudition,** *noun* (ehr–oo–DISH–un).

eschew, *verb* (es–CHOO). To avoid with care; to abstain from or shun. EXAMPLE: It is wise to eschew any sign of favoritism when dealing with your children.

esoteric, *adjective* (es–uh–TEHR–ik). Intelligible to only a few; taught only to a select group. Also, confidential. EXAMPLE: A book of such an esoteric nature rarely has a large market. RELATED WORD: **esoterically,** *adverb* (es–uh–TEHR–ih–kul–lee).

espouse, *verb* (es–POWZ). To advocate or support, usually referring to a course of action or a doctrine. EXAMPLE: The congressman announced his decision to espouse the abolition of the Electoral College. RELATED WORD: **espousal,** *noun* (es–POWZ–'l).

euphemism, *noun* (YOO–fuh–mizm). A less accurate but "nicer" word or phrase which is substituted for one that is more precise but considered offensive. Also, the act of such a substitution. EXAMPLE: "Inner city" is the current euphemism for "slum." RELATED WORDS: **euphemist,** *noun* (YOO–fem–ist); **euphemistic,** *adjective* (yoo–fem–ISS–tik), **euphe-**

mistically, *adverb* (yoo–fem–ISS–tih–kul–lee) and **euphemize,** *verb* (YOO–fem–ize).

euphoria, *noun* (yoo–FOR–ee–uh). A feeling of extreme well-being, great comfort or elation, often inexplicable. EXAMPLE: In view of the task that lay ahead of him, he was amazed at the euphoria he felt. RELATED WORD: **euphoric,** *adjective* (yoo–FOR–ik).

evoke, *verb* (eh–VOHK). To call forth; to draw out. EXAMPLE: "Every slight movement in the street evoked a casual curiosity in him." (Richard Wright). RELATED WORDS: **evocable,** *adjective* (EV–uh–kuh–b'l), **evocation,** *noun* (ev–uh–KAY–shun), **evocative,** *adjective* (eh–VOK–uh–tiv) and **evocatively,** *adverb* (eh–VOK–uh–tiv–lee).

exacerbate, *verb* (eg–ZASS–er–bayt). To aggravate; to intensify the severity of. EXAMPLE: The problems of reaching an equitable settlement of the strike were exacerbated by the violent tactics some of the strikers used. RELATED WORD: **exacerbation,** *noun* (eg–zass–er–BAY–shun).

excoriate, *verb* (eks–KOR–ee–ayt). To strip off or wear off the skin. By extension, to tongue-lash; to rebuke scathingly. EXAMPLE: The soapbox speaker excoriated the heckler for his defense of the Establishment. RELATED WORD: **excoriation,** *noun* (eks–kor–ih–AY–shun).

exemplary, *adjective* (eg–ZEM–pluh–ree). Deserving to be imitated; or to serve as a model. Also, serving as a warning, as in "exemplary punishment." EXAMPLE: His courtroom behavior could not have been more exemplary. RELATED WORDS: **exemplar,** *noun* (eg–ZEM–pl'r), **exemplarily,** *adverb* (eg–ZEM–pluh–rih–lee) and **exemplariness,** *noun* (eg–ZEM–pluh–rih–nus).

expiation, *noun* (ek–spee–AY–sh'n). Atonement; amends, either the act or the means. EXAMPLE: The boys were ordered to clean up the entire school grounds as expiation for their vandalism. RELATED WORDS: **expiate,** *verb* (EK–spee–ayte), **expiator,** *noun* (EK–spee–uh–tohr) and **expiatory,** *adjective* (EK–spee–uh–tohr–ee).

exigency, *noun* (EKS–uh–jun–see). An urgent need requiring immediate attention or action. Usually used in the plural in referring to a situation. EXAMPLE: A special session of the assembly was called to deal with the exigencies of the school situation. RELATED WORDS: **exigent,** *adjective* (EKS–uh–j'nt) and **exigently,** *adverb* (EKS–uh–j'nt–lee).

extant, *adjective* (ek–STANT or EKS–tant). Continuing to exist or live; not destroyed or lost. EXAMPLE: In an effort to keep the species extant, many furriers are refusing to use leopard hides.

facetious, *adjective* (fuh–SEE–shus). Joking, lightly witty or humorous. EXAMPLE: The comedies of Noel Coward are notable for their facetious dialogue. RELATED WORDS: **facetiously,** *adverb* (fuh–SEE–shus–lee) and **facetiousness,** *noun* (fuh–SEE–shus–nus).

facile, *adjective* (FASS–'l). Easy, skillful, fluent, dexterous. EXAMPLE: The glib-tongued orator was notably facile in his choice of words. RELATED WORDS: **facilitate,** *verb* (fuh–SIL–ih–tayt) and **facility,** *noun* (fuh–SIL–ih–tee).

fallacious, *adjective* (fuh–LAY–shus). False, untrue, misleading, not based in fact. EXAMPLE: The attempt to eliminate the consumption of alcohol by the prohibition amendment was based upon fallacious reasoning. RELATED WORD: **fallacy,** *noun* (FAL–uh–see).

fallible, *adjective* (FAL–ih–b'l). Prone to error, likely to fail. EXAMPLE: Even the best-intentioned mortal is fallible, for "to err is human." RELATED WORDS: **fallibility,** *noun* (fal–ih–BIL–ih–tee) and **fallibly,** *adverb* (FAL–ib–lee).

farcical, *adjective* (FAR–sih–k'l). Hilariously funny, ridiculous, ludicrous. EXAMPLE: The president's pompous promises fell farcically short of fulfillment after his election. RELATED WORD: **farce,** *noun* (FARSS).

fastidious, *adjective* (fas–TID–ee–us). Very neat, meticulous. Also squeamish; hard to please. EXAMPLE: The woman was dressed with fastidious attention to the smallest detail. RELATED WORDS: **fastidiousness,** *noun* (fas–TID–ee–us–ness) and **fastidiously,** *adverb* (fas–TID–ee–us–lee).

fatuous, *adjective* (FAT–choo–us). Silly, empty, smugly stupid. EXAMPLE: We were bored to tears by her fatuous prattle. RELATED WORDS: **fatuously,** *adverb* (FAT–choo–us–lee) and **fatuousness,** *noun* (FAT–choo–us–ness).

feasible, *adjective* (FEE–zih–b'l). Practicable, workable, possible. EXAMPLE: "Coal, oil and waterfalls are the most feasible sources of power." (J. C. Furnas). RELATED WORDS: **feasibility,** *noun* (fee–zih–BIL–ih–tee), **feasibleness,** *noun* (FEE–zih–b'l–ness) and **feasibly,** *adverb* (FEE–zih–blee).

fecund, *adjective* (FEE–kund or FEK–und). Productive, fertile, fruitful. EXAMPLE: The writings of Shakespeare have proved a fecund source of literary quotations. RELATED WORDS: **fecundate,** *verb* (FEE–kun–dayt), **fecundation,** *noun* (fee–kun–DAY–shun) and **fecundity,** *noun* (fih–KUN–dih–tee).

fetid, *adjective* (FET–id). Foul-smelling, stinking. EXAMPLE: "The ship, full of fetid port air and swarming with mosquitoes, got underway." (Katherine Anne Porter).

fetish, *noun* (FET–ish). An object believed to have magical properties or mysterious powers; anything receiving unreasoning attention or devotion. EXAMPLE: "Public opinion, the fetish of the nineteenth century . . ." (James Russell Lowell).

fiasco, *noun* (fee–ASS–koh). Disastrous failure; ignominious end to an ambitious project. EXAMPLE: The scheme for a one-hundred-story skyscraper far outside the city limits proved an absolute fiasco.

fiat, *noun* (FY–at). Command, order, decree. EXAMPLE: In wartime a military governor may rule a captured province simply by fiat.

filch, *verb* (FILCH). To steal, pilfer, especially items of slight value. EXAMPLE: While the storekeeper's attention was elsewhere, he filched some peanuts from the display. RELATED WORD: **filcher,** *noun* (FIL–cher).

filial, *adjective* (FIL–ee–ul). Pertaining to a son or daughter, especially in his or her relationship to his parents. EXAMPLE: "My filial obedience was natural and easy." (Edward Gibbon).

finite, *adjective* (FY–nite). Having specific boundaries; limited. Also, impermanent, transient. EXAMPLE: "Rigid are the boundaries of this, our finite world." (William Morris). RELATED WORD: **finitely,** *adverb* (FY–nite–lee).

flamboyant, *adjective* (flam–BOY–unt). Splashy, gaudy, ornate, garish, richly colored. EXAMPLE: Few spectacles can match the flamboyant circus parade on the march. RELATED WORDS: **flamboyance,** *noun* (flam–BOY–unss), **flamboyancy,** *noun* (flam–BOY–un–see) and **flamboyantly,** *adjective* (flam–BOY–unt–lee).

foible, *noun* (FOY–b'l). Human failing, weakness of character. EXAMPLE: We love Micawber as much for his foibles as for his inherent integrity.

folderol, *noun* (FOL–der–ol). Nonsense; foolish talk. EXAMPLE: We had to wade through a lot of windy folderol before we could cut through to the essence of the argument. NOTE: The first *folderol* was incorporated in popular songs sung in English music halls in the early nineteenth century. It was a sort of infectious gibberish not unlike "Hut Sut on the Rillerah" and "Mairsy Doats," silly songs of a generation ago.

foment, *verb* (foh–MENT). To stir up, provoke, instigate, arouse. EXAMPLE: His only purpose in taking up the cause of the downtrodden and oppressed was to foment violent outbreaks and eventual revolution. RELATED WORDS: **fomentation,** *noun* (foh–men–TAY–shun) and **fomenter,** *noun* (foh–MEN–ter).

fortuitous, *adjective* (for–TYOO–ih–tus). Accidental, providential, happening by chance. EXAMPLE: Our encounter in Rome was entirely fortuitous. Neither of us knew the other was within three thousand miles of the Eternal City. RELATED WORDS: **fortuitously,** *adverb* (for–TYOO–ih–tus–lee), **fortuitousness,** *noun* (for–TYOO–ih–tus–ness) and **fortuity,** *noun* (for–TYOO–ih–tee).

friable, *adjective* (FRY–uh–b'l). Easily crushed or pulverized. EXAMPLE: Unlike most pills, these tablets are readily friable. Simply grasp between thumb and forefinger and squeeze. RELATED WORDS: **friability,** *noun* (fry–uh–BIL–ih–tee) and **friableness,** *noun* (FRY–uh–b'l–ness).

fulsome, *adjective* (FUL–sum). Disgustingly excessive; offensive, loathsome. EXAMPLE: "The oratory of the senator was so fulsome, so sloppily sentimental that it merited the adjective 'maudlin'." (Bruce Bohle). RELATED WORDS: **fulsomely,** *adverb* (FUL–sum–lee) and **fulsomeness,** *noun* (FUL–sum–ness). NOTE: This word is commonly misused, especially in phrases like "fulsome praise" and "fulsome oratory," by people who think it simply means "full" or "abundant." In its true sense, obviously, it is far from a flattering adjective.

furtive, *adjective* (FER–tiv). Stealthy, undercover, secretive, sly, surreptitious. EXAMPLE: Sneak thieves are notable for their furtive behavior. RELATED WORDS: **furtively,** *adverb* (FER–tiv–lee) and **furtiveness,** *noun* (FER–tiv–ness).

futile, *adjective* (FYOO–til or FYOO–tile). Ineffectual, vain, useless, unproductive. EXAMPLE: By the end of the first inning, we knew that the team's effort to win the championship would prove futile. RELATED WORDS: **futilely,** *adverb* (FYOO–til–lee), **futileness,** *noun* (FYOO–til–ness) and **futility,** *noun* (fyoo–TIL–ih–tee).

gamut, *noun* (GAM–ut). A complete course, series or range. EXAMPLE: "She ran the gamut of emotions from A to B." (Dorothy Parker, reviewing Katherine Hepburn's Broadway debut).

garble, *verb* (GAR–b'l). To distort, to mutilate, especially in retelling a story or an account of an incident. EXAMPLE: After passing through several layers of censorship, the account of the disaster was badly garbled.

garish, *adjective* (GAIR–ish). Flashy, gaudy, showy, excessively ornamented. EXAMPLE: "Hide me from Dad's garish eye." (John Milton).

garrulous, *adjective* (GAIR–uh–lus). Exceedingly talkative, loquacious, wordy. EXAMPLE: There are few things more boring than a garrulous old war veteran bent on proving how brave he was.

gauche, *adjective* (GOHSH). Awkward, lacking in social grace, tactless. EXAMPLE: His loud voice and gauche overtipping proved that he had not been reared as a gentleman. NOTE: *Gauche* is a borrowing from the French where it means simply "left." Compare this with *dexterous.*

genocide, *noun* (JEN–uh–side). The calculated extermination of masses of people, even of an entire race or religion. EXAMPLE: When accused of genocide at the Nuremberg trials, many Nazi officers claimed that they had merely been following orders.

geriatrics, *noun* (plural in form but taking a singular verb) (jer–ee–AT–rix). The science and treatment of old age and its ills. EXAMPLE: Certain areas of the West Coast of Florida are known as the "geriatrics belt," because of the many aged people who live there. RELATED WORDS: **geratric,** *adjective* (jer–ee–AT–rik) and **geriatrician,** *noun* (jer–ee–uh–TRISH–un).

germane, *adjective* (jer–MAYN). Relevant, closely related, pertinent. EXAMPLE: To keep the discussion from wandering, the chairman refused to admit any subjects not germane to the matter under discussion.

gist, *noun* (JIST). Essence, main point, central idea. EXAMPLE: The very gist of the Declaration of Independence may be found in the dedication to life, liberty and the pursuit of happiness.

glib, *noun* (GLIB). Smooth-speaking, fluent, especially when insincere. EXAMPLE: The senator was seldom more glib than when assuring his colleagues that he was innocent of any conflict of interest. RELATED WORDS: **glibly,** *adverb* (GLIB–lee) and **glibness,** *noun* (GLIB–ness).

gregarious, *adjective* (greh–GAIR–ee–us). Moving easily in crowds, liking company, enjoying the fellowship of others. EXAMPLE: An absolute requirement for a political candidate is that he must be gregarious by nature. RELATED WORD: **gregariously,** *adverb* (greh–GAIR–ee–us–lee).

hackneyed, *adjective* (HAK–need). Trite, over-worked, banal. EXAMPLE: Although the phrase is hackneyed, it's perfectly true that there's no place like home.

harbinger, *noun* (HAR–bin–jer). Prophet of things to come, forerunner, precursor. EXAMPLE: "In a few minutes would appear the train's harbinger . . . a puff of white smoke." (Vladimir Nabokov). NOTE: The first *harbingers* were royal servants or emissaries who traveled ahead of the royal party to make sure that lodging was prepared in advance.

hedonism, *noun* (HEE–dun–ism). Belief in pleasure for pleasure's own sake. EXAMPLE: In an atmosphere of license and extreme permissiveness, the cult of hedonism seems to have won many adherents. RELATED WORDS: **hedonistic,** *adjective* (hee–duh–NISS–tik) and **hedonist,** *noun* (HEE–dun–nist).

heinous, *adjective* (HAY–nus). Hateful, monstrous, atrocious, grossly wicked. EXAMPLE: Few events in literature are more heinous than Macbeth's cold-blooded slaying of Macduff's wife and children. RELATED WORDS: **heinously,** *adverb* (HAY–nus–lee) and **heinousness,** *noun* (HAY–nus–ness).

heretical, *adjective* (heh–RET–ih–kul). Unorthodox, nonconformist, disruptive. EXAMPLE: The judges of ancient Salem found the alleged witches guilty of heretical thoughts. RELATED WORDS: **heresy,** *noun* (HEH–reh–see) and **heretic,** *noun* (HEH–reh–tik).

hiatus, *noun* (hy–AY–tus). Gap, opening; pause, interruption. EXAMPLE: When the mayor appeared, there was a brief hiatus in the announced program so that he could make a few remarks to the group.

hierarchy, *noun* (HY–er–ar–kee). The various ranks in which persons in authority are grouped; a body so organized, especially of religious or church leaders. EXAMPLE: Until the advent of Pope John XXIII, the Roman Catholic hierarchy had been very rigidly structured for centuries. RELATED

WORDS: **hierarch,** *noun* (HY–er–ark), **hierarchic,** *adjective* (hy–er–AR–kik) and **hierarchical,** *adjective* (hy–er–AR–kik–al).

hirsute, *adjective* (HER–soot). Hairy, covered with hair. EXAMPLE: One of the more interesting phenomena of late twentieth century America is the return to favor of elaborate hirsute facial adornment among men.

histrionics, *noun* (his–tree–ON–ix). Theatrical entertainment, especially that of an elaborate, formal or pompous nature; dramatics; melodrama. EXAMPLE: The members of the legendary Barrymore clan were noted for histrionics, both on stage and off.

holocaust, *noun* (HOL–uh–kost). Great disaster, especially one accompanied by great loss of life and by fire. EXAMPLE: Historians debate whether the fire bombing of Dresden or the atom bombing of Hiroshima was the greatest holocaust of World War II. RELATED WORDS: **holocaustal,** *adjective* (hol–uh–KOSS–t'l); **holocaustic,** *adjective* (hol–uh–KOSS–tik).

homily, *noun* (HOM–ih–lee). Sermon or admonition, especially one intended as moral instruction and uplift. EXAMPLE: The sage old schoolteacher bored his pupils stiff with antiquated homilies.

homogeneous, *adjective* (hoh–muh–JEEN–ee–us). Composed of similar elements, uniform, alike in nature and kind. EXAMPLE: Thanks to the bussing of pupils from one school district to another the previously homogeneous racial patterns were disrupted.

honorarium, *noun* (hon–uh–RAIR–ee–um). Fee, stipend, especially one paid for professional consultation. EXAMPLE: An honorarium is what a publisher calls the fee when he wants to make it appear that he's doing you an honor to let you be associated with the work. It also enables him to offer you less money.

hypocrite, *noun* (HIP–uh–krit). One who pretends to beliefs or virtues he does not possess; an insincere person. EXAMPLE: "I swear he is no hypocrite but prays from the heart." (William Shakespeare).

ignominy, *noun* (IG–nuh–min–ee). Disgrace or dishonor, especially when widely publicized. Also, the act which brings the disgrace. EXAMPLE: The ignominy he suffered when the

swindle was exposed brought great anguish to his family.
RELATED WORDS: **ignominious**, *adjective* (ig–nuh–MIN–ee–us),
ignominiously, *adverb* (ig–nuh–MIN–ee–us–lee) and **igno-
miniousness**, *noun* (ig–nuh–MIN–ee–us–nus).

immure, *verb* (im–YOOR). To enclose within walls; to im-
prison. (Often used figuratively.) Also, to build into or en-
tomb within a wall. EXAMPLE: "Love lives not alone im-
mured in the brain." (William Shakespeare). RELATED WORD:
immurement, *noun* (ih–MYOOR–ment).

impasse, *noun* (IM–pass or im–PASS). A dead-end road or
passage. Also, a predicament or dilemma for which no solution is apparent. EXAMPLE: The negotiations seemed to have
reached an impasse since neither side was willing to yield on
one basic question.

impecunious, *adjective* (im–peh–KYOO–nee–us). Penniless;
habitually poverty-stricken. EXAMPLE: His father disinherited
him, and he seemed doomed to an impecunious existence.
RELATED WORDS: **impecuniosity**, *noun* (im–peh–kyoo–nee–
OSS–ih–tee), **impecuniously**, *adverb* (im–peh–KYOO–nee–
us–lee) and **impecuniousness**, *noun* (im–peh–KYOO–nee–
us–nus).

impinge, *verb* (im–PINJ). To strike or dash upon or against;
to encroach or invade; to infringe. EXAMPLE: The man
brought suit against the neighborhood association on the
grounds that a chain across the road impinged on his right
of free access to his own property. RELATED WORDS: **impinge-
ment**, *noun* (im–PINJ–m'nt) and **impinger**, *noun* (im–
PINJ–'r).

imponderable, *adjective* (im–PON–der–uh–b'l). Not capable of
being weighed, measured or evaluated; intangible. EXAMPLE:
In an effort to arrive at a decision, he listed the imponderable
as well as the tangible elements in the situation. RELATED
WORDS: **imponderableness**, *noun* (im–PON–der–uh–b'l–nus)
and **imponderably**, *adverb* (im–PON–der–uh–blee).

importune, *verb* (im–por–TYOON). To beg or plead; to request repeatedly. EXAMPLE: The lawyer importuned the bank
for a time extension on the loan but without success. RELATED
WORDS: **importunate**, *adjective* (im–POR–choo–nit), **impor-
tunately**, *adverb* (im–POR–choo–nit–lee), **importunateness**,
noun (im–POR–choo–nit–nus), **importunely**, *adverb* (im–
por–TYOON–lee), **importuner**, *noun* (im–por–TYOON–'r)
and **importunity**, *noun* (im–por–TYOON–ih–tee).

imprecation, *noun* (im–preh–KAY–shun). A curse; the act of invoking a curse. EXAMPLE: The angry father hurled imprecations at the man whose car had struck his daughter. RELATED WORDS: **imprecate,** *verb* (IM–preh–kayt) and **imprecatory,** *adjective* (IM–preh–kuh–tor–ee).

impute, *verb* (im–PYOOT). To lay blame or responsibility for, sometimes without cause. Also, to give credit to; to attribute. EXAMPLE: "How dare you . . . impute such monstrous intentions to me?" (George Bernard Shaw). RELATED WORDS: **imputable,** *adjective* (im–PYOO–tuh–b'l), **imputably,** *adverb* (im–PYOO–tuh–blee), **imputation,** *noun* (im–pyoo–TAY–shun), **imputative,** *adjective* (im–PYOO–tuh–tiv) and **imputatively,** *adverb* (im–PYOO–tuh–tiv–lee).

inane, *adjective* (in–AYN). Senseless or pointless; without meaning or significance; silly. EXAMPLE: The woman was a master of the inane comment. RELATED WORDS: **inanely,** *adverb* (in–AYN–lee) and **inanity,** *noun* (in–AN–ih–tee).

indigenous, *adjective* (in–DIJ–ih–nus). Native to a particular region, country or state; born and/or growing naturally in such a place (said of animals and plants). EXAMPLE: "No horses I have ever seen are so hardy as those little animals which are indigenous to the Kirghis steppes." (F. C. Burnaby). RELATED WORDS: **indigent,** *noun* (IN–dih–jent), **indigenously,** *adverb* (in–DIJ–ih–nus–lee) and **indigenousness,** *noun* (in–DIJ–ih–nus–nes).

indolent, *adjective* (IN–dul–l'nt). Lazy, disinclined to work. EXAMPLE: The new typist approached her task in such an indolent manner that her employer realized immediately that she would have to be replaced. RELATED WORD: **indolence,** *noun* (IN–duh–lunss).

infinitesimal, *adjective* (in–fin–ih–TESS–ih–mul). Minute; inmeasurably small. EXAMPLE: He prided himself on the infinitesimal amount of vermouth he used in making martinis. RELATED WORD: **infinitesimally,** *adverb* (in–fin–ih–TESS–ih–mul–lee).

inherent, *adjective* (in–HEER–'nt). Inborn; basic, usually referring to a characteristic or quality; belonging by nature. EXAMPLE: I never doubted his word because he had long since proved his inherent honesty. RELATED WORDS: **inhere,** *verb* (in–HEER), **inherence,** *noun* (in–HEER–'ns), **inherency,** *noun* (in–HEER–en–see) and **inherently,** *adverb* (in–HEER–'nt–lee).

innocuous, *adjective* (in–NOK–yoo–us). Harmless; producing no injury or bad effect; lacking in real meaning or significance; insipid. EXAMPLE: Most April Fool jokes are innocuous. RELATED WORDS: **innocuously,** *adverb* (in–NOK–yoo–us–lee) and **innocuousness,** *noun* (in–NOK–yoo–us–nus).

inordinate, *adjective* (in–ORD–in–it). Excessive, immoderate; irregular or disordered. EXAMPLE: He took an inordinate pride in his piano playing, although he had only modest ability. RELATED WORDS: **inordinacy,** *noun* (in–ORD–in–uh–see), **inordinately,** *adverb* (in–ORD–in–it–lee) and **inordinateness,** *noun* (in–ORD–in–it–nus).

inscrutable, *adjective* (in–SCROO–tih–b'l). Enigmatic; not capable of being understood. EXAMPLE: An inscrutable countenance is invaluable to a diplomat. RELATED WORDS: **inscrutability,** *noun* (in–scroo–ta–BIL–ih–tee), **inscrutableness,** *noun* in–SCROO–tih–b'l–nus) and **inscrutably,** *adverb* (in–SCROO–tih–blee).

insensate, *adjective* (in–SEN–sit). Lacking physical awareness or sensation; without feeling or understanding; inhuman. EXAMPLE: Many accused the president of being insensate to the wishes of the people. RELATED WORD: **insensately,** *adverb* (in–SEN–sit–lee).

intractable, *adjective* (in–TRAK–tuh–b'l). Unruly; not easily managed, governed or dealt with. EXAMPLE: When I was in school, pupils who proved intractable in the classroom were sent to the principal's office for punishment. RELATED WORDS: **intractability,** *noun* (in–trak–tih–BIL–ih–tee), **intractableness,** *noun* (in–TRAK–tih–b'l–nus) and **intractably,** *adverb* (in–TRAK–tuh–blee).

inveigh, *verb* (in–VAY). To make bitter or vehement protest; to rail. EXAMPLE: The mothers inveighed against the construction of a parking lot on a site they had hoped would become a playground. RELATED WORD: **inveigher,** *noun* (in–VAY–er).

inveigle, *verb* (in–VEE–g'l or in–VAY–g'l). To persuade by flattery or deceit; to entice. EXAMPLE: Within a month she had inveigled him into marrying her. RELATED WORDS: **inveiglement,** *noun* (in–VEE–g'l–m'nt) and **inveigler,** *noun* (in–VEE–gler).

inveterate, *adjective* (in–VET–er–it). Habitual, confirmed, deep-rooted as the result of habit or practice of long standing. EXAMPLE: All his associates knew him to be an inveterate gambler. RELATED WORDS: **inveteracy,** *noun* (in–VET–er–uh–see), **inveterateness,** *noun* (in–VET–er–it–nus) and **inveterately,** *adverb* (in–VET–er–it–lee).

invidious, *adjective* (in–VID–ee–us). Tending to provoke animosity or resentment. EXAMPLE: She was deeply hurt by his invidious comparison of her to the younger woman. RELATED WORDS: **invidiously,** *adverb* (in–VID–ee–us–lee) and **invidiousness,** *noun* (in–VID–ee–us–nus).

irascible, *adjective* (ih–RASS–ih–b'l). Easily provoked to anger. EXAMPLE: As grandfather grew older, he seemed to become more and more irascible. RELATED WORDS: **irascibility,** *noun* (ih–rass–ih–BIL–ih–tee), **irascibleness,** *noun* (ih–RASS–ih–b'l–nus) and **irascibly,** *adverb* (ih–RASS–ih–blee).

jack-a-napes, *noun* (JAK–uh–nayps). Upstart; an impertinent person or a mischievous child. EXAMPLE: ". . . dressing him out like a jack-a-napes and giving him money to play the fool with." (Lord Chesterfield).

jaded, *adjective* (JAY–ded). Worn out or satiated as the result of excessive indulgence. EXAMPLE: ". . . the sickening sweet life of the amoral, jaded, bored upper classes." (John Simon). RELATED WORDS: **jadedly,** *adverb* (JAY–ded–lee) and **jadedness,** *noun* (JAY–ded–nus).

jape, *noun* (JAYP). A joke, quip, jest. EXAMPLE: The salesman's awkward japes did little to put the customer in a mood for purchase. RELATED WORDS: **jape,** *verb* and **japery,** *noun* (JAYP–er–ee).

jargon, *noun* (JAR–gun). The special language of a trade or profession; argot; cant. EXAMPLE: "She could not follow the ugly academic-jargon." (Virginia Woolf).

jaundiced, *adjective* (JAWN–diss'd). Marked with emotion such as distaste, satiety, prejudice or hostility; embittered. EXAMPLE: He took a jaundiced view of the elaborate plans that had been made for the festivities. RELATED WORD: **jaundice,** *noun* (JAWN–diss).

jaunty, *adjective* (JAWN–tee). Sprightly, referring to dress or manner; gay and care-free. EXAMPLE: The girl completed her costume with a jaunty hat of bright red straw. RELATED WORDS: **jauntily,** *adverb* (JAWN–tih–lee) and **jauntiness,** *noun* (JAWN–tih–nus).

jeer, *verb* (JEER). To deride, scoff, mock, taunt. EXAMPLE:

The crowd began to jeer when the officer told them to disperse. RELATED WORDS: **jeerer**, *noun* (JEER–er) and **jeeringly**, *adverb* (JEER–ing–lee).

jejune, *adjective* (jeh–JOON). Insipid, barren, dull, arousing no enthusiasm. EXAMPLE: "There pour forth jejune words and useless, empty phrases." (Anthony Trollope).

jeopardy, *noun* (JEP–er–dee). Hazard, danger, peril, vulnerability. EXAMPLE: Even a slight error in timing puts a trapeze artist's life in jeopardy. RELATED WORDS: **jeopardize**, *verb* (JEP–er–dize) and **jeopardous**, *adjective* (JEP–er–dus).

jeremiad, *noun* (jer–uh–MY–ad). Lamentation; long drawn-out tale of woe. EXAMPLE: Mets fans, weary of season-end jeremiads, were elated to cheer their conquering heroes. NOTE: This word is derived from the name of the Old Testament prophet Jeremiah, author of the Book of Lamentations.

jerry-built, *adjective* (JEH–ee–BILT). Built flimsily with cheap materials. EXAMPLE: With mortgage money so scarce, it is difficult to buy even a jerry-built house.

jettison, *verb* (JET–ih–sun). To cast off or discard, abandon. EXAMPLE: The publisher decided to jettison the magazine as an unprofitable venture.

jezebel, *noun* (JEZ–uh–bel). A wicked, shameless woman. NOTE: The first Jezebel was the infamous wife of Ahab, king of Israel, and was notorious for her wickedness. (I Kings 16:31 et seq.) EXAMPLE: Four of the witnesses at the divorce hearing testified that she was a true jezebel.

jingo, *noun* (JING–goh). One who believes in an aggressive foreign policy for his country; a chauvinist. EXAMPLE: It can be dangerous to have a jingo as head of the Department of State. RELATED WORDS: **jingoism**, *noun* (JING–goh–izm), **jingoist**, *noun* (JING–goh–ist) and **jingoistic**, *adjective* (JING–goh–ist–ik).

jocose, *adjective* (joh–KOHS). Joking, funny, given to jest; facetious. EXAMPLE: Nothing brightens a speech better than a jocose introduction. RELATED WORDS: **jocosely**, *adverb* (joh–KOHS–lee), **jocular**, *adjective* (JOK–yoo–ler), **jocularity**, *noun* (jok-yoo–LAIR–ih–tee) and **jocularly**, *adverb* (JOK–yoo–lar–lee).

jocund, *adjective* (JOK–und). Gay, cheerful, jolly; mirthful. EXAMPLE: A jocund salesman is usually a successful one. RELATED WORDS: **jocundly**, *adverb* (JOK–und–lee) and **jocundity**, *noun* (joh–KUN–dih–tee).

jostle, *verb* (JOSS–'l). To push or shove; to come into contact with; to contend with. EXAMPLE: Early Christmas shopping makes it unnecessary to jostle one's way through last-minute crowds.

joust, *verb* (JOWST). To engage in a duel of lances while on horseback; hence, to engage in competition with another. EXAMPLE: "Car manufacturers jousting like surly giants over the business of making and selling millions of motor cars . . ." (A. W. Baum).

judicious, *adjective* (joo–DISH–uss). Based on sound judgment. EXAMPLE: By judicious handling of its finances, a family can usually avoid going into debt. RELATED WORDS: **judiciously,** *adverb* (joo–DISH–uss–lee) and **judiciousness,** *noun* (joo–DISH–uss–nus).

jugular, *noun* (JUG–yuh–ler). One of the large veins in the neck. (Also used figuratively.) EXAMPLE: A participant in cut-throat competition can be said to have an instinct for the jugular.

junket, *noun and verb* (JUN–ket). As a noun, **junket** initially meant a custardlike dessert. Then it extended its meaning to cover picnics and feasts at which such a dessert might be served. Then, in recent years, it has come to mean a kind of free-loading excursion, often by politicians at taxpayers' expense. This has led also to the creation of the verb meaning to take such a trip. EXAMPLE: The legislators' trip to inspect European air bases was little more than a junket to various spas and resorts—all paid for by air force funds. RELATED WORDS: **junketer,** *noun* (JUNK–et–er) and **junketeer,** *noun* (jun–keh–TEER).

jurisdiction, *noun* (joor–iss–DIK–shun). Legal authority or control; the extent or scope of such authority or control. EXAMPLE: The students contended that the matters of skirt and hair length lay in their parents' jurisdiction. RELATED WORDS: **jurisdictional,** *adjective* (joor–iss–DIK–shun–'l) and **jurisdictionally,** *adverb* (joor–iss–DIK–shun–uh–lee).

jurisprudence, *noun* (joor–iss–PROO–d'nss). The science or philosophy of law; a system of law. Also, the course of court decisions as distinguished from legislation. EXAMPLE: The numerous court cases relating to interpretation of the Selective Service Act have resulted in a whole new area of jurisprudence. RELATED WORDS: **jurist,** *noun* (JOOR–ist), **jurispru-**

dent, *noun* (joor–iss–PROO–d'nt), **jurisprudential,** *adjective* (joor–iss–proo–DEN–shul) and **jurisprudentially,** *adverb* (joor–iss–proo–DEN–shuh–lee).

kaleidoscope, *noun* (kuh–LY–duh–skohp). A tube in which a considerable variety of color patterns are created which may be rapidly changed if the viewer twists the tube. Hence, any constantly changing scene or experience. EXAMPLE: Today's three-ring circus provides a veritable kaleidoscope of colorful faces, animals and exciting stunts. RELATED WORDS: **kaleidoscopic,** *adjective* (kuh–ly–duh–SKOP–ik) and **kaleidoscopically,** *adverb* (kuh–ly–duh–SKOP–ik–uh–lee).

kaput, *adjective* (kah–POOT). Destroyed, out of commission, wrecked. EXAMPLE: Despite the investment of millions, the highly touted swingwing plane went kaput.

karma, *noun* (KAR–muh). Destiny, fate, the end result of existence. EXAMPLE: "As our desires shape themselves, so we act and build up our coming fate, our karma." (Paul Elmer More).

keelhaul, *verb* (KEEL–haul). To punish a person by dragging him under the keel of a boat from one side to the other. EXAMPLE: Once the jury was safely out of earshot, the judge keelhauled both the defendant and his attorney in some of the most biting language ever heard in a court of law. NOTE: This kind of punishment is, of course, long obsolete, but the word is still used figuratively in the sense of to castigate or to abuse with words.

ken, *noun* (KEN). Knowledge, understanding; range of perception. EXAMPLE: The finer points of the new math are simply beyond my ken.

kibitzer, *noun* (KIB–it–ser). A meddler; an unwanted onlooker and commentator; one who gives gratuitous advice. EXAMPLE: In the great drama of international power politics, we all tend to be kibitzers. RELATED WORD: **kibitz,** *verb* (KIB–itz).

kibosh, *noun* (KY–bosh). An end to something, a sudden termination; a squelching. It is used chiefly in the expression "put the kibosh on." EXAMPLE: The arrival of the police quickly put the kibosh on the riotous street brawl.

kindred, *adjective* (KIN–dred). Pertaining to one's relatives, family, clan; similar in origin, nature or character. EXAMPLE: "The youth studied the faces of his companions, ever on the watch to detect kindred emotions." (Stephen Crane).

kiosk, *noun* (KEE–osk). Originally an open summer-house in Turkey or elsewhere in the Middle East; now a cylindrical structure housing a news-stand, subway exit or the like. EXAMPLE: "The kiosk in the center of Harvard Square was surrounded by milling students and townies aching for a fight." (C. L. Whipple).

kismet, *noun* (KIZ–met). Destiny, fate, fortune. EXAMPLE: The bank foreclosed the mortgage. His son wrecked the family car. His wife ran off with his best friend. But he was philosophical. "You can't win them all," he murmured. "It's kismet."

kleptomania, *noun* (klep–toh–MAY–nee–uh). An irresistible desire to steal; a compulsion toward theft. EXAMPLE: The banker's wife, of all people, was driven so by kleptomania that she was several times picked up for shoplifting. RELATED WORD: **kleptomaniac,** *noun* (klep–toh–MAY–nee–ak).

kosher, *adjective* (KOH–sher). Prescribed according to Jewish dietary ritual; by extension, correct, proper, permissible, legitimate. EXAMPLE: Before making any investment in the project, he insisted on proof that it would be entirely kosher.

kowtow, *verb* (KOW–tow). To defer to, to bow before, to show deference to. EXAMPLE: The imperious lexicographer would brook no contradiction from his subeditors. He insisted that they kowtow to his every whim.

kudos, *noun* (KYOO–doss). Praise, acclaim, honor, glory. EXAMPLE: "All the kudos of the Presidency of the United States . . ." (Eric Goldman) NOTE: This word is very widely misused by people who don't realize that *kudos* is a singular noun. It is NOT the plural of "kudo"—a word which simply does not exist. Properly speaking, one should say "Kudos IS (not ARE) due him for his achievement."

lachrymose, *adjective* (LAK–rih–mohs). Tearful, sad, mournful, weeping. EXAMPLE: When she emerged from the theater, her red-rimmed eyes proved that she had spent a lachrymose hour or two. RELATED WORD: **lacrimosely,** *adverb* (lak–rih–MOHS–lee).

laconic, *adjective* (luh–KON–ik). Terse, succinct, short, concise. EXAMPLE: The early prose of Ernest Hemingway was noted for its short, punchy sentences and generally laconic style. RELATED WORDS: **laconically,** *adverb* (luh–KON–ih–kuh–lee); **laconism,** *noun* (LAK–uh–nism).

lagniappe, *noun* (lan–YAP). A trifling gift, especially one given to close a deal or cement a bargain. EXAMPLE: In the traditional "baker's dozen" the thirteenth doughnut may be considered the lagniappe.

lambent, *adjective* (LAM–bent). Gleaming, softly radiant, twinkling, flickering. EXAMPLE: ". . . his eyes soft and lambent." (Katherine Anne Porter).

languid, *adjective* (LANG–wid). Lacking vigor and vitality; indifferent; without interest or spirit. EXAMPLE: ". . . the Irish had been languid in their demands for autonomy." (Sean O'Faolain) RELATED WORDS: **languidly,** *adverb* (LANG–wid–lee), **languor,** *noun* (LANG–er) and **languish,** *verb* (LANG–wish).

larcenous, *adjective* (LAR–sen–us). Thieving, inclined to or guilty of stealing. EXAMPLE: Merchants take substantial losses annually because of larcenous clerks. RELATED WORDS: **larcenist,** *noun* (LAR–sen–ist); **larceny,** *noun* (LAR–sen–ee).

largesse, *noun* (lar–JESS). Generous gift, generosity, liberality in gift-giving. EXAMPLE: For years she subsisted on the largesse of a well-to-do aunt.

latent, *adjective* (LAY–tent). Potential, concealed, not apparent or manifest. EXAMPLE: The challenge of athletic competition sometimes reveals latent abilities in high-school pupils. RELATED WORDS: **latency,** *noun* (LAY–ten–see) and **latently** *adverb* (LAY–tent–lee).

lectern, *noun* (LEK–tern). Reading stand or desk, usually with a slanted top, where the speaker can place his speech or notes. EXAMPLE: As the speaker strode to the lectern, a hush fell over the audience. NOTE: The word *podium* is frequently used when *lectern* is meant. A *podium* is a raised platform that a lecturer or conductor must mount, while a *lectern* is merely the desk or stand described above.

lethal, *adjective* (LEE–thul). Deadly, fatal, capable of causing death. EXAMPLE: The bottle contained a lethal poison. RELATED WORD: **lethality,** *noun* (lee–THAL–ih–tee).

lethargic, *adjective* (leh–THAR–jik). Slow-moving, easy-going, lazy, drowsy, dull, sluggish, sleepy. EXAMPLE: Midday in a small town of the antebellum South always produced a mood of lethargic somnolence. RELATED WORD: **lethargy,** *noun* (LETH–er–jee).

levity, *noun* (LEV–ih–tee). Light-heartedness, gaiety, frivolousness, lightness. EXAMPLE: "My method is to take the utmost trouble to find the right thing to say, and then to say it with the utmost levity." (George Bernard Shaw).

lexicon, *noun* (LEX–ih–kon). Glossary, dictionary, the vocabulary of a trade or profession. EXAMPLE: He was familiar with "imprint," "out-of-print," "quantity discount"—indeed with the entire lexicon of the book wholesaler.

liaison, *noun* (lee–AY–zun). Close relationship; means of communication between two persons or groups; intimate relationship between male and female, especially when illicit. EXAMPLE: He had served as liaison between French and American units during the invasion.

limbo, *noun* (LIM–boh). Place of exile or detention; oblivion; place to which are relegated things or persons no longer wanted. EXAMPLE: Refused further promotion or increases in pay, the subeditor finally realized that he had been shunted into a sort of limbo. NOTE: The original religious sense of *limbo* was of a resting place for souls inadmissible to heaven because they had not been baptized.

limpid, *adjective* (LIM–pid). Transparent, clear, lucid; serene. EXAMPLE: "The early mornings and evenings were limpid and restful." (Isak Dinesen). RELATED WORDS: **limpidity,** *noun* (lim–PID–ih–tee), **limpidness,** *noun* (LIM–pid–ness) and **limpidly,** *adverb* (LIM–pid–lee).

lissome, *adjective* (LIS–sum). Supple, graceful, flexible, lithe. EXAMPLE: The danseuse moved with lissome elegance. RELATED WORDS: **lissomely,** *adverb* (LIS–sum–lee) and **lissomeness,** *noun* (LIS–sum–ness).

logistics, *noun* (loh–JISS–tix). Procurement and maintenance of men, supplies and equipment. EXAMPLE: Effective deployment of military manpower and firepower is an impossibility without careful attention to all the details of logistics. NOTE: Though plural in form, *logistics* is construed as singular: logistics IS (not ARE) a prime concern of the military.

loquacious, *adjective.* (loh–KWAY–shus). Talkative, garrulous, given to incessant chatter. EXAMPLE: I could have slept through the whole flight except for the loquacious female directly behind me. RELATED WORDS: **loquaciously,** *adverb* (loh–KWAY–shus–lee) and **loquacity,** *noun* (loh–KWASS–it–tee).

lucid, *adjective* (LOO–sid). Clear, intelligible, sane, rational. EXAMPLE: Between spells of delirium, the patient had absolutely lucid periods. RELATED WORDS: **lucidly,** *adverb* (LOO–sid–lee) and **lucidity,** *noun* (loo–SID–ih–tee).

malefactor, *noun* (MAL–eh–fak–ter). One who breaks the law; a criminal. EXAMPLE: The police proved that a prominent businessman was the malefactor. RELATED WORDS: **malefaction,** *noun* (mal–uh–FAK–shun) and **malefactress,** *noun* (MAL–eh–fak–tress).

malign, *verb* (muh–LYNE). To speak evil of without basis in fact; to slander. To injure another's reputation by false insinuations or statement. EXAMPLE: The lawyer informed him that unless he ceased to malign his neighbor he would face legal action. RELATED WORDS: **malignance,** *noun* (muh–LIG–nunss), **malignancy,** *noun* (muh–LIG–nun–see), **malignant,** *adjective* (muh–LIG–nunt), **maligner,** *noun* (muh–LYNE–er), **malignity,** *noun* (muh–LIG–nih–tee) and **malignly,** *adverb* (muh–LYNE–lee).

maudlin, *adjective* (MAWD–lin). Excessively and effusively sentimental, sometimes as the result of drunkenness. EXAMPLE: He dreaded the maudlin reminiscences which were always a part of his class reunion. RELATED WORDS: **maudlinly,** *adverb* (MAWD–lin–lee) and **maudlinness,** *noun* (MAWD–lin–nus).

mayhem, *noun* (MAY–hem). The deliberate maiming or permanent crippling or disfiguring of a person. Also, wanton destruction of something. EXAMPLE: He gave the boy a beating that was just short of mayhem. RELATED WORD: **maim,** *verb* (MAYM).

megalomania, *noun* (meg–uh–lo–MAY–nee–uh). Mental disorder characterized by exaggerated notions of omnipotence. EXAMPLE: Every dictator in history has probably suffered from megalomania. RELATED WORDS: **megalomaniac,** *noun* (meg–uh–lo–MAY–nee–ak) and **megalomaniacal,** *adjective* (meg–uh–lo–MAY–nee–ak–'l).

mendacious, *adjective* (men–DAY–shus). Dishonest, untruthful, lying. EXAMPLE: The historian's memoirs were mendacious and also dull. RELATED WORDS: **mendaciously,** *adverb* (men–DAY–shus–lee) and **mendaciousness,** *noun* (men–DAY–shus–nus).

mentor, *noun* (MEN–ter). A trusted teacher, tutor or counselor. EXAMPLE: He became successful in local politics because he had the former senator as his mentor.

mercenary, *adjective* and *noun* (MER–s'n–ehr–ee). Motivated only by the desire for money or gain. Also, as a noun it means one who works solely for pay, as a hired soldier in the service of a foreign country. EXAMPLE: He felt it necessary to keep a close eye on his associate whom he thought far too mercenary for total honesty. The senate acted to bar use of Loatian mercenaries in the Indochina conflict. RELATED WORDS: **mercenarily,** *adverb* (MER–s'n–ehr–uh–lee) and **mercenariness,** *noun* (MER–s'n–ehr–ee–nus).

meretricious, *adjective* (mer–uh–TRISH–us). Pertaining to a prostitute. Hence, insincere; tawdry; deceptively attractive. EXAMPLE: "There is no pomp of words; there is an entire lack of even the attempt at meretricious adornment." (T. R. Loussbury). RELATED WORDS: **meretriciously,** *adverb* (mer–uh–TRISH–us–lee) and **meretriciousness,** *noun* (mer–uh–TRISH–us–nus). NOTE: Do not confuse *meretricious* with *meritorious,* which has the opposite meaning.

metamorphosis, *noun* (met–uh–MOR–fuh–sis). Transformation; a change in shape, structure, appearance, character or circumstance. EXAMPLE: "His visage changed as from a mask to a face. I know not that I have ever seen in any other human face an equal metamorphosis." (Charlotte Brontë). RELATED WORDS: **metamorphic,** *adjective* (met–uh–MOR–fik), **metamorphism,** *noun* (met–uh–MOR–fizm) and **metamorphose,** *verb* (met–uh–MOR–fohz).

misogynist, *noun* (mih–SOJ–ih–nist). A hater of women. EXAMPLE: Life with his first wife had been almost enough to turn him into a misogynist. RELATED WORDS: **misogynistic,** *adjective* (mih–SOJ–uh–nis–tik), **misogynous,** *noun* (mih–SOJ–uh–nus) and **misogyny,** *noun* (mih–SOJ–uh–nee).

mitigate, *verb* (MIT–ih–gayt). To make less painful or harsh; to alleviate. EXAMPLE: The mother's grief at her son's departure was mitigated by the knowledge that he would be in good hands. RELATED WORDS: **mitigation,** *noun* (MIT–ih–gay–shun), **mitigative,** *adjective* (MIT–uh–gay–tiv), **mitiga-**

tor, *noun* (MIT–uh–gay–tor) and **mitigatory,** *adjective* (MIT–ih–guh–tor–ee).

mollify, *verb* (MOL–ih–fy). To pacify, placate or appease; to soften. EXAMPLE: The man managed to mollify his disappointed wife by presenting her with theater tickets for the following night. RELATED WORDS: **mollifiable,** *adjective* (MOL–uh–fy–uh–b'l); **mollification,** *noun* (mol–uh–fuh–KAY–shun); **mollifier,** *noun* (MOL–uh–fy–er) and **mollifyingly,** *adverb* (MOL–uh–fy–ing–lee).

morass, *noun* (muh–RASS). A bog or swamp; low, marshy ground. Hence, a confused or difficult situation or condition. EXAMPLE: One problem you face after a long vacation is finding important letters in the morass of accumulated and unsorted mail that has arrived in your absence.

moribund, *adjective* (MOR–ih–bund). Dying. Coming to an end or going out of existence. EXAMPLE: "The wail of a moribund world . . ." (Thomas Carlyle). RELATED WORDS: **moribundity,** *noun* (mor–ih–BUN–dih–tee) and **moribundly,** *adverb* (MOR–ih–bund–lee).

morose, *adjective* (muh–ROHSS). Sullen; gloomy. EXAMPLE: After hearing the doctor's diagnosis of her illness, she became very morose and uncommunicative. RELATED WORDS: **morosely,** *adverb* (muh–ROHSS–lee) and **moroseness,** *noun* (muh–ROHSS–nus).

motley, *adjective* (MOT–lee). Multi-colored. Also, made up of diversified elements. EXAMPLE: The auction drew a strange and motley collection of people, many of whom came only out of curiosity.

multifarious, *adjective* (mul–tih–FAIR–ee–us). Having great variety or diversity. EXAMPLE: The minister's multifarious community activities left him little time for his family. RELATED WORDS: **multifariously,** *adverb* (mul–tih–FAIR–ee–us–lee) and **multifariousness,** *noun* (mul–tih–FAIR–ee–us–nus).

mundane, *adjective* (mun–DAYN). Secular rather than spiritual; worldly. Also, relating to the practical or ordinary. EXAMPLE: The mundane problems of keeping house can be very stifling to the creative mind. RELATED WORD: **mundanely,** *adverb* (mun–DAYN–lee).

munificent, *adjective* (myoo–NIH–fih–sent). Extremely generous or liberal in giving; showing evidence of such generosity. EXAMPLE: Many private schools depend on munificent gifts from former students. RELATED WORDS: **munificence,** *noun* (myoo–NIH–fih–senss) and **munificently,** *adverb* (myoo–NIH–fih–sent–lee).

nabob, *noun* (NAY–bob). Originally, a native ruler in India but now any man of extreme wealth. EXAMPLE: Nob Hill in San Francisco got its name from the fact that local nabobs built palatial homes there.

narcissism, *noun* (NAHR–siss–izm). Excessive love of one's self; great concern with one's physical appearance, importance and comfort. EXAMPLE: A woman who displays considerable narcissism is not likely to make a good marriage partner. NOTE: The original Narcissus was a youth in Greek myth who fell in love with his own image in a pool of water and was transformed into the flower narcissus, also popularly called jonquil and daffodil. RELATED WORDS: **narcissist,** *noun* (NAHR–sih–sist) and **narcissistic,** *adjective* (nahr–sih–SISS–tik).

narcosis, *noun* (nahr–KOH–sis). A comatose state brought on by the use of a narcotic. EXAMPLE: The doctors in the emergency room quickly identified his condition as narcosis. RELATED WORD: **narcotic,** *noun* and *adjective* (nahr–KOT–ik).

nebulous, *adjective* (NEB–yoo–luss). Unclear; vague, hazy; cloudy, indistinct. EXAMPLE: Their plans for the summer are still quite nebulous since a lot will depend on how much money is available. RELATED WORDS: **nebula,** *noun* (NEB–yoo–luh), **nebular,** *adjective* (NEB–yoo–lahr), **nebulously,** *adverb* (NEB–yoo–luss–lee) and **nebulousness,** *noun* (NEB–yoo–luss–nuss).

nefarious, *adjective* (neh–FAIR–ee–us). Characterized by villainy or evil. EXAMPLE: "A white cat, stealing with wary look and stealthy pace towards the stables, as if on some nefarious expedition." (Washington Irving). RELATED WORDS: **nefariously,** *adverb* (neh–FAIR–ee–us–lee) and **nefariousness,** *noun* (neh–FAIR–ee–us–nus).

nemesis, *noun* (NEM–ih–siss). Retribution or justifiable vengeance; the person who so avenges. Also, a victorious foe. EXAMPLE: "We carry our nemesis within us: yesterday's self-admiration is the legitimate father of today's feeling of guilt." (Dag Hammerskjold). NOTE: The word comes from Nemesis, the Greek goddess of vengeance.

neologism, *noun* (nee–OL–uh–jizm). The name for a newly-coined word, phrase or expression; a new meaning for an old word, phrase or expression. Also, the act of coining words or changing meanings. EXAMPLE: The almanac features a list of the previous year's neologisms. RELATED WORDS: **neologist,** *noun* (nee–OL–oh–jist); **neologistic,** *adjective* (nee–ol–oh–JISS–tik), **neologistical,** *adjective* (nee–ol–oh–JISS–tih–k'l) and **neology,** *noun* (nee–OL–oh–jee).

neophyte, *noun* (NEE–uh–fyte). A beginner. In the Roman Catholic Church, a newly ordained priest or a novice in a convent. EXAMPLE: As a neophyte on the newspaper staff, he could not expect to get important assignments.

nepotism, *noun* (NEP–uh–tizm). The practice by officials, either in public or private office, of showing favoritism to relatives, especially in terms of employment. EXAMPLE: When the charges of nepotism were investigated, the congressman was found to have a sister and a niece on his payroll. NOTE: The word comes from the Latin "nepos," nephew, because rulers of the Church were often said to give preference to their nephews in making appointments. RELATED WORDS: **nepotist,** *noun* (NEP–uh–tist), **nepotistic,** *adjective* (nep–uh–TISS–tik) and **nepotistical,** *adjective* (nep–uh–TISS–tih–k'l).

nihilism, *noun* (NY–ul–izm). This word has numerous shades of meaning, ranging fɪ ʰn nothingness to belief in the need for complete destruction of social institutions as the only means of progress. EXAMPLE: Nihilism is the credo of "a man who does not bow to any authorities, who does not take any principle on trust, no matter with what respect that principle is surrounded." (I. S. Turgenev). RELATED WORDS: **nihilist,** *noun* (NY–uh–list), **nihilistic,** *adjective* (NY–uh–liss–tik) and **nihility,** *noun* (ny–HIL–ih–tee).

noisome, *adjective* (NOY–sum). Offensive, disgusting, foul, malodorous. EXAMPLE: "Surely he shall deliver thee from the snare of the fowler, and from the noisome pestilence." (Psalms 91:3). NOTE: While the word bears a resemblance to *noise,* they have different origins and meanings, with *noisome* coming from the Middle English word for annoy.

nomadic, *adjective* (noh–MAD–ik). Given to wandering; having no permanent home or fixed abode. EXAMPLE: It is amazing how many young men from middle class homes have taken up a nomadic existence, at least temporarily. RELATED WORDS: **nomad,** *noun* (NOH–mad), **nomadical,** *adjective* (noh–MAD–ih–k'l) and **nomadically,** *adverb* (noh–MAD–ih–k'l–lee).

nonce, *noun* (NONSS). The present; a particular purpose or occasion. EXAMPLE: "For the nonce, conditions were reasonably normal." (P. G. Wodehouse).

nonplus, *verb* (non–PLUSS). To puzzle or perplex to a degree that precludes further speech, action or thought; to baffle completely. EXAMPLE: After all the details had been worked out and the papers drawn up, the lawyer was nonplussed by her change of mind about selling the house.

nostalgic, *adjective* (noss–TAL–jik). Full of longing for something long ago or far away, may refer to persons, things or situations). Also, homesickness. EXAMPLE: Her birthday brought a nostalgic letter from her daughter, recalling other birthdays they had spent together. RELATED WORD: **nostalgia,** *noun* (noss–TAL–juh).

nostrum, *noun* (NOSS–trum). A medicine of undisclosed composition, especially a quack medicine. Also, a pet scheme of questionable value in solving a problem. EXAMPLE: The Food and Drug Administration has made it virtually impossible for a nostrum to get on the market today.

noxious, *adjective* (NOK–shus). Injurious to health or morals; pernicious; poisonous; unwholesome. EXAMPLE: He refused to eat the stew, calling it "a noxious mess." RELATED WORDS: **noxiously,** *adverb* (NOK–shus–lee) and **noxiousness,** *noun* (NOK–shush–nuss).

nuance, *noun* (NOO–ahnss). A slight shade of difference or variation in meaning, quality or color. EXAMPLE: ". . . the jazz world's increasing preoccupation with melodic and harmonic nuances." (Wilder Hobson).

nubile, *adjective* (NOO–b'l). Of marriageable age, said of women. EXAMPLE: The daughter of the house turned out to be a very pretty nubile girl. RELATED WORD: **nubility,** *noun* (noo–BIL–ih–tee).

nullify, *verb* (NUL–ih–fy). To make ineffective or to invalidate; to annul, cancel or strip of legal force. EXAMPLE: The ruling by the appeals court nullified the sentence the lower court had imposed. RELATED WORDS: **nullification,** *noun* (nul–ih–fuh–KAY–shun) and **nullifier,** *noun* (NUL–ih–fy–er).

nurture, *verb* (NER–cher). To cause or help to grow or thrive; to nourish or promote the development of. EXAMPLE: "Your lovers' feeble eyes you feed, but starve their hearts that needeth nurture most." (Edmund Spenser). RELATED WORD: **nurturer,** *noun* (NER–cher–er).

obdurate, *adjective* (OB–dyoor–it). Refusing to repent. Hard-hearted; unyielding; intractable. EXAMPLE: ". . . obdurate conscience of the old sinner." (Sir Walter Scott). RELATED WORDS: **obduracy,** *noun* (OB–dyoor–uh–see), **obdurately,** *adverb* (OB–dyoor–it–lee) and **obdurateness,** *noun* (OB–dyoor–it–nus).

obeisance, *noun* (oh–BAY–sunss). A gesture or movement of the body that expresses reverence, respect or submission, such as a bow or curtsy. Also, an attitude of such respect or reverence. EXAMPLE: ". . . a throne to which conquered nations yielded obeisance." (Richard Steele). RELATED WORD: **obeisant,** *adjective* (oh–BAY–s'nt).

objurgate, *verb* (OB–jer–gayt). To scold or rebuke harshly; to censure. EXAMPLE: The critic objurgated the prima donna's use of needless trills. RELATED WORDS: **objurgation,** *noun* (ob–jer–GAY–shun), **objugatorily,** *adverb* (ob–jer–guh–TOHR–ih–lee) and **objugatory,** *adjective* (ob–JUG–uh–tohr–ee).

oblivious, *adjective* (ob–LIV–ee–us). Unmindful, lacking knowledge of, unaware; forgetful. EXAMPLE: Whenever she was reading, she was completely oblivious to anything else that was happening in the room. RELATED WORDS: **obliviously,** *adverb* (ob–LIV–ee–us–lee) and **obliviousness,** *noun* (ob–LIV–ee–us–nus).

obsequious, *adjective* (ob–SEE–kwee–us). Servile; excessively deferential. EXAMPLE: His manner was so obsequious as to be offensive. RELATED WORDS: **obsequiously,** *adverb* (ob–SEE–kwee–us–lee) and **obsequiousness,** *noun* (ob–SEE–kwee–us–nus).

obstreperous, *adjective* (ob–STREP–er–us). Boisterous; noisily unruly or defiant, unmanageable. EXAMPLE: Because the children were obstreperous at the luncheon table, they were denied dessert. RELATED WORDS: **obstreperously,** *adverb* (ob–STREP–er–us–lee) and **obstreperousness,** *noun* (ob–STREP–er–us–nus).

obtrusive, *adjective* (ob–TROO–siv). Protruding or thrust out. Hence, pushing or intrusive; undesirably conspicuous or showy. EXAMPLE: We resent the obtrusive behavior of a spoiled child. RELATED WORDS: **obtrude,** *verb* (ob–TROOD),

obtrusively, *adverb* (ob–TROO–siv–lee) and **obtrusiveness,** *noun* (ob–TROO–siv–nus).

obtuse, *adjective* (ob–TOOSS). Blunt in formation; not pointed. Also, imperceptive; lacking in understanding. EXAMPLE: He seemed very obtuse regarding the needs of the community. RELATED WORDS: **obtusely,** *adverb* (ob–TOOSS–lee) and **obtuseness,** *noun* (ob–TOOSS–nus).

obviate, *verb* (OB–vee–ayt). To make unnecessary by preventive action; to avert. EXAMPLE: ". . . the remedies and means to obviate these dangers." (Oliver Cromwell). RELATED WORDS: **obviation,** *noun* (ob–vee–AY–sh'n) and **obviator,** *noun* (OB–vee–ay–tor).

officious, *adjective* (oh–FISH–us). Meddlesome, offering unwelcome advice or help; unduly bossy. EXAMPLE: All the committee chairmen avoided her because she was officious. RELATED WORDS: **officiously,** *adverb* (oh–FISH–us–lee) and **officiousness,** *noun* (oh–FISH–us–ness).

oligarchy, *noun* (OL–ih–gar–kee). Government by a small group or a particular class or clique; the state so ruled; the group in power. EXAMPLE: Our democracy was designed to prevent the creation of an oligarchy in this country. RELATED WORDS: **oligarchal,** *adjective* (ol–ih–GAR–kul), **oligarchic,** *adjective* (ol–ih–GAR–kik) and **oligarchical,** *adjective* (ol–ih–GAR–ih–kul).

onerous, *adjective* (OH–ner–us). Burdensome; oppressive. EXAMPLE: He complained that he was always given the most onerous task. RELATED WORDS: **onerously,** *adverb* (OH–ner–us–lee) and **onerousness,** *noun* (OH–ner–us–nus).

opportune, *adjective* (op–er–TOON). Favorable; appropriate; timely. EXAMPLE: He decided to wait for a more opportune moment to present his request for a raise. RELATED WORDS: **opportunely,** *adverb* (op–er–TOON–lee), **opportuneness,** *noun* (op–er–TOON–nus) and **opportunist,** *noun* (op–er–TOON–ist).

opprobrium, *noun* (uh–PROH–bree–um). Disgrace resulting from shameful acts; scorn and reproach relating to such disgrace; the acts from which disgrace arose. EXAMPLE: The so-called witches of Salem were subjected to much undeserved opprobrium. RELATED WORDS: **opprobriously,** *adverb* (uh–PROB–bree–us–lee) and **opprobriousness,** *noun* (uh–PROB–bree–us–nus).

optimum, *noun* (OP–tih–mum). The best condition possible;

the maximum amount or degree. Also used as an adjective to mean maximum or best. EXAMPLE: Heirs usually need legal advice in handling estates to optimum advantage. RELATED WORDS: **optimal,** *adjective* (OP–tih–mul) and **optimally,** *adverb* (OP–tih–mul–lee).

opulence, *noun* (OP–yoo–lenss). Wealth, abundance, luxury. EXAMPLE: "Here in an atmosphere of private opulence and public squalor, the private goods have full sway." (John Kenneth Galbraith). RELATED WORDS: **opulent,** *adjective* (OP–yoo–l'nt) and **opulency,** *noun* (OP–yoo–len–see).

orthodox, *adjective* (OR–thuh–doks). Adhering to established beliefs and doctrines, especially in religion. Traditional; conventional. EXAMPLE: Many students today are not willing to accept orthodox views of what constitutes an education. RELATED WORDS: **orthodoxly,** *adverb* (OR–thuh–doks–lee) and **orthodoxy,** *noun* (OR–thuh–doks–ee).

osmosis, *noun* (oz–MOH–sis). The passage of a solvent through a porous membrane separating it from a solution. Hence, assimilation of knowledge effortlessly and sometimes unconsciously. EXAMPLE: He had never had any instruction in photography but seemed to have acquired his skill by osmosis. RELATED WORDS: **osmose,** *verb* (oz–MOHZ), **osmotic,** *adjective* (oz–MOT–ik) and **osmotically,** *adverb* (oz–MOT–ih–kul–lee).

ostensible, *adjective* (oss–TEN–sih–b'l). Seeming; outwardly apparent; professed. EXAMPLE: The ostensible reason for building the fence was to protect the dunes; the real purpose was to make work for his brother. RELATED WORDS: **ostensibly,** *adverb* (oss–TEN–sih–blee), **ostensibility,** *noun* (oss–ten–sih–BIL–ih–tee) and **ostentation,** *noun* (see below).

ostentation, *noun* (oss–ten–TAY–shun). Pretentious display; flamboyant exhibition. EXAMPLE: The use of sterling silver forks at a picnic is a ridiculous example of ostentation. RELATED WORDS: **ostentatious,** *adjective* (oss–ten–TAY–shus) and **ostentatiously,** *adverb* (oss–ten–TAY–shus–lee).

ostracism, *noun* (OSS–truh–sizm). Rejection or exclusion from a group or from society as a whole. EXAMPLE: "The American impeachment resembles the Athenian ostracism, which was likewise a political, not a penal, institution." (Francis Lieber). RELATED WORD: **ostracize,** *verb* (OSS–truh–size).

overt, *adjective* (oh–VERT). Manifest; open to observation; not concealed. EXAMPLE: The real estate broker claimed he had never committed an overt act of discrimination. RELATED WORD: **overtly,** *adverb* (oh–VERT–lee).

paltry, *adjective* (PAWL–tree). Trifling; insignificant. Also, worthless; contemptible or despicable. EXAMPLE: "With me poetry has not been a purpose but a passion; and the passions should be held in reverence . . . they cannot at will be excited with an eye to the paltry compensations of mankind." (Edgar Allan Poe). RELATED WORDS: **paltrily,** *adverb* (PAWL–trih–lee) and **paltriness,** *noun* (PAWL–trih–nus).

paragon, *noun* (PAIR–uh–gon). A model of perfection or excellence. EXAMPLE: A secretary should be a paragon of punctuality.

pecuniary, *adjective* (peh–KYOO–nee–er–ee). Pertaining to or consisting of money, financial. Also, involving the payment of money. EXAMPLE: The president of the company had only a pecuniary interest in the factory and no concern for the quality of the product.

penchant, *noun* (PEN–chant). Strong leaning or inclination; great liking. EXAMPLE: Justice William O. Douglas, over the years, has exhibited a penchant for hiking.

penury, *noun* (PEN–yoor–ee). Destitution; extreme poverty. Also, extreme insufficiency or inadequacy. EXAMPLE: The congressional investigation proved that many families in the state were living in penury. RELATED WORDS: **penurious,** *adjective* (pen–YOOR–ee–us); **penuriously,** *adverb* (pen–YOOR–ee–us–lee) and **penuriousness,** *noun* (pen–YOOR–ee–us–nus).

perfidious, *adjective* (per–FID–ee–us). Traitorous; deliberately faithless or disloyal. EXAMPLE: "The Informer" is a classic story of a perfidious friend. RELATED WORDS: **perfidiously,** *adverb* (per–FID–ee–us–lee), **perfidiousness,** *noun* (per–FID–ee–us–nus) and **perfidy,** *noun* (PER–fih–dee).

permeate, *verb* (PER–mee–ayt). To spread throughout; to saturate. EXAMPLE: A spirit of gloom permeated the room as they listened to the reports of the stock market crash. RELATED WORDS: **permeability,** *noun* (per–mee–uh–BIL–ih–tee) and **permeable,** *adjective* (PER–mee–uh–b'l).

pernicious, *adjective* (per–NISH–us). Deadly; highly injurious or ruinous. Also, evil in the sense of undermining morals. EXAMPLE: "No doctrine, involving more pernicious consequences, was ever invented by the wit of man than that any of the Constitution's provisions can be suspended during any of the great exigencies of government. (David Davis). RE- LATED WORDS: **perniciously,** *adverb* (per–NISH–us–lee) and **perniciousness,** *noun* (per–NISH–us–nus).

perspicacity, *noun* (per–spih–KASS–ih–tee). Keenness of dis- cernment or understanding. EXAMPLE: It takes considerable perspicacity to handle an emotionally disturbed person. RE- LATED WORDS: **perspicacious,** *adjective* (per–spih–KAY–shus); **perspicaciously,** *adverb* (per–spih–KAY–shus–lee) and **per- spicaciousness,** *noun* (per–spih–KAY–shus–nus).

pertinacious, *adjective* (per–tih–NAY–shus). Steadfast in belief or purpose; stubbornly or perversely persistent. EXAMPLE: "As pertinaceous as ivy climbing a wall." (Oxford English Dictionary). RELATED WORDS: **pertinaciously,** *adverb* (per– tih–NAY–shus–lee) and **pertinaciousness,** *noun* (per–tih– NAY–shus–nus).

platitudinous, *adjective* (plat–ih–TYOOD–ih–nus). Trite; lack- ing in originality; characterized by common-place remarks. EXAMPLE: All too often, commencement speakers give the graduates nothing but platitudinous advice. RELATED WORDS: **platitude,** *noun* (PLAT–ih–tyood) and **platitudinize,** *verb* (plat–ih–TYOOD–ih–nize).

poignant, *adjective* (POYN–yunt). Keenly painful, physically or emotionally; moving or appealing. Also piercing or as- tute. EXAMPLE: Family photographs often serve to bring back poignant memories of many happy occasions. RE- LATED WORDS: **poignance,** *noun* (POYN–yunss), **poignancy,** *noun* (POYN–yun–see) and **poignantly,** *adverb* (POYN– yunt–lee).

portend, *verb* (por–TEND). To serve as a warning or omen; to presage. EXAMPLE: A darkening sky usually portends a storm. RELATED WORDS: **portent,** *noun* (POR–tent), **porten- tious,** *adjective* (por–TEN–shus), **portentiously,** *adverb* (por– TEN–shush–lee) and **portentiousness,** *noun* (por–TEN–shus– nus).

pragmatic, *adjective* (prag–MAT–ik). Concerned with the fac- tual or practical aspects; also, meddlesome. EXAMPLE: The pragmatic solution to their financial problems would be to sell the house. RELATED WORDS: **pragmatical,** *adjective* (prag– MAT–ih–kul), **pragmatically,** *adverb* (prag–MAT–ih–kul–ee) and **pragmatism,** *noun* (PRAG–muh–tiz–'m).

prerogative, *noun* (preh–ROG–uh–tiv). An exclusive or peculiar right, privilege or power, especially one stemming from position or rank. EXAMPLE: Taking two-hour lunches may be the prerogative of an executive but certainly not of a secretary or typist.

prestigious, *adjective* (press–TEEJ–ee–us). Possessing or conferring renown, fame, prominence or influence. EXAMPLE: The presidency of a college is a prestigious post, but a difficult one, too. RELATED WORDS: **prestige,** *noun* (press–TEEZH), **prestigiously,** *adverb* (press–TEEG–ee–us–lee) and **prestigiousness,** *noun* (press–TEEJ–ee–us–nus).

primacy, *noun* (PRY–muh–see). The state of having priority or precedence over all others. EXAMPLE: ". . . the primacy of the deed over word and thought." (Gilbert Highet).

pristine, *adjective* (pris–TEEN). Unsullied, in original condition, unaltered, pure, primitive. EXAMPLE: The first settlers in the Bay Colony found a land of pristine natural beauty.

proclivity, *noun* (proh–KLIV–ih–tee). Inclination, tendency, predisposition. EXAMPLE: The child had to repress his natural proclivities before he could be accepted into polite society.

procrastination, *noun* (proh–krass–tih–NAY–shun). Laziness, putting off, dawdling. EXAMPLE: "Procrastination is the thief of time." (Edward Young). RELATED WORDS: **procrastinate,** *verb* (pro–KRASS–tih–nayt) and **procrastinator,** *noun* (pro–krass–tih–NAYT–er).

prodigal, *noun* (PROD–ih–gul). One who wastes his talents; spendthrift; one given to extravagance. EXAMPLE: One of the great talents of the American theater was John Barrymore, truly a prodigal, financially as well as artistically. RELATED WORDS: **prodigal,** *adjective* (PROD–ih–gul) and **prodigality,** *noun* (prod–ih–GAL–ih–tee).

prodigy, *noun* (PROD–ih–gee). A person with extraordinary natural talent; something that stirs wonder or disbelief. EXAMPLE: The Grand Canyon is one of the prodigies of nature. RELATED WORDS: **prodigious,** *adjective* (proh–DIJ–us), **prodigiously,** *adverb* (proh–DIJ–us–lee) and **prodigiousness,** *noun* (proh–DIJ–us–ness).

profligate, *noun* (PROF–lih–gayt). Rake, debauchee; ne'er-do-well; wastrel. EXAMPLE: Born with riches, charm and talent, he dissipated them all, living the life of a profligate. RELATED WORDS: **profligate,** *adjective* (PROF–lih–gayt), **profligacy,**

noun (PROF–lig–uh–see) and **profligateness,** *noun* (PROF–lih–gayt–ness).

progeny, *noun* (PROJ–eh–nee). Offspring, descendants, children collectively of one family. EXAMPLE: At their fiftieth wedding anniversary, their progeny numbered more than thirty. RELATED WORDS: **progenitive,** *adjective* (proh–JEN–ih–tiv); **progenitor,** *noun* (pro–JEN–ih–tor).

prognosis, *noun* (prog–NOH–sis). Forecast; prediction, especially of the course of a disease and treatment indicated. EXAMPLE: In view of the church's financial plight, the prognosis indicated either a sharp cutback in the rector's salary or his replacement by a better qualified fund-raiser. RELATED WORDS: **prognosticate,** *verb* (prog–NOS–tih–kate) and **prognostication,** *noun* (prog–nos–tih–KAY–shun).

proliferate, *verb* (proh–LIF–er–ate). To multiply in rapid succession; to reproduce rapidly. EXAMPLE: One reason office files are so cluttered is that memoranda proliferate, thanks to duplicating machines. RELATED WORDS: **proliferation,** *noun* (proh–lif–er–AY–shun) and **proliferous,** *adjective* (proh–LIF–er–us).

prolific, *adjective* (proh–LIF–ik). Fruitful, highly productive, producing many works. EXAMPLE: Erle Stanley Gardner may not have been the greatest writer of his generation, but he certainly was among the most prolific. RELATED WORDS: **prolificacy,** *noun* (proh–LIF–ih–kuh–see), **prolifically,** *adverb* proh–LIF–ik–uh–lee) and **prolificness,** *noun* (proh–LIF–ik–ness).

prolix, *adjective* (proh–LIX). Tedious, long-winded, wordy, verbose. EXAMPLE: Dictated letters are almost always more prolix than handwritten ones. RELATED WORD: **prolixity,** *noun* (proh–LIX–ih–tee).

promulgate, *verb* (PROM–ul–gayt). To announce a decree or law publicly; to announce officially. EXAMPLE: Many an act has become the law of the land without ever being promulgated by the President or by the press. RELATED WORDS: **promulgation,** *noun* (prom–ul–GAY–shun) and **promulgator,** *noun* (prom–ul–GAY–ter).

propensity, *noun* (pruh–PEN–sih–tee). Tendency, natural inclination, bent. EXAMPLE: Unfortunately for his acting career, he had a strong propensity towards alcohol.

propitious, *adjective* (proh–PISH–us). Favorable, helpful, indicating good fortune, auspicious. EXAMPLE: Bright sunlight, a moderate temperature, and favorable winds marked a propitious beginning for the yacht race. RELATED WORD: **propitiate,** *verb* (proh–PISH–ee–ate).

propriety, *noun* (proh–PRY–ih–tee). Correctness, circumspectness, social decorum, conformity to prevailing customs. EXAMPLE: Few acts are more calculated to violate propriety than the use of four-letter words in tea-party conversation.

prosaic, *adjective* (proh–ZAY–ik). Run-of-the-mill, unimaginative, dull, commonplace, matter of fact. EXAMPLE: The best we could get from the policeman was a prosaic recital of statistics—the time of the accident, location, and names of the participants. RELATED WORDS: **prosaically,** *adverb* (proh–ZAY–ic–lee) and **prosaicness,** *noun* (proh–ZAY–ik–ness).

protagonist, *noun* (proh–TAG–uh–nist). Leading figure, leader, hero. EXAMPLE: Lyndon Baines Johnson was the protagonist in a drama that engaged the interest of every citizen. NOTE: The sense of protagonist as "hero," while very common, is frowned on by careful speakers and writers. In Greek drama, where the term was originally used, and still, among knowledgeable users of the language, *protagonist* means merely "leader in a matter of importance." He may be villain as well as hero.

protégé, *noun* (PROH–teh–zhay). A person whose career is sponsored by another. EXAMPLE: Leonard Bernstein was initially a protégé of the great Serge Koussevitsky, conductor of the Boston Symphony Orchestra.

prowess, *noun* (PROW–ess). Superior skill, bravery, valorous achievement, great ability. EXAMPLE: A shelf of trophies was testimony to his golfing prowess.

puerile, *adjective* (PYOO–er–il). Childish, foolish, trifling, immature, juvenile. EXAMPLE: When a man passes thirty he should give up such puerile sports as girl-watching . . . Well, would you believe eighty? NOTE: *Puerile* is directly derived from the Latin word for boy, "puer." RELATED WORDS: **puerilely,** *adverb* (PYOO–er–il–lee), **puerileness,** *noun* (PYOO–er–il–ness) and **puerility,** *noun* (pyoo–er–IL–ih–tee).

punctilious, *adjective* (punk–TIL–ee–us). Extremely proper; insisting on strict conformance to social proprieties; scrupulous. EXAMPLE: The baron was punctilious in observing all the rules of dueling. RELATED WORDS: **punctiliously,** *adverb*

(punk–TIL–ee–us–lee) and **punctiliousness,** *noun* (punk–
TIL–ee–us–ness).

pusillanimous, *adjective* (pyoo–sih–LAN–ih–mus). Cowardly,
extremely timid, faint-hearted. EXAMPLE: Perhaps the most
pusillanimous creature in all movie history was the Cowardly Lion in *The Wizard of Oz* portrayed by the immortal
Bert Lahr. RELATED WORDS: **pusillanimity,** *noun* (pyoo–sil–
uh–NIM–ih–tee); **pusillanimously,** *adverb* (pyoo–sih–LAN–
ih–mus–lee).

querulous, *adjective* (KWER–uh–lus). Complaining, fault-finding, fretful, peevish, plaintive. EXAMPLE: He dreaded returning home at night; he knew he was sure to be greeted with
a querulous account of all the day's minor disasters. RELATED
WORDS: **querulously,** *adverb* (KWER–uh–lus–lee) and **queru-
lousness,** *noun* (KWER–uh–lus–ness).

quibble, *verb* (KWIB–'l). To haggle over petty details; to find
fault over minor matters, especially when a matter of importance is involved. EXAMPLE: The publication was delayed
because of quibbling over the inclusion of the names of long-
forgotten vice presidents. RELATED WORDS: **quibble,** *noun*
(KWIB–'l); **quibbler,** *noun* (KWIB–ler).

quintessence, *noun* (kwint–ESS–enss). The perfect essence of a
quality or thing; the pure embodiment of something. EXAM-
PLE: "Thou fiery-faced quintessence of all that is abomi-
nable!" (Edgar Allen Poe). RELATED WORD: **quintessential,**
adjective (kwint–ess–EN–shul).

quixotic, *adjective* (kwix–OT–ik). Idealistic; foolishly romantic;
visionary and unworldly. EXAMPLE: The politician who starts
his career full of quixotic plans to better the lot of his fellow
men soon learns that reality is a very different and often quite
sordid thing. RELATED WORDS: **quixotical,** *adjective* (kwix–
OT–ih–kul), **quixotically,** *adverb* (kwix–OT–ih–kuh–lee) and
quixotism, *noun* (KWIX–uh–tizm).

rabid, *adjective* (RAB–id). Violent, raging, furious, irrationally
irate. EXAMPLE: The late senator was a rabid foe of com-
munism. RELATED WORDS: **rabidly,** *adverb* (RAB–id–lee) and
rabidness, *noun* (RAB–id–ness).

raconteur, *noun* (rak–on–TER). Story teller, anecdotist, narrator. EXAMPLE: The master of ceremonies doesn't have to be a good raconteur—but it helps if he is.

raillery, *noun* (RAYL–er–ee). Good-humored ridicule; teasing, banter, ribbing. EXAMPLE: At the bachelor's dinner, the groom was subjected to much good-natured raillery.

rambunctious, *adjective* (ram–BUNK–shus). Obstreperous, wild, unruly, boisterous, uproarious, disorderly. EXAMPLE: Andy Jackson's buddies did not need whiskey to become rambunctious.

rancor, *noun* (RANK–er). Abiding hatred; deep-seated resentment; intense malice; enmity. EXAMPLE: The famous feud between the Hatfields and McCoys was fed by generations-old rancor. RELATED WORD: **rancorous,** *adjective* (RANK–er–us).

rapacious, *adjective* (ruh–PAY–shus). Plundering, thieving, predatory, greedy, taking by force. EXAMPLE: The Huns under Attila were rapacious in their sack of Rome. RELATED WORDS: **rapaciously,** *adverb* (ruh–PAY–shus–lee), **rapaciousness,** *noun* (ruh–PAY–shus–ness) and **rapacity,** *noun* (ruh–PASS–ih–tee).

raucous, *adjective* (RAW–kus). Harsh, grating, rough-sounding. EXAMPLE: The proposal that the returning golfers celebrate with iced tea and cookies was greeted with hoots of raucous laughter. RELATED WORDS: **raucity,** *noun* (RAW–sih–tee), **raucously,** *adverb* (RAW–kus–lee) and **raucousness,** *noun* (RAW–kus–ness).

ravenous, *adjective* (RAV–eh–nus). Extremely hungry, starving, famished, voracious; greedy for gratification. EXAMPLE: When the dinner finally arrived, the children were simply ravenous. RELATED WORDS: **ravenously,** *adverb* (RAV–en–us–lee) and **ravenousness,** *noun* (RAV–en–us–ness).

recalcitrant, *adjective* (rih–KAL–sih–trunt). Unmanageable, unruly, perversely obstinate, refractory. EXAMPLE: Try as she would, the teacher could not control her recalcitrant pupils. RELATED WORDS: **recalcitrant,** *noun* (rih–KAL–sih–trunt) and **recalcitrance,** *noun* (rih–KAL–sih–trunss).

recant, *verb* (rih–KANT). To renounce, disavow, retract. EXAMPLE: Many politicians find it impossible to recant claims of military victory even in face of clear-cut evidence that it will not come. RELATED WORDS: **recantation,** *noun* (rih–kan–TAY–shun) and **recanter,** *noun* (rih–KAN–ter).

recapitulate, *verb* (ree–kuh–PIT–choo–layt). To summarize; re-state, especially in shorter form. EXAMPLE: At the end of the briefing, one of the junior officers offered to recapitulate the reports. NOTE: In newspaper jargon *recap,* a shortened form, serves as both noun and verb. RELATED WORDS: **recapitulation,** *noun* (ree–kuh–pit–choo–LAY–shun) and **recapitulatory,** *adjective* (ree–kuh–PITCH–uh–luh–tor–ee).

recondite, *adjective* (REK–un–dite). Profound, abstruse, beyond ordinary comprehension, hard to understand. EXAMPLE: Even for physicists, Einstein's theory of relativity poses some recondite problems. RELATED WORDS: **reconditely,** *adverb* (REK–un–dite–lee) and **reconditeness,** *noun* (REK–un–dite–ness).

recoup, *verb* (rih–KOOP). To regain, retrieve, make up for. EXAMPLE: Two hours at the gaming tables were not enough to enable her to recoup the previous night's losses. RELATED WORD: **recoupment,** *noun* (rih–KOOP–m'nt).

recrimination, *noun* (rih–krim–ih–NAY–shun). A counter-charge; replying to one accusation with another. EXAMPLE: Before the trial ended, the courtroom was the scene of many violent recriminations. RELATED WORDS: **recriminate,** *verb* (rih–KRIM–ih–nayt); **recriminatory,** *adjective* (rih–KRIM–ih–nuh–tor–ee).

redoubtable, *adjective* (rih–DOUT–uh–b'l). Valiant, formidable, fearsome, meriting respect. EXAMPLE: In the early years of the Revolution, the Redcoats proved a redoubtable and re-sourceful foe. RELATED WORDS: **redoubtableness,** *noun* (rih–DOUT–uh–b'l–ness) and **redoubtably,** *adverb* (rih–DOUT–uh–blee).

redundant, *adjective* (rih–DUN–d'nt). Superfluous, excessive, unnecessary, needlessly repetitive, verbose. EXAMPLE: "The modern car of today" is clearly redundant. RELATED WORDS: **redundance,** *noun* (rih–DUN–d'nss), **redundancy,** *noun* (rih–DUN–d'n–see) and **redundantly,** *adverb* (rih–DUN–d'nt–lee).

reiterate, *verb* (ree–IT–er–ate). To repeat, say or do again. EXAMPLE: The fire marshal emphasized the danger by re-iterating his warning. RELATED WORDS: **reiteration,** *noun* (ree-it–er–AY–shun) and **reiterative,** *adjective* (ree–IT–er–uh–tiv).

relegate, *verb* (REL–uh–gate). To move to an obscure or in-ferior position; to banish. EXAMPLE: After missing four passes, the flanking end was relegated to the second team.

repartee, *noun* (rep–ar–TEE). Witty response, quick and clever retort. EXAMPLE: Sparkling conversation depends on ready repartee.

reprisal, *noun* (rih–PRY–zul). Retaliation; attack on an enemy with intent to damage him as much as he has you. EXAMPLE: The Dresden fire bomb attack was considered suitable reprisal for the German bombings of Coventry and London.

reprobate, *noun* (REP–ruh–bate). An unprincipled, depraved chap; a morally deficient person; a profligate. EXAMPLE: After many bouts with the demon rum, he was little more than a dissolute old reprobate. RELATED WORDS: **reprobation,** *noun* (rep–ruh–BAY–shun) and **reprobative,** *adjective* (rih–PROH–buh–tiv).

repugnant, *adjective* (rih–PUG–n'nt). Offensive, distasteful, objectionable, repelling. EXAMPLE: "Characters in comedy which involve some notion repugnant to the moral sense . . ." (Charles Lamb). RELATED WORDS: **repugnance,** *noun* (rih–PUG–nunss); **repugnancy,** *noun* (rih–PUG–nun–see).

requisite, *noun* (REK–wiz–it). Something required or indispensable. EXAMPLE: The first requisite for a marriage is a groom. Having a bride helps, too.

requite, *verb* (reh–KWITE). To repay for past favors; to give or do in return; to retaliate; to avenge. EXAMPLE: One way to requite a neighbor for past kindnesses is to have a party for him.

reticent, *adjective* (RET–ih–s'nt). Reserved, quiet, not talkative. EXAMPLE: The lad proved surprisingly reticent when asked about the disturbances at his school. RELATED WORDS: **reticently,** *adverb* (RET–ih–sent–lee) and **reticence,** *noun* (RET–ih–senss).

reverie, *noun* (REV–er–ee). Daydream, musing, visionary thinking. EXAMPLE: The lad was so lost in reverie that he didn't hear the teacher's question.

ribald, *adjective* (RIB–'ld). Racy, improper, vulgarly humorous, coarsely jesting. EXAMPLE: Chaucer's "Miller's Tale" abounds in ribald jest. RELATED WORD: **ribaldry,** *noun* (RIB–ul–dree).

riposte, *noun* (rih–POST). A quick thrust, whether physical or verbal; a swift retort, sharp response. EXAMPLE: The mayor's criticism brought a swift riposte from the district attorney.

roseate, *adjective* (ROHS–ee–it). Optimistic, hopeful, cheerful, rosy. EXAMPLE: The investors basked in roseate dreams of affluence until the bottom dropped out of the market. RELATED WORD: **roseately,** *adverb* (ROHS–ee–it–lee).

rotund, *adjective* (roh–TUND). Plump, chubby, round-shaped. EXAMPLE: Dickens' Mr. Pickwick sported a comfortably rotund figure. RELATED WORDS: **rotundity,** *noun* (roh–TUN–dih–tee) and **rotundness,** *noun* (roh–TUND–ness).

ruminate, *verb* (ROOM–ih–nayt). To ponder, turn over in the mind, meditate, muse, chew the cud. EXAMPLE: He ruminated a long, long time before accepting the terms he had been offered. NOTE: "Chewing the cud" is not only a popular expression but the literal meaning of *ruminate.* Indeed, an entire order of mammals, including cattle, sheep, goats, deer and giraffes, are known as *ruminants,* because they all chew a cud of partially digested food. So if the next cow you see looks especially thoughtful, it's because she's ruminating. RELATED WORDS: **rumination,** *noun* (room–ih–NAY–shun) and **ruminative,** *adjective* (ROOM–ih–nay–tiv).

sacrosanct, *adjective* (SAK–roh–sankt). Very sacred, most holy; inviolable. EXAMPLE: In earlier years university libraries were considered as sacrosanct as cathedrals. RELATED WORD: **sacrosanctity,** *noun* (sak–roh–SANK–tih–tee).

sanguine, *adjective* (SAN–gwin). Confident, hopeful, cheerful. Also, having the color of blood. EXAMPLE: Despite early season defeats, the team was still sanguine about winning the pennant. NOTE: The seeming disparity between the two meanings "cheerful" and "of the color of blood" may be traced to the medieval belief that people with ruddy complexions were likely to be cheerful. RELATED WORDS: **sanguinarily,** *adverb* (san–gwin–AIR–ih–lee), **sanguinariness,** *noun* (san–gwin–AIR–ih–ness), and **sanguineous,** *adjective* (san–GWIN–ee–us).

sapient, *adjective* (SAY–pee–ent). Wise, all-knowing, discerning, often used sarcastically. EXAMPLE: The head of research may not be very bright, but one must admit he looks sapient. RELATED WORDS: **sapience,** *noun* (SAY–pee–enss), **sapiency,** *noun* (SAY–pee–en–see) and **sapiential,** *adjective* (say–pee–EN–shul).

sententious, *adjective* (sen–TEN–shus). Pompous, moralizing, stuffy; given to the overuse of proverbs, maxims and quotations. EXAMPLE: The good impression the minister made on the congregation was soon dispelled by his tediously sententious sermon. RELATED WORDS: **sententiously,** *adverb* (sen–TEN–shus–ly) and **sententiousness,** *noun* (sen–TEN–shus–ness).

shibboleth, *noun* (SHIB–uh–leth). Password, countersign, slogan; custom or practice distinguishing one class or group from others. EXAMPLE: The hot-potato-in-the-mouth accent was once practically the shibboleth of Groton men at Harvard. NOTE: This word is borrowed from the Hebrew where it means ear of corn. It was used by the Gileadites (Judges 12) as a password because their enemies, the Ephraimites, could not pronounce it correctly. In the words of the Bible: "They said to him 'Say you now Shibboleth,' and he said 'Sibboleth,' for he could not frame to pronounce it right. Then they took him and slew him . . ."

simulate, *verb* (SIM–yoo–layt). To pretend, feign, imitate. EXAMPLE: "There is no disguise which can for long conceal love where it exists or simulate it where it does not." (La Rochefoucauld). RELATED WORDS: **simulation,** *noun* (sim-yoo–LAY–shun), **simulative,** *adjective* (SIM–yoo–lay–tiv) and **simulator,** *noun* (SIM–yoo–lay–ter).

sinecure, *noun* (SY–neh–kyoor). A job with few duties but good pay. EXAMPLE: After election the party faithful were rewarded with suitable sinecures on the public payroll. RELATED WORDS: **sinecurism,** *noun* (SY–neh–kyoor–ism) and **sinecurist,** *noun* (SY–neh–kyoor–ist).

sinister, *adjective* (SIN–iss–ter). Evil or threatening evil; ominous; presaging trouble. EXAMPLE: A sinister atmosphere pervades most so-called Gothic novels. NOTE: Compare *sinister,* which comes from the Latin word for "left," with *dexterous* for further evidence of the way language discriminates against left-handedness. RELATED WORDS: **sinisterly,** *adverb* (SIN–iss–ter–lee) and **sinisterness,** *noun* (SIN–iss–ter–ness).

sinuous, *adjective* (SIN–yoo–us). Bending, winding, undulating, having many curves or bends. EXAMPLE: The river followed a sinuous course on its way to the sea. RELATED WORDS: **sinuously,** *adverb* (SIN–yoo–us–lee) and **sinuosity,** *noun* (sin-yoo–OSS–ih–tee).

sophistry, *noun* (SOF–iss–tree). A believable but false and misleading argument or method of reasoning. EXAMPLE: The prosecutor's summation was sharply criticized as nothing but a maze of legal sophistries. RELATED WORDS: **sophism,** *noun*

(SOF–izm), **sophist,** *noun* (SOF–ist) and **sophistic,** *adjective* (suh–FIS–tik).

soporific, *adjective* (sop–uh–RIF–ik). Inducing sleep; sleepy, drowsy. EXAMPLE: The lecturer's monotonous tone had a markedly soporific effect on his audience. RELATED WORD: **soporiferous,** *adjective* (sop–uh–RIF–er–us).

specious, *adjective* (SPEE–shus). Deceptive; seemingly true but not actually so. EXAMPLE: "Daydreaming bears a specious resemblance to the workings of the creative imagination." (Cyril Connolly). RELATED WORDS: **speciosity,** *noun* (spee–she–OSS–ih–tee), **speciously,** *adverb* (SPEE–shus–lee) and **speciousness,** *noun* (SPEE–shus–ness).

spontaneous, *adjective* (spon–TAY–nee–us). Without plan, unpremeditated, self-generated; unconstrained. EXAMPLE: The speaker was surprised, then delighted, by the burst of spontaneous applause. RELATED WORDS: **spontaneity,** *noun* (spon–tuh–NEE–ih–tee), **spontaneously,** *adverb* (spon–TAY–nee–us–lee) and **spontaneousness,** *noun* (spon–TAY–nee–us–ness).

sporadic, *adjective* (spuh–RAD–ik). Intermittent, occasional; irregular. EXAMPLE: The rebels responded with sporadic outbursts of gunfire. RELATED WORD: **sporadically,** *adverb* (spuh–RAD–ik–uh–lee).

spurious, *adjective* (SPYOOR–ee–us). Fake, phony, false, counterfeit; illegitimate. EXAMPLE: The "baron" was unmasked. His title was completely spurious. RELATED WORDS: **spuriously,** *adverb* (SPYOOR–ee–us–lee) and **spuriousness,** *noun* (SPYOOR–ee–us–ness).

stereotyped, *adjective* (STER–ee–oh–typd). Trite; hackneyed, unoriginal; banal. EXAMPLE: Political speeches tend to be full of stereotyped cliches. RELATED WORD: **stereotype,** *noun* (STER–ee–oh–type).

strident, *adjective* (STRY–dent). Shrill, harsh, grating. EXAMPLE: "His bluff strident words struck the note sailors understand." (J. M. Barrie). RELATED WORDS: **stridently,** *adverb* (STRY–dent–lee) and **stridency,** *noun* (STRY–den–see).

suave, *adjective* (SWAHV). Smooth, urbane, gracious. EXAMPLE: "He was a man of commanding appearance, and of suave and courteous manners." (J. H. Shorthouse). RELATED WORDS: **suavely,** *adverb* (SWAHV–lee), **suaveness,** *noun* (SWAHV–ness) and **suavity,** *noun* (SWAHV–ih–tee).

subtle, *adjective* (SUT–'l). Delicate, ingenious, clever; quietly skillful. EXAMPLE: "The Lord God is subtle, but malicious he is not." (Albert Einstein). RELATED WORDS: **subtleness,** *noun* (SUT–'l–ness), **subtlety,** *noun* (SUT–'l–tee) and **subtly,** *adverb* (SUT–lee).

succinct, *adjective* (suk–SINKT). Terse; brief and clear; concise; pithy. EXAMPLE: The editor praised the reporter for his succinct account of the riot. RELATED WORDS: **succinctly,** *adverb* (suk–SINKT–lee) and **succinctness,** *noun* (suk–SINKT–ness).

sultry, *adjective* (SUL–tree). Hot and humid, torrid; voluptuous, passionate. EXAMPLE: August in the lowlands has more than its share of sultry days. RELATED WORD: **sultriness,** *noun* (SUL–tree–ness).

supercilious, *adjective* (soo–per–SIL–ee–us). Haughty, contemptuous, disdainful. EXAMPLE: The defendant's plea for mercy drew only a supercilious look from the presiding justice. NOTE: This word means quite literally "with lifted eyebrow," since it comes from the Latin words "super," upper, and "cilium," eyebrow or eyelid. RELATED WORDS: **superciliously,** *adverb* (soo–per–SIL–ee–us–lee); **superciliousness,** *noun* (soo–per–SIL–ee–us–ness).

surfeit, *noun* (SER–fit). Overabundance, excessive amount; disgust caused by excess. EXAMPLE: "As a surfeit of the sweetest things/ The deepest loathing to the stomach brings." (William Shakespeare). RELATED WORDS: **surfeit,** *verb* (SER–fit) and **surfeiter,** *noun* (SER–fit–er).

surreptitious, *adjective* (ser–rep–TISH–us). Stealthy, underhanded, furtive, secret. EXAMPLE: Shoplifters are skilled at the surreptitious concealment of objects in their garments. RELATED WORDS: **surreptitiously,** *adverb* (ser–rep–TISH–us–lee); **surreptitiousness,** *noun* (ser–rep–TISH–us–ness).

sycophant, *adjective* (SIK–uh–f'nt). Hanger-on; toady; servile flatterer or self-seeker. EXAMPLE: "The king appeared with his dogs and sycophants behind him." (Kathleen Winsor). RELATED WORDS: **sycophancy,** *noun* (SIK–uh–f'n–see) and **sycophantic,** *adjective* (sik–uh–FAN–tik).

taciturn, *adjective* (TASS–ih–tern). Uncommunicative; habitually silent; reserved in speech. EXAMPLE: Like many gifted writers, he was moody and taciturn in person. RELATED WORD: **taciturnity,** *noun* (tass–ih–TER–nih–tee).

tangible, *adjective* (TAN–jih–b'l). Real, solid, material; capable of being touched. EXAMPLE: The only tangible asset of the corporation was a barren plot of land. RELATED WORDS: **tangibility,** *noun* (tan–jih–BIL–ih–tee), **tangibleness,** *noun* (TAN–jih–b'l–ness) and **tangibly,** *adverb* (TAN–jih–blee).

tantamount, *adjective* (TANT–uh–mount). Having the same value or effect; equivalent. EXAMPLE: Receiving the equivalency diploma is tantamount to graduation from school.

temerity, *noun* (teh–MEHR–ih–tee). Brashness, boldness, audacity, effrontery, recklessness. EXAMPLE: "Bravery is the mean between cowardice and temerity." (Friedrich Ueberweg). RELATED WORDS: **temerarious,** *adjective* (tem–er–AIR–ee–us) and **temerariously,** *adverb* (tem–er–AIR–ee–us–lee).

tenacious, *adjective* (ten–AY–shus). Holding tight; dogged; stubborn; retentive; persistent. EXAMPLE: The bulldog clung to the man's ankle with a tenacious grip. RELATED WORDS: **tenaciously,** *adverb* (ten–AY–shus–lee), **tenaciousness,** *noun* (ten–AY–shus–ness) and **tenacity,** *noun* (ten–ASS–ih–tee).

terse, *adjective* (TERSS). Brief, pithy, concise, free of excess verbiage. EXAMPLE: "Sighted sub; sank same" is a model of terse reporting. RELATED WORDS: **tersely,** *adverb* (TERSS–lee) and **terseness,** *noun* (TERSS–ness).

travesty, *noun* (TRAV–ess–tee). Ludicrous parody; grotesque or absurd imitation; caricature. EXAMPLE: Adding songs and dances to Hamlet resulted in a travesty of Shakespeare's drama. RELATED WORD: **travesty,** *verb* (TRAV–ess–tee).

treatise, *noun* (TREE–tiss). Detailed, scholarly account, usually in written form; thorough analysis of a subject. EXAMPLE: There are many scholarly treatises on linguistics—most of them unreadable.

trenchant, *adjective* (TREN–chent). Cutting, biting, incisive, penetrating, vigorous, clear-cut. EXAMPLE: When the debaters finished, the chairman delivered a trenchant summation of the arguments. RELATED WORDS: **trenchancy,** *noun* (TREN–chen–see) and **trenchantly,** *adverb* (TREN–chent–lee).

trepidation, *noun* (trep–ih–DAY–shun). Hesitancy, fear, apprehension, dread. EXAMPLE: A mood of trepidation seized the wanderers as they approached the haunted house. RELATED WORD: **trepid,** *adjective* (TREP–id).

truculent, *adjective* (TRUK–yoo–lent). Antagonistic, harsh; rude, cruel; scathing; defiant. EXAMPLE: The sight of the oncoming bulldozers stirred the villagers to truculent defiance.

RELATED WORDS: **truculence,** *noun* (TRUK–yoo–lenss), **truculency,** *noun* (TRUK–yoo–len–see) and **truculently,** *adverb* (TRUK–yoo–lent–lee).

turgid, *adjective* (TER–jid). Swollen, bloated; pompous, bombastic. EXAMPLE: The senator from Illinois was a master of the pompous phrase, the trite turgid prose. RELATED WORDS: **turgidity,** *noun* (ter–JID–ih–tee), **turgidly,** *adverb* (TER–jid–lee) and **turgidness,** *noun* (TER–jid–ness).

tyro, *noun* (TY–roh). Beginner, amateur, inexperienced person. EXAMPLE: Even a golfing tyro can break 100—for nine holes.

ubiquitous, *adjective* (yoo–BIK–wih–tus). Omnipresent; seemingly present everywhere at the same time. EXAMPLE: Every lecturer, sooner or later, learns to loathe the ubiquitous creamed chicken and peas. NOTE: This adjective, logically enough, comes from the Latin adverb "ubique," meaning everywhere, on all sides. RELATED WORDS: **ubiquitously,** *adverb* (yoo–BIK–wih–tus–lee), **ubiquitousness,** *noun* (yoo–BIK–wih–tus–ness) and **ubiquity,** *noun* (yoo–BIK–wih–tee).

umbrage, *noun* (UM–brij). Displeasure; resentment; offense. EXAMPLE: The headmaster took umbrage when the pupils presented a list of "non-negotiable" demands. RELATED WORDS: **umbrageous,** *adjective* (um–BRAY–jus) and **umbrageously,** *adverb* (um–BRAY–jus–lee).

unctuous, *adjective* (UNK–choo–us). Oily, slippery; smooth-spoken, suavely pretending concern; insincere. EXAMPLE: The hypocritical Uriah Heep in Dickens' *David Copperfield* is one of the most unctuous villains in all literature. RELATED WORDS: **unctuously,** *adverb* (UNK–choo–us–lee), **unctuosity,** *noun* (unk–choo–OSS–ih–tee) and **unctuousness,** *noun* (UNK–choo–us–ness).

unmitigated, *adjective* (un–MIT–ih–gayt–ed). Without modification, absolute, unlimited, unconscionable. EXAMPLE: With his rambling, twice-told anecdotes, he soon became an unmitigated bore. RELATED WORD: **unmitigatedly,** *adverb* (un–MIT–ih–gayt–ed–lee).

urbane, *adjective* (er–BAYN). Civilized, elegant, courteous. EXAMPLE: "Urbane and pliant, he was at ease even in the drawing rooms of Paris." (R. R. Palmer). RELATED WORDS: **urbanely,** *adverb* (er–BANE–lee) and **urbanity,** *noun* (er–BAN–ih–tee).

utopian, *adjective* (yoo–TOHP–ee–un). Idealistic, visionary, impractical. EXAMPLE: Dollar-conscious businessmen care little for utopian schemes. NOTE: This word comes from the name Sir Thomas More chose for the title of his book *Utopia,* describing an imaginary island where the moral, social and political life was absolutely perfect. It's made up of two Greek words meaning "no place." RELATED WORD: **utopianism,** *noun* (yoo–TOHP–ee–uh–nizm).

vacillate, *verb* (VASS–ih–layt). To fluctuate, sway to and fro; to waver between opinions, be indecisive. EXAMPLE: The true executive must have decision-making ability; he must not vacillate. RELATED WORDS: **vacillating,** *adjective* (VASS–ih–layt–ing), **vacillation,** *noun* (vass–ih–LAY–shun) and **vacillatory,** *adjective* (vass–il–uh–tor–ee).

vacuous, *adjective* (VAK–yoo–us). Devoid of ideas, mentally slow, stupid. EXAMPLE: Many a maiden who seems shy and modest, is actually simply vacuous. RELATED WORD: **vacuity,** *noun* (vuh–KYOO–ih–tee).

vapid, *adjective* (VAP–id). Stale, insipid, tasteless, dull, uninteresting. EXAMPLE: For connoisseurs of vapid prose, there's nothing quite to equal the society pages. RELATED WORDS: **vapidity,** *noun* (vuh–PID–ih–tee); **vapidness,** *noun* (VAP–id–ness).

venal, *adjective* (VEE–nul). Easily bribed, corrupt, mercenary, unscrupulous. EXAMPLE: Every police scandal involves at least a few completely venal cops, often in the higher ranks. RELATED WORDS: **venality,** *noun* (vee–NAL–ih–tee); **venally,** *adverb* (VEE–nuh–lee).

venerate, *verb* (VEN–er–ate). To worship, idolize, regard with deep respect and reverence. EXAMPLE: In all the long history of the papacy, few pontiffs have been so venerated as Pope John XXIII. RELATED WORDS: **veneration,** *noun* (ven–er–AY–shun) and **venerator,** *noun* (VEN–er–ay–tor).

venomous, *adjective* (VEN–uh–mus). Poisonous, malicious, spiteful. EXAMPLE: The producer reacted angrily to the critic's comments, which he regarded as venomous. RELATED WORDS: **venomously,** *adverb* (VEN–uh–mus–lee) and **venomousness,** *noun* (VEN–uh–mus–ness).

veracity, *noun* (ver–ASS–ih–tee). Truthfulness; accuracy, precision. EXAMPLE: There could be no doubt about the veracity of the points the prosecution lawyers made. RELATED WORDS: **veracious**, *adjective* (ver–AY–shus) and **veraciousness**, *noun* (ver–AY–shus–ness).

verbatim, *adjective* and *adverb* (ver–BAY–tim). Word for word; in precisely the same words. EXAMPLE: The court reporter read back the testimony verbatim.

verbose, *adjective* (ver–BOHSS). Talky, wordy, using too many words. EXAMPLE: The orator was so long-winded and verbose that he lost his audience long before he finished. RELATED WORDS: **verbosity**, *noun* (ver–BOSS–ih–tee), **verboseness**, *noun* (ver–BOHSS–ness) and **verbosely**, *adverb* (ver–BOHSS–lee).

vernacular, *noun* (ver–NAK–yoo–ler). Popular speech, common everyday language. EXAMPLE: Many American authors have written in the vernacular, but the acknowledged masterpiece of this genre is Mark Twain's *Huckleberry Finn.* RELATED WORDS: **vernacularism**, *noun* (ver–NAK–yoo–ler–ism) and **vernacularly**, *adverb* (ver–NAK–yoo–ler–lee).

versatile, *adjective* (VER–suh–til). Multi-talented, capable of performing many tasks with skill and ease. EXAMPLE: Among popular musicians few are as versatile as Bobby Hackett, whose musical mastery extends to the cornet, the guitar and the piano. RELATED WORDS: **versatility**, *noun* (ver–suh–TIL–ih–tee) and **versatilely**, *adverb* (VER–suh–til–lee).

vestige, *noun* (VESS–tij). Trace, very small amount; mark of something no longer existing. EXAMPLE: When boasting of his talents, he displayed no slightest vestige of modesty. RELATED WORDS: **vestigial**, *adjective* (ves–TIJ–ul) and **vestigially**, *adverb* (ves–TIJ–ul–lee).

vicarious, *adjective* (vih–KAIR–ee–us). Acting in place of someone else; enjoyed through imagined, rather than actual experience. EXAMPLE: Millions of Americans shared the suspense of the astronauts' trip through space, as vicarious participants in the feat. RELATED WORDS: **vicariously**, *adverb* (vih–KAIR–ee–us–lee) and **vicariousness**, *noun* (vih–KAIR–ee–us–ness).

vicissitude, *noun* (vih–SISS–ih–tyood). One of life's ups and downs; an alteration in fortune. EXAMPLE: Robert E. Lee shared all the vicissitudes of war, from near-victory to ultimate defeat.

vitiate, *verb* (VISH–ee–ayt). To make imperfect, impair; to nullify. EXAMPLE: All the governor's good intentions were vitiated by his wife's unfortunately outspoken insult to the guest from overseas.

vituperate, *verb* (vy–TOO–per–ayt). To abuse, revile, slander, insult in abusive fashion, berate. EXAMPLE: The sharp-tongued fishwife roundly vituperated the policeman, even though he was trying to help her. RELATED WORDS: **vituperation,** *noun* (vy–tyoo–per–AY–shun) and **vituperative,** *adjective* (vy–TYOOP–er–uh–tiv).

vivacious, *adjective* (vih–VAY–shus). Sprightly, animated, spirited. EXAMPLE: The film, "Golddiggers of Broadway," was notable for the vivacious dancing of its principals. RELATED WORDS: **vivaciously,** *adverb* (vih–VAY–shus–lee), **vivaciousness,** *noun* (vih–VAY–shus–ness) and **vivacity,** *noun* (vih–VASS–ih–tee).

vociferous, *adjective* (voh–SIF–er–ous). Shouting or talking loudly; clamorous; noisily talkative. EXAMPLE: The vociferous lady was famous for approaching every new problem with an open mouth. RELATED WORDS: **vociferate,** *verb* (voh–SIF–er–ate) and **vociferously,** *adverb* (voh–SIF–er–us–lee).

wanton, *adjective* (WON–tun). Extravagant, excessive, unrestrained, overabundant, merciless, cruel. EXAMPLE: "The wanton troopers riding by have shot my faun and it will die." (Andrew Marvell). RELATED WORDS: **wantonly,** *adverb* (WON–tun–lee) and **wantonness,** *noun* (WON–tun–ness).

welter, *noun* (WEL–ter). Confusion, turmoil, jumble. EXAMPLE: ". . . the welter of workaday annoyances which all of us meet with." (James Thurber).

whim, *noun* (HWIM). Sudden fancy, capricious idea, arbitrary impulse: EXAMPLE: "My wife has a whim of iron." (Oliver Herford).

writhe, *verb* (RYTHE). To twist about, as in pain. EXAMPLE: "He writhed himself quite off his stool." (Charles Dickens).

zeal, *noun* (ZEEL). Fervor, diligent devotion to a goal, enthusiasm. EXAMPLE: The indispensable characteristic of the long-distance runner is zeal. RELATED WORD: **zealous,** *adjective* (ZEL–us).

9. Test Your Vocabulary

THE A–TO–Z WORD GAME

The following multiple-choice word game is based on a random selection of fifty words from those you have just been reading about. It serves two purposes—to challenge your wits and memories and to send you straight back (I hope) to any words you may miss. Please bear in mind one point: the meanings given in this game are not phrased in precisely the same words as the definitions used in the list. There is a very good reason for this. Words are really not much use to you if you have memorized them by rote. You must become truly familiar with them if you are to use them with ease.

Therefore, in this word quiz, you are asked to choose the sense *closest in meaning* to the one you have just learned. The form in which the word is given may differ slightly. For instance, the quiz may use one of the words given in this chapter under the heading RELATED WORDS. But that should not matter. It will merely add a modest element of trickery to the game—and, after all, what's a game without challenges and tricks?

Right on, then, reader. Choose the lettered word or phrase closest in meaning to the numbered word. If (c) means just about the same as 5, your answer is 5c. You will find a list of the answers on page 182. And, of course, you can always get a fuller explanation by referring back to the list.

1. **Adipose:** (a) fatty; (b) stubborn; (c) lazy.
2. **Antonym:** (a) nickname; (b) word of opposite meaning; (c) new word.
3. **Bailiwick:** (a) bail bondsman; (b) area of influence; (c) deodorant.
4. **Carnage:** (a) decoration; (b) slaughter; (c) two-wheeled carriage.
5. **Chicanery:** (a) poultry farm; (b) admiration; (c) trickery.
6. **Complicity:** (a) abetment; (b) international agreement; (c) lawsuit.

7. **Culpable:** (a) not capable; (b) deserving blame; (c) evasive.

8. **Eschew:** (a) chew carefully; (b) shun; (c) demand repayment.

9. **Euphemism:** (a) flowery writing; (b) mild word for blunt one; (c) cheerfulness.

10. **Euphoric:** (a) early-blooming; (b) in a state of well-being; (c) sleepy.

11. **Exacerbate:** (a) enchant; (b) make bitter; (c) ridicule.

12. **Fetid:** (a) magical charm; (b) gala party; (c) bad-smelling.

13. **Fetish:** (a) passion; (b) witch's wand; (c) object of blind reverence.

14. **Fiat:** (a) trivial falsehood; (b) absolute order; (c) complete flop.

15. **Heinous:** (a) full of shame; (b) obscure; (c) extremely wicked.

16. **Heretical:** (a) slanting; (b) witchlike; (c) opposed to orthodox beliefs.

17. **Honorarium:** (a) token payment; (b) rare musical instrument; (c) honorary degree.

18. **Japery:** (a) joking; (b) table linens; (c) milk-white glassware.

19. **Jocosity:** (a) jesting remark; (b) serious excess weight; (c) stuffiness.

20. **Kismet:** (a) fate; (b) lovers' embrace; (c) Oriental temple.

21. **Lagniappe:** (a) napping; (b) trifling gift; (c) native dancer.

22. **Lambent:** (a) baby lamb; (b) radiant; (c) soft and cuddly.

23. **Languid:** (a) speaking several languages; (b) presumptuous; (c) exhausted.

24. **Lectern:** (a) rare wild bird; (b) platform; (c) reading desk.

25. **Lethal:** (a) considerate; (b) very powerful; (c) causing death.

26. **Lethargic:** (a) dynamic; (b) infernal; (c) lacking energy.

27. **Lissome:** (a) supple; (b) beautiful; (c) glamorous.

28. **Procrastination:** (a) enforced conformity; (b) dawdling; (c) overwriting.

29. **Prognosis:** (a) analysis; (b) extremely long nose; (c) forecast.

30. **Proliferate:** (a) embezzle; (b) make holes in; (c) multiply rapidly.

31. **Prolix:** (a) over-weight; (b) over-wordy; (c) over-complex.

32. **Promulgate:** (a) forbid; (b) publish decree;
    (c) involve in lawsuit.
33. **Propensity:** (a) inclination toward; (b) lust;
    (c) state of well-being.
34. **Propitious:** (a) favorable; (b) feeling pity; (c) appeasing.
35. **Punctilious:** (a) prompt; (b) dapper; (c) precise in conduct.
36. **Quibble:** (a) evasive argument; (b) mason's tool;
    (c) leak in tire.
37. **Recalcitrant:** (a) stubbornly defiant; (b) cooking slowly;
    (c) breathing fast.
38. **Recant:** (a) tip over; (b) renounce beliefs;
    (c) trot horse rapidly.
39. **Recapitulate:** (a) surrender; (b) summarize;
    (c) recapitalize business.
40. **Recondite:** (a) rare mineral; (b) profound;
    (c) build over again.
41. **Recoup:** (a) get back; (b) pen up chickens;
    (c) gain power over.
42. **Redundant:** (a) growing fast; (b) more than enough;
    (c) murky.
43. **Sententious:** (a) sentimental; (b) high-sounding;
    (c) sensitive.
44. **Succinct:** (a) concise; (b) helpless; (c) fresh-tasting.
45. **Travesty:** (a) wall hanging; (b) parody;
    (c) Mongolian monastery.
46. **Treatise:** (a) special treat; (b) learned argument;
    (c) formal essay.
47. **Ubiquitous:** (a) quarrelsome; (b) everywhere at once;
    (c) pretentious.
48. **Venal:** (a) coming in Spring; (b) mercenary; (c) bloody.
49. **Vicarious:** (a) French song; (b) pertaining to victory;
    (c) performed by another.
50. **Whimsy:** (a) sudden chill; (b) caprice;
    (c) taste for fine wine.

THE WILLIAM MORRIS SELF-SCORING
VOCABULARY TEST

For nearly twenty years thousands of teachers, pupils and just
plain word addicts have tried their hands at various forms of
this word test, one which not only challenges the limits of your

word knowledge but pays an added bonus at the end by enabling you to figure out how many words there are in your vocabulary.

Before raising your hopes too high, though, let me assure you that the figure you will wind up with may well be smaller than you expect. That results from two causes. First, this is a very tricky test, indeed. Second, there has been more hogwash written about the size of the average literate man's vocabulary than almost any other topic in the world of linguistics. One well-known and self-styled "word expert" solemnly preached that the average college graduate could be expected to have about 120,000 words in his vocabulary. He based this on the claim of the *Webster's Second New International Dictionary* that it contained 600,000 entries. So our "expert" figured that his average alumnus would have acquired about one-fifth of that number while passing through the groves of academe.

What he failed to realize was that the 600,000 "entries" claimed—and quite justly claimed—by the Merriam editors included many thousands of variant forms and undefined compounds. So an entry like this example (from the *American Heritage Dictionary*), **escape,** *v.* **-caped, -caping, -capes,** followed by various definitions, does not count as *one* entry but as *four.* Furthermore, since this verb has both transitive and intransitive senses, and the undefined words **escapable,** *adj.* and **escaper,** *n.* are also listed in the entry, the total count is *seven,* not *one.* So the very least that must be done is to scale down sharply the estimated number of words in the vocabulary of the average literate American.

Henry L. Mencken, in his *The American Language,* exploded some of the myths that had long been propagated about vocabulary size and concluded that ". . . even the most stupid adults know at least 5,000 [words]. The average American, indeed, probably knows nearly 5,000 nouns. As for the educated, their vocabularies range from 30,000 words to maybe as many as 70,000." My own researches, spanning some thirty years, fully corroborate his finding.

So when you take the test that follows, do not be surprised if your score, computed according to the instruction on pages 146–7, falls somewhere within this range.

The American Language, fourth edition (A. A. Knopf, N.Y., 1946) page 426.

And now for the test itself. First, in Section I, you are asked to pair words *similar* in meaning to each other. For each numbered word in the left-hand column, there is a lettered word in the right-hand column with virtually the same meaning, a *synonym*. If numbered word 5 means practically the same thing as lettered word h, your answer is 5h. Place h in the space following 5. When you work your way down the list, you will find it helpful to strike out the words in the second column, as you use their letters in the first column. The answers are on page 182.

SECTION I

1. Choleric	a. Ineffective
2. Poignant	b. Legendary
3. Benign	c. Incipient
4. Austere	d. Craven
5. Heinous	e. Macabre
6. Ancestral	f. Enthusiastic
7. Futile	g. Fragrant
8. Enigmatic	h. Inherent
9. Deft	i. Lawful
10. Ebullient	j. Ingenuous
11. Slovenly	k. Stubborn
12. Immanent	l. Insipid
13. Inchoate	m. Monstrous
14. Jejune	n. Lugubrious
15. Obdurate	o. Affecting
16. Licit	p. Cryptic
17. Inane	q. Ascetic
18. Naive	r. Carping
19. Redolent	s. Dexterous
20 Dolorous	t. Splenetic
21 Pusillanimous	u. Unkempt
22. Captious	v. Wandering
23. Fabulous	w. Benevolent
24. Gruesome	x. Vacuous
25. Peripatetic	y. Hereditary

SECTION II

This section is played and scored exactly like Section I with one very important difference. This time you are to find words *opposite* in meaning, *antonyms*. You will find this much more challenging.

1. Mulish	a. Brawny
2. Temporal	b. Evasive
3. Patriotic	c. Accidental
4. Licentious	d. Rash
5. Ornate	e. Austere
6. Pernicious	f. Disloyal
7. Obese	g. Pale
8. Premeditated	h. Flaccid
9. Supercilious	i. Blamed
10. Authoritative	j. Lighthearted
11. Indefatigable	k. Careful
12. Reticent	l. Vociferous
13. Resilient	m. Innocuous
14. Monotonous	n. Doubtful
15. Candid	o. Opaque
16. Heedless	p. Scrawny
17. Despondent	q. Lively
18. Puny	r. Humble
19. Eulogized	s. Contemptible
20. Gracious	t. Chaste
21. Rubicund	u. Lazy
22. Estimable	v. Tractable
23. Transparent	w. Unsociable
24. Taciturn	x. Eternal
25. Discreet	y. Outgoing

SECTION III

Here is another of the multiple choice tests with which you are now very familiar. But again there is a slight difference. Now you have four words and phrases to choose from, instead of three. You will find rules for scoring all three sections of this self-scoring quiz on pages 146-7. Now press on—and good luck.

1. **Banal:** (a) vivid; (b) imaginative; (c) folksy;
  (d) commonplace.
2. **Farrow:** (a) row made by plow; (b) wrinkle on brow;
  (c) litter of pigs; (d) military leave.

3. **Diffident:** (a) unusual; (b) unconfident; (c) various;
   (d) routine.

4. **Quixotic:** (a) swift; (b) insane; (c) practical;
   (d) romantically idealistic.

5. **Potable:** (a) drinkable; (b) transportable; (c) elementary;
   (d) poisonous.

6. **Mundane:** (a) pecuniary; (b) worldly;
   (c) happening on the first weekday; (d) municipal.

7. **Necropolis:** (a) large city; (b) cemetery; (c) lovers' lane;
   (d) site of gallows.

8. **Didactic:** (a) poetic; (b) entertaining; (c) instructive;
   (d) pertaining to dietary restrictions.

9. **Truculent:** (a) portable; (b) amiable; (c) stiffly formal;
   (d) fiercely resentful.

10. **Opulent:** (a) wealthy; (b) industrious; (c) overweight;
    (d) impoverished.

11. **Effulgent:** (a) filling to overflowing; (b) feeding till fat;
    (c) shining brilliantly; (d) reticent.

12. **Euphony:** (a) repetitious sound; (b) musical variation;
    (c) chamber music group; (d) sweet sound.

13. **Prescience:** (a) preliminary investigation;
    (b) ancient science; (c) clarity; (d) foresight.

14. **Postulate:** (a) protest; (b) reply to statement;
    (c) student priest; (d) proposition taken for granted.

15. **Ephemeral:** (a) effeminate; (b) lasting; (c) interesting;
    (d) short-lived.

16. **Garble:** (a) pervert in meaning; (b) chatter unceasingly;
    (c) refuse; (d) dress a mannequin.

17. **Desultory:** (a) dreary; (b) designing; (c) aimless;
    (d) lonely.

18. **Profligate:** (a) set fire to; (b) extravagant; (c) humdrum;
    (d) hateful.

19. **Blatant:** (a) dark; (b) bland; (c) flattering; (d) noisy.

20. **Foment:** (a) extinguish; (b) smooth over; (c) nurse to life;
    (d) make bubble-like.

21. **Soporific:** (a) dreamy; (b) sleep-inducing; (c) very swift;
    (d) viscous.

22. **Collate:** (a) eat a meal; (b) gather and compare; (c) clot;
    (d) add.

23. **Uxorious:** (a) devoted to one's wife; (b) urgent;
    (c) usurping; (d) wearying.

24. **Pariah:** (a) Polish papa; (b) outcast; (c) ancient;
    (d) politician.
25. **Vestige:** (a) official power; (b) trace; (c) sprouting seed;
    (d) sign of destruction.
26. **Accolade:** (a) award; (b) court verdict;
    (c) international diplomat; (d) special dispensation.
27. **Icon:** (a) TV picture tube; (b) religious image;
    (c) pledge of self-belief; (d) vertical icicle.
28. **Anomalous:** (a) like another; (b) routine; (c) diminutive;
    (d) out of the ordinary.
29. **Hebdomadal:** (a) happening weekly;
    (b) pertaining to the stomach; (c) worshipping idols;
    (d) varying seasonally.
30. **Insensate:** (a) underdeveloped; (b) small in size;
    (c) with keen sensory perception;
    (d) devoid of sensation.
31. **Calumny:** (a) catastrophe; (b) false accusation;
    plea of "nolo contendere"; (d) settling of guilt.
32. **Porcine:** (a) hoggish; (b) round-bodied; (c) high-handed;
    (d) listless.
33. **Olfactory:** (a) ancient factory; (b) oleomargarine maker;
    (c) menacing; (d) pertaining to smell.
34. **Recalcitrant:** (a) fatty; (b) distended; (c) stubborn;
    (d) lazy.
35. **Enucleate:** (a) tie together; (b) raze structure;
    (c) peel from shell; (d) break something.
36. **Verisimilar:** (a) closely resembling;
    (b) related mathematically; (c) contrary to reality;
    (d) appearing to be true.
37. **Depurate:** (a) appoint deputy; (b) free of impurities;
    (c) delegate power; (d) form rock group.
38. **Lustrate:** (a) make pure by offerings;
    (b) point out something; (c) show by illustration;
    (d) pay homage to.
39. **Cozenage:** (a) family relations; (b) humorous play;
    (c) organized choral singing; (d) practice of fraud.
40. **Polyandry:** (a) mischievous ghost;
    (b) having more than one husband;
    (c) having more than one wife; (d) having many names.
41. **Ominous:** (a) thunderous; (b) portentious; (c) vacillating;
    (d) faithful.

42. **Asterisk:** (a) kind of flower; (b) symbol of peace;
    (c) footnote; (d) printing symbol.
43. **Flatulent:** (a) stereotyped; (b) without plan;
    (c) pretentious; (d) flat.
44. **Pother;** (a) make a fuss; (b) be contrary; (c) plan;
    (d) organize.
45. **Fecund:** (a) sourish; (b) hateful; (c) miserly; (d) prolific.
46. **Apostatize:** (a) proclaim sainthood; (b) request;
    (c) renounce one's faith; (d) petition.
47. **Carnivorous:** (a) meat-eating; (b) festive; (c) juicy;
    (d) ravenous.
48. **Chromatic:** (a) optical; (b) of colors; (c) irritable;
    (d) dissonant.
49. **Pertinacious:** (a) loosely held; (b) tending to give up;
    (c) pertaining to corn; (d) stubborn.
50. **Tumid:** (a) swollen; (b) dampish; (c) enormous;
    (d) characterized by tumult.

HOW TO SCORE THIS TEST

To score Sections I and II: Find the number of *correct* answers
and multiply by 800. (Thus, if you had 40 correct answers,
your score would be 32,000 for Sections I and II.)

To score Section III: Count the number of *mistakes* you
made and multiply this figure by 533. Deduct the total from
20,000. This is your score for Section III. (Thus, if you had 10
mistakes, you should deduct 5,330 from 20,000, giving you a
score of 14,670 for Section III.)

Then add the scores for both sections to find the approximate
number of words in your recognition vocabulary. These are
the words you understand when you come upon them in reading. Your speaking vocabulary may be assumed to be between
one-half and two-thirds the size of your recognition vocabulary.

Please note: This test takes no account of the number of
proper names and place names that may be part of your vocabulary. This element of one's vocabulary varies so greatly
from person to person that no attempt to evaluate it is practicable. Furthermore, most of us use, in addition to our general
vocabulary, the jargon of our trade or profession, which may
run from as few as fifty words to as many as a thousand or

more words in the case of doctors, lawyers and journalists. It is safe, therefore, to say that a professional man's vocabulary will be substantially larger than this test may indicate.

On this test a rating of 15,000 words or better is excellent for a high-school pupil, while an adult high-school graduate should score above 25,000 to rate "excellent." According to a recent Brown University study, newspapermen have wider and more versatile vocabularies than professors, so a college-educated journalist should score well above 40,000.

10. Words to Watch For

During the time from the publication of Dr. Johnson's Dictionary in 1755 until the early years of this century grammarians and dictionary editors demonstrated a strong inclination to dictate the "rights" and "wrongs" of language. You must never end a sentence with a preposition. You must never intrude an adverb between the two parts of an infinitive. The word "ain't" is forever taboo. And so on. As recently as 1913 one distinguished American lexicographer, Frank Vizetelly of Funk and Wagnalls, could solemnly state that "*Raise* should never be used of bringing human beings to maturity: it is a misuse common in the southern and western United States. Cattle are *raised;* human beings are *brought up* or, in an older phrase, *reared.*"

This same distinguished dictionary editor was given to pontificating on "the general principles determining correctness in English speech and writing, with their application to some of the more common instances of violation."

Well, that was more than a half-century ago and we're happy to report that no one today would attempt to lay down such rules for grammar and usage. Winston Churchill, certainly one of the great writers and orators of this century, never hesitated to violate the rules when he could gain greater emphasis by so doing. One of his most celebrated wartime speeches began: "This is me, Churchill speaking"—and, although purists might have shuddered at that *me,* the soldiers listening to him were properly impressed. On another occasion, questioned about a sentence in one of his speeches which ended with a preposition, the great man simply snorted that the taboo was "nonsense up with which I will not put."

This, incidentally, brings us to another matter which was once of great concern to the self-styled purists who laid down the rules for language—*shall* and *will.* Our old friend Vizetelly once created an elaborate chart headed "Shall and Will . . . To use these words correctly apply the rules in the accompanying table" and then ran on for another page and a half giving such solemn advice as "Will in the first person expresses determination. . . . Shall expresses a simple future." That ridiculous distinction received its death blow when General Douglas MacArthur—as language-conscious as he was uniform-conscious—announced on his departure from Bataan: "I *shall* return."

Well, there's not much point in beating dead horses—and most of these old-fashioned rules of grammar are long dead. But what should take their place? People still want guidance in the use of language—not stern, unbending rules, but guidance.

When the Merriam-Webster editors issued their *Webster's Third New International Unabridged Dictionary* in 1961, many critics and reviewers noted with dismay that warning labels like "slang," "colloquial" and "vulgar" had been almost entirely eliminated. Moreover, all of the words, except *God*, were spelled without initial capital letters, even words like *Washingtonian* and *Miamian* which never appear in print any other way. Similarly all periods were omitted and various other stylistic quirks marred this newest edition of what had long been regarded as America's greatest dictionary. But the chief complaint was that the editors had virtually eliminated observations on how the language is used and, of the comments they did include, at least a few seemed of dubious merit.

What raised the greatest commotion was the editorial comment that "ain't [is] used orally in most parts of the United States by many cultivated speakers, especially in the phrase 'ain't I?' " One critic was moved to wonder just where Merriam cultivated such speakers. Others cried out in protest, for the taboo on "*ain't*"—especally in writing—remains virtually ironclad.

One result of all the controversy caused by the appearance of what many called "this permissive dictionary" was a decision by the editors of *American Heritage Magazine* to produce a dictionary which would not content itself merely with recording the language but would also include guidance on how it might most effectively be used. As editor-in-chief of the work, I assembled a panel of more than one hundred talented writers and speakers, men and women who had demonstrated their abiilty to use the language with skill, care and grace (to aid the editors in determining levels of usage.)

Poets such as John Ciardi, Marianne Moore, and Langston Hughes; journalists like Walter Lippmann, Vermont Royster and Russell Baker; public figures like Senators Eugene McCarthy, Mark Hatfield and Maureen Neuberger; historians like Bruce Catton, Barbara Tuchman and Gerald Carson—these and many other talented people contributed over a period of several years to the compilation of guidelines, in the form of Usage Notes, on how they actually use the language. (These notes provide guidance to the dictionary reader on how he may best use particular words and phrases.) The spirit motivating these panelists was perhaps most winningly set forth by Miss Tuchman who wrote: "English is a language of marvelous properties. I like to see it properly used, just as one likes to see a shirt properly laundered or a dinner table properly set."

The results of the many questions we put to the panelists—questions like "are *bimonthly* and *semimonthly* synonymous?" and "do you draw a distinction between *imply* and *infer?*"—are fully recorded in the *American Heritage Dictionary of the English Language* and many of the same usage notes are reported in the Dell paperback edition of that dictionary. This chapter will not report in detail on the work of the panel. Rather, we will look at some of the thorny problems of usage that confront writers and speakers today, with my suggestions for their solution. These suggestions may not always agree with those of the panel, for we are all individuals and, indeed, there was almost never complete unanimity on any one topic. Herewith, then, some of the problems—and my own suggestions for their solution.

ain't. There is no simple answer to the implications of *ain't,* as the editors at Merriam-Webster learned to their sorrow. To a very substantial percentage of the great American public, *ain't* is a commonplace part of everyday speech. Yet generations of schoolteachers have damned it as "illiterate," "vulgar" or "ignorant." To most college-educated Americans, *ain't* is never permissible in writing—except in fiction where it is used to indicate character—and it is very much frowned upon in speech.

Still, and perhaps surprisingly, *ain't* has its apologists and among them may be found some outstanding authorities on language. Henry W. Fowler, in his *Modern English Usage,* for example, wrote: "*Ain't* is merely colloquial and, as used for *isn't* is an uneducated blunder and serves no useful purpose. But it is a pity that *ain't* for *am not,* being a natural contraction and supplying a real want, should shock us as though tarred with the same brush." And Porter Perrin in his *Writers' Guide and Index to English* sounds almost wistful when he writes that *ain't* "could be an economical single form for *am not, is not, are not, has not, have not* if the social objection could be relaxed."

So the advice from here is to avoid *ain't* absolutely in writing and restrict its use in speech to deliberately humorous sentences like "I *ain't* about to object to *ain't* from a truck-driver."

aren't I. This expression, more common in England than in the United States, is an effort to avoid *ain't* and the virtually unpronounceable *amn't I.* But it sounds stilted and, what's worse, it utterly violates grammatical propriety, as is transparently clear when the phrase is reversed. Who but a complete ignoramus would say *I are not!*

author. In recent years, particularly on TV talk shows, guests are introduced in this fashion: "So-and-so has *authored* a new book"—and every time I hear this my hackles rise. *Author* is a noun, not a transitive verb—and we're not persuaded by the argument that it was a verb many centuries ago. According to the respected *Oxford Dictionary* this use of *author* as a verb is obsolete—and we feel it should remain that way. What's wrong with the good old verb *to write?* As one who has committed far too many words to print, I aver that I *write* books, not *author* them.

bad; badly. The question is repeatedly raised as to whether one feels *bad* or feels *badly.* The latter phrase has a touch of phony elegance about it which makes it appeal to the kind of person who says *aren't I?* and *between you and I.* In this particular case, *feel* is what linguists call a "linking verb," like *to be,* and customarily it is followed by a predicate adjective. So *feel bad* is the preferred form. Say I *feel badly* only when you wish to indicate that your tactile sense is below par.

balding. This is a coinage of the Luce empire, like *tycoon, socialite* and other Timestyle inventions from the early years of the news magazine. Unlike most of them, however, this one seems to serve a useful purpose and objections to it on the grounds that *bald* is an adjective, not a verb, and that *balding* is therefore unacceptable seem a bit wide of the mark. Mark this one acceptable in all except the most formal contexts.

between you and I. Phony genteelism is the only label for this particular monstrosity. The word *between* is a preposition. Objects of prepositions should be in the objective case. The objective case of the first personal pronoun is *me,* not *I.* So *between you and me* is the only correct form for this phrase. As one critic has remarked, "America sometimes seems full of people who were taught early in life that *me* is a dirty word." It isn't.

bring; take. There is a useful distinction to be made between these two often misused words. *Bring* implies transporting something from a distance to where the speaker is. *Take* means transporting something away from where the speaker is. So "*bring* the paper in from the front step" but "*take* the report down to the office when you go."

bimonthly; semimonthly. The prefixes *bi* and *semi* should have clearly distinguished meanings, but far too many dictionaries define them as interchangeable. *Bimonthly* means every two months. *American Heritage* is a *bimonthly* magazine. *Look* is a *biweekly* magazine. *Semimonthly* means twice a month; *semiweekly* means twice a week. While we're on the subject, *biennial* means every two years, while *biannual* means twice a year.

burgeon. This word has had great vogue in recent years, almost exclusively at the hands of writers and speakers who don't know what it means. Almost invariably you hear terms like "our *burgeoning* population" or "the *burgeoning* economy." What these people are trying to say is "mushrooming" or "expanding" or "thriving." *Burgeoning* simply means "budding"—and it should be restricted in use to that meaning.

cohort. Here's another word much misused in recent years. Many people seem to think any companion or associate is a *cohort.* He isn't. A *cohort,* properly speaking, is a group, or association, especially such a group working collectively towards a common goal.

contact. The use of *contact* as a verb—"I'll *contact* him after the meeting"—originated in business parlance and for a number of years was frowned upon by those who felt it lacked precision. Many felt, and some still do, that more specific

YOUR HERITAGE OF WORDS 153

words like *telephone* or *write* were preferable. However, language changes and yesterday's prejudices have a way of becoming today's accepted phrases. So it's now pretty well agreed that *contact* both as a verb and as a noun—"He's my *contact* at I.B.M."—is acceptable in all except the most formal contexts.

data. Properly speaking *data* is the plural form of the Latin word *datum* and should require a plural verb—"the *data* are inconclusive." However, this distinction is not widely observed, especially on informal levels and in business, technical and scientific writing, one frequently encounters "The *data* is inconclusive." In defense of this usage, a parallel may be drawn to *agenda,* likewise technically a plural, but almost invariably regarded as a collective unit and hence as taking a singular verb.

different from; different than. Both of these expressions appear commonly in the works of talented and careful writers. My own preference generally is for *different from* as being more direct and rather less affected than *different than.* This is especially true when the second item in the pair being compared is a simple noun: "The new paper was radically *different from* the old." However, if the second item would lead into a lengthy or awkward clause, *different than* may be preferable: "How *different* his condition seems now *than* yesterday" rather than "How *different* his condition seems now *from* what it was yesterday." In sum, though, this comes down pretty much to what strikes your own ear as the better form to use.

disinterested; uninterested. There is a valuable distinction to be drawn between these two words. A person who is *uninterested* is simply not concerned with the matter, probably even bored by it. On the other hand a judge in a legal action can and should be deeply interested in the cause before him— but truly *disinterested* in the sense that he is utterly impartial, not interested on behalf of either litigant but very much interested in seeing that the cause of justice is served.

enthuse. This is a back-formation, as the linguists say, from the noun enthusiasm and it's one of fairly recent vintage. It was disapproved of by many careful users of language but seems to be making its way into the speech and writing of literate people. Certainly it is simpler to say "I *enthused* over the film" than to say "I was very *enthusiastic* about the film."

Nonetheless, it should still be restricted to informal conversation and avoided in writing, especially writing of a formal nature.

farther; further. In careful speech and writing *farther* should be used in reference to physical distance: "The astronauts traveled *farther* than any other humans." *Further* should be reserved for references to degree or time: "Let's discuss the matter *further* tomorrow."

fewer; less. The distinction here, which Madison Avenue's advertising copywriters have done much to blur in recent years, is that *fewer* should be used in reference to things that can be counted, while *less* should be used in reference to quantities that can be measured. "*Fewer* people attended the dinner, so the revenue was *less* than had been expected."

finalize. Many careful writers stigmatize this word on the grounds that it is merely a rather pretentious-sounding synonym for end, conclude, or complete. I have had correspondence with bureaucrats, particularly in the armed services, who contend that there is a subtlety of difference here and that to *finalize* means more than simply to terminate. However, the distinctions have been so subtle that they have eluded me completely. The suggestion from this quarter, then —and this disregards the fact that both presidents Eisenhower and Kennedy seemed fond of *finalize*—is to use the simpler words and leave this one for the bureaucrats.

flaunt; flout. This pair is so often scrambled that even a brace of Supreme Court justices had trouble with them. According to the *Washington Post,* on one historic Monday, Justices Black and White penned opinions in which one used *flaunt* when he meant *flout* and the other wrote *flout* when he meant *flaunt.* So the mistake is common in high places and it might be well for us to settle the issue once and for all—spell it out in black and white, if you will forgive the pun.

To *flaunt* something is to display it ostentatiously: "As the parade moved up the avenue, flags were *flaunted* throughout the ranks."

To *flout* something is to show contempt for it, to scorn it. "The young people *flouted* convention with their long hair, sandals and bizarre attire."

A magazine editor summed it up rather neatly in a memorable phrase: "He who *flaunts* his mistress *flouts* his wife."

And another sage put it this way: "He who *flouts* grammar *flaunts* his ignorance."

flounder; founder. More than one writer has come to grief using *flounder* when he meant *founder* or vice versa. Perhaps this is not surprising, since the etymologists tell us that *flounder*, the newer of the two words, was clearly influenced in its origin by *founder*. When one *flounders* about, he is moving clumsily, almost convulsively, as if in an effort to regain lost balance: "The new foreman *floundered* about making hasty and unwise decisions." One might bear in mind that a fish out of water *flounders* about a good bit, although *flounder*, the fish, and the act of *floundering* are actually two quite different words. The person or thing that *founders*, however, is in much worse straits. He or it has failed utterly. When a ship *founders*, it sinks beneath the surface of the water. When a horse *founders*, it goes lame.

fulsome. Few words are so frequently and mistakenly used. All too many people think that *fulsome* is a word of flattery when actually it is one that borders on contempt. The true meaning of *fulsome* is disgusting or offensive to good taste. So when one speaks of a senator's *fulsome* oratory, you may be using the adjective correctly. But don't expect him to be flattered by it— not if he is familiar with its dictionary meaning.

gourmand—gourmet. The distinction between these two words is a nice one, but one worth preserving, especially in these days when *gourmet* seems to be applied to everything from galloping chefs to frozen packaged meals. *A gourmet*, properly speaking, is an authority on the selection and preparation of fine foods; and he is almost invariably also a connoisseur of fine vintage wines. But he is not usually a very heavy eater. Indeed, his careful discrimination in foods and his desire to keep his taste buds fresh and alert usually lead to his eating rather sparingly.

The *gourmand*, on the contrary, loves food and sizeable helpings of it. *Gourmand*, indeed, was originally a French word meaning "gluttonous"—and a trace of this notion carries over in our use of the word today.

graduate. "He graduated high school last year" is simply illiterate, an unforgiveable solecism. One *graduates from* a school or college. In years past, to raise the ghost of Frank Vizetelly one more time, purists used to insist on "was *graduated* from"—but this has passed.

healthful; healthy. There's a nice distinction to be drawn here. A person in good health is *healthy*. A climate or a particular part of the country may be described as *healthful*, that is, conducive to good health.

hopefully. "*Hopefully* things will get better" is an expression one hears on every side, even from people normally careful in their speech. What is intended, of course, is something along the lines of "It is to be hoped" or, less formally, "I hope that." Despite its current vogue, *hopefully* in this context is frowned upon by many authorities and, if you haven't already succumbed to its pervasive lure, I hope you won't.

host; cohost. The conversion of the noun *host* to a transitive verb, "He is *hosting* the late-night show this week," seems so complete that objection to it would be futile. It would still be wise to avoid it in formal speech or writing, however, and *cohost,* for example, "Tom and Jerry *cohosted* the luncheon," is simply an abomination.

illiterate. Strictly interpreted, *illiterate* describes a person who can neither read nor write. It comes from the Latin word, "illiteratus," unlettered. As used by educators and sociologists in such sentences as "A shocking percentage of sixth-graders are functionally *illiterate,*" this is pretty much the sense in which it was used. Certainly a case could be made for restricting its use to that precise meaning, for there are plenty of workable synonyms, like "ignorant" and "stupid," to use in describing people who can read but are still not notably intelligent.

However, that's not the way language works. It seldom stays in carefully marked channels and *illiterate* is one word that has acquired meanings rather far afield from its original one. Nowadays it has come to be used to describe people who are uncultured, ignorant, or uneducated in any single aspect of our culture. Thus you might describe a moon-walking astronaut as being politically *illiterate*. What's more, the word has been widely used, in a pejorative sense, to refer to people perfectly capable of reading but incapable of absorbing the content or meaning of what they have read. One famous university administrator remarked not long ago: "It is common knowledge that our professional students and candidates for the Ph.D. are *illiterate*." Granting that he almost certainly was indulging in hyperbole, this word serves to indicate the extended sense in which *illiterate* may be used even by a man who himself is highly literate.

imply; infer. It would be difficult to think of a more common error in our language than the use of *infer* when *imply* is intended. It's a bit difficult to understand why this should be so, since the difference between the two is obvious when clearly stated. When I make a statement, I may *imply* (that is, suggest or hint) that things may not be precisely what they seem to be. Listening to the tone of my voice, you may *infer* that I am making such a suggestion.

One commentator on current usage notes: "*Infer* has been used so much with the meaning of *imply* that it is given as a secondary sense of the word in some dictionaries." That puts me in mind of a story told by Alistair Cooke about C. P. Scott, the first great editor of the *Manchester Guardian*. Finding the phrase "from whence" in some news copy, he called in and reprimanded the reporter who had written it. "But sir," replied the reporter, "Henry Fielding used 'from whence' in *Tom Jones*." Replied Scott: "Mr. Fielding would not have used 'from whence' in MY newspaper." In the same spirit, *imply* and *infer* are not given as synonyms in MY dictionary.

irregardless. There is a school of thought that contends that there simply is no such word as *irregardless*. Unfortunately, this is not the case and we cannot simply deny the existence of a word which is far too prevalent in various American dialects. However, we can say it is both wrong and unnecessary, since it says nothing that *regardless* alone does not say. It is simply a rather silly duplication of negatives: *ir*—a variation of *in*—and *less*. A college teacher of my acquaintance used to make this marginal comment whenever he found *irregardless* on a student's paper: "Why not go all the way and make it *disirregardless*?" He reported that, over many years of teaching, no pupil had failed to get the point.

It's me. As noted earlier, Winston Churchill made this formulation completely acceptable to all save a few stuffy diehards. Actually, Sir Winston was merely ratifying a decision that most grammarians had arrived at decades earlier. In theory, of course, the verb *to be* should be followed by the same case that precedes it—that is by the nominative case. However, even Henry W. Fowler, writing in 1926, was able to say: "*Me* is technically wrong in '*It wasn't me*' etc., but the phrase being of its very nature colloquial, such a lapse is of no importance . . . there is more danger of using *I* for *me* —'between you and I,' 'let you and I try' are not uncommon." Still other grammarians, notably Prof. C. C. Fries of the University of Michigan, theorize that the use of nominative or objective cases of pronouns rests chiefly on whether they fall in "subjective territory" (ahead of the verb) or "objective territory" (after the verb). Looked at this way, there's no difficulty in accepting the logic of *It's me,* because *me* is clearly in "objective territory."

As a sort of footnote, we might note that the contraction *it's,* once restricted to use as a shortened form of *it is* is now widely accepted as a contraction for *it has.* So you can say with complete propriety both "It's a hot day today" and "It's been a long winter."

like. Few advertising campaigns have created such a furor as the one involving the use of *like* as a conjunction in the phrase "tastes good like a cigarette should." Curiously enough, nobody questioned the use of "good"—although one might have anticipated that the self-styled purists who insist on "feel badly" and "go slowly" might have been expected to push for "taste well." But the sensibilities of even non-purists were outraged by *like* instead of *as.* As it happens, your author is to be numbered among those who much prefer *as* in constructions where a verb is involved. However, there can be no gainsaying the fact that *like* as a conjunction— "he behaved *like* he was told to"—is increasingly heard even in the speech of literate, educated people. Some authorities even report it to be "now within the range of Standard English." The suggestion from here, however, is that it should be carefully avoided in writing, except in fiction where it may be needed to delineate character.

One cautionary note; a few people, horrified by the "bad grammar" of the cigarette commercial overreacted to the extent that they became suspicious of any use of the word *like.* I know of one young editor who went through a manuscript carefully changing every *like* to *as,* even when it resulted in such obvious lunacies as "he writes as Hemingway."

The calculated vulgarities of tobacco advertising have a long history, going back to the cigarette that "*travels* the smoke further" and culminating, let us hope, in the one about "*us* XXX smokers would rather fight than switch." Someone on Madison Avenue is convinced that the shock value of such illiteracies pays off. We doubt it and certainly hope that these devastating assaults on our language will cease.

media. This is, of course, a plural form of *medium*, but it has been so widely used and abused by advertisers and their agents that such expressions as "try another *media*" have become commonplace. There are, of course, various advertising *media*—newspapers, magazines, radio and television, to name only a few. Still the misuse of *media* as a singular (and even of *medias* as a plural) persists. We suspect that the underlying cause, besides sheer ignorance, is the fact that to some Madison Avenue types *media* simply sounds more elegant.

myself. This is correctly used as the intensive or reflexive form of the pronouns *I* and *me*. In such a statement as "I cannot trust him to do the job. I must do it *myself*," the word is correctly used as an intensifier. Similarly "I hurt *myself*" is a satisfactory example of its use as a reflexive. However, such formulations as "Mary and *myself* are to be dinner guests" and "He sold the car to Tom and *myself*" are increasingly common and, while not actually wrong, should be avoided as stilted and awkward. Almost certainly sentences such as these result from the speaker's uncertainty about whether to use *I* or *me*. In both cases the simpler form is preferable —"Mary and I" and "Tom and me."

muchly. Forget this one. You may have heard the expression "Thank you *muchly*"—though we rather hope for your sake that you haven't. In any event, it's artificial elegance, to be avoided like the plague.

personality. In the sense of the qualities that make a man an individual, the characteristics that make him either attractive or unattractive to his fellow men, *personality* is a word that has been in the lexicon for centuries. In recent years, however, it has acquired a new meaning, a "notable" or a "celebrity," originally confined to show business but now spreading broadly through other areas of our culture. We find little objection to this usage in popular media—the press, radio and the like. However, it should still be avoided in formal contexts.

phase. This word has been widely and loosely used of late as though it meant no more than "part": "This *phase* of the editorial review is completed." Actually, and correctly, *phase* should be used to refer to a distinct stage in an evolutionary process: "Preparations for blast-off fell into three successive *phases*."

preposition at end of sentence. As noted earlier, this is another item that dies hard in the folklore of traditional grammar. Actually it had its origin in the attempts of nineteenth century grammarians to force the modes and characteristics of Latin grammar on English. That's where the "It is I" nonsense came from, too. Few sentences in Latin—with the exception of some verse—end in prepositions for the reason that practically all Latin prose has a verb at the end of the sentence. So if you want to say "I certainly have a lot to put up with" or "What's all the shouting about?"—go right ahead. Any revamping of such sentences would result in awkwardness up with which you'd not want to put.

preventative. This is simply an error, like *irregardless* but perhaps even more common. The correct, and simpler, form is *preventive*.

principal; principle. These words cause trouble for many people. *Principal* as an adjective means chief or most important. It is also used as a noun—most frequently with reference to the *principal* of a school but also to describe leaders in almost any operation: "Before floating the bond issue, it was necessary to being the *principals* together." *Principle* means a basic truth or law or an essential element: "The *principles* of religious faith are inculcated at an early age."

raise; rear. The outmoded stricture that cattle are *raised* while humans are *reared* has been commented on earlier. Today it is merely amusing and millions more Americans *raise* children than *rear* them.

Reverend. This, we suspect, belongs in our department of lost causes but, because many clergymen dislike being saluted with "Hello, Reverend," we'll take one more tilt at this particular windmill. The problem arises from the fact that *reverend* is properly an adjective, like *holy*. One would scarcely think of approaching a cleric with "Hello, Holy"— but that, in effect, is what the laity does at millions of church doors every Sunday. Something more than forty years ago an anonymous Anglican divine dashed off a bit of verse on the subject—whose refrain is still quoted on divinity school campuses:

Call me *Brother*, if you will;/Call me *Parson*—better still.

Or if, perchance the Catholic frill/Doth your heart with
longing fill,

Though plain *Mister* fills the bill,/Then even *Father* brings
no chill

Of hurt or rancor or ill-will.

To no D. D. do I pretend,/Though some with *Doctor*
honor lend.

Preacher, Pastor, Rector, Friend,/Titles almost without end

Never grate and ne'er offend;/A loving ear to all I bend.

But how the man my heart doth rend,/Who blithely calls
me *Reverend!*"

sick; ill. These two words are used practically interchangeably
in the United States, although *sick* is by far the commoner.
In England, however, *sick* is restricted to physical nausea,
the feeling we generally describe as "*sick* to (or at) one's
stomach."

slow; slowly. A very common misconception is that all adverbs
must end in *-ly* and that, therefore, road signs that say "Go
Slow" or "Drive *Slow*" are in error. The fact is that both
slow and *slowly* are adverbs and the choice of which to use
depends chiefly on the context. In the matter of road signs, the
imperative need is to communicate swiftly to a fast-driving
motorist, and there seems no doubt that "Drive *Slow*" is
preferable to "Drive *Slowly*." Similarly there are instances
where the idiom requires one or the other. You wouldn't
say "My watch runs *slowly*." The idiom demands "My watch
runs *slow*." On the other hand, in formal writing or speech,
slowly is preferred: "The funeral cortege moved *slowly* towards Arlington Cemetery."

split infinitive. Here is another pedant's bogey, carried over
from the Latinate prescriptions of the nineteenth century.
There was no such thing as a split infinitive in Latin for the
simple reason that each Latin infinitive was a single word.
Our "to hold" is expressed in Latin simply by "tenere." So
such a construction as "to fully hold the water" was quite
literally impossible in Latin. Therefore the schoolmarms rea-
soned that both elements of an English preposition should be
considered as fused into one—unsplittable and sacrosanct.
Only that's not the way the English language works. But
there remain no hard-and-fast rules as to when one may
and when one may not *split an infinitive*. The general con-

sensus is that *split infinitives* should be unsplit when too many adverbial elements intrude and by their very number cause the reader perplexity. Such a sentence as: "The leader undertook to forcefully, firmly, fully and systematically advise the members of their rights" leaves even the attentive reader or listener a bit baffled. The remedy is simple: transpose all those adverbs to the end of the sentence: "The leader undertook to advise the members of their rights—forcefully, firmly, fully and systematically." That sentence still is not a model of clarity—but it's much more comprehensible than the other.

However, if the intrusion of one or at most two adverbs between the parts of an infinitive sounds right to your ear and if it aids in clarity, feel free to *split the infinitive*. "He wanted to really help his mother" sounds much less stilted than "He wanted really to help his mother"—and "he wanted to help his mother really" is just meaningless.

The definitive analysis, not of *split infinitives* but of *infinitive-splitters*, comes from the pen of Henry W. Fowler who wrote in *Modern English Usage*: "The English-speaking world may be divided into (1) those who neither know nor care what a *split infinitive* is; (2) those who do not know but care very much; (3) those who know and condemn; (4) those who know and approve; and (5) those who know and distinguish . . . Those who neither know nor care are the vast majority and are a happy folk to be envied by most of the minority classes."

stationary; stationery. This duo shouldn't cause any trouble but somehow it does. The distinction is really quite elementary. A thing that is *stationary* is fixed, immoveable. *Stationery* is what you write letters on.

surprise; astonish. Practically the only reason for bringing this pair up for consideration is to reprise the story that has been told about every dictionary editor—excepting only Dr. Johnson—from Cawdrey to Morris. It seems that the lexicographer's wife comes home unannounced and unexpected to find the editor in what used to be called a compromising position with the serving wench. "I am surprised," she exclaims. "Not so," he replies, "I am surprised. You are astonished." But today the distinction is seldom observed.

theft. Here is another instance, like *author,* of a noun being converted into a verb for no apparent reason. "He *thefted* the bankroll" says no more, and says it much less well, than "he stole the bankroll."

Thusly. See comments on *muchly*. This is just more of the same.

Unique and other incomparable adjectives. With increasing frequency, especially in the fields of fashion and show business, we hear phrases like *more unique* and *most unique*. These chill the marrow of anyone with any feeling for the language. A thing that is *unique* is precisely that—one of a kind. Julian Huxley once wrote that "Man's language is *unique* in consisting of words." Not only is that true but it should serve as a cautionary note to us to preserve the *uniqueness* of *unique*. If one wants merely to qualify an adjective of approbation with "more" or "most," there are plenty available: remarkable, exceptional, and unusual, for starters.

There are a number of other absolute or "incomparable" adjectives and precision in their use is one mark of a careful speaker or writer. Among them are: contemporary, eternal, everlasting, incessant, inevitable, omniscient, simultaneous, universal, and basic.

whence. The expression *from whence,* though appearing in literature from the King James Bible down to the present day, is considered redundant, since the idea of *from* is already contained in *whence,* which means "from where" or "from what place." So *from whence* should be avoided except in deliberately humorous contexts, as in the chorus girl's complaint in Frank Loesser's *Guys and Dolls:*

"Take back your mink to *from whence* it came
And tell them to Hollanderize it for some other dame!"

whose. The last of the strict-constructionist grammarians' phobias to come under our scrutiny is the theory that *whose* must be used only in reference to humans, not to animals and much less to inanimate objects. Careful following of this nonexistent "rule" results in things like this: "The classical drama the precepts *of which* had been established by Sophocles . . ." instead of "The classical drama *whose* precepts had been established by Sophocles." Ignore this so-called rule. If you feel the need to cite a notable precedent for your use of *whose* in reference to inanimate objects, you need look no further than our national anthem: "Whose broad stripes and bright stars . . . were so gallantly streaming."

11. Your Very Own Heritage of Words

The purpose of this book has been, of course, to interest you in Your Heritage of Words, to encourage you to an awareness of the richness and excitement that await you as you extend your command of the language. The word histories and word games that have been spread before you have been designed to add to your working vocabulary. But I have had another idea, as well. That, put simply, is to get you hooked on words, to persuade you that a continuing interest in words will almost certainly lead not only to financial rewards but also to something that, in the long run, will prove even more important—a lifelong addiction to words.

If the approach has seemed somewhat lighthearted, even occasionally casual, that too is part of the plan. For language can be fun and vocabulary building need not be dull. That's why there are so many word quizzes interspersed throughout this book. There's a saying that the greatest scholars are those who "wear their learning lightly," and, while none of us will qualify as among the greatest of scholars, there's not a reason in the world why we can't enjoy ourselves, even as we add to our knowledge of the richness and variety that characterize our language. Samuel Johnson once remarked that "curiosity is one of the permanent and certain characteristics of a vigorous mind." If this book succeeds in stimulating your curiosity about language and the pleasures you will enjoy from knowing it better, it will have succeeded in its aim.

Because we are all somewhat self-centered, the best place to start is with yourself. Stop for a moment of self-assessment. Who are you? What is your station in life? What is your job? What are your hobbies? Who are your favorite associates?

Then ask yourself what bearing each of these facts has on the language you speak, write and read. If you are a high-school pupil, you undoubtedly share several enthusiasms with your classmates—sports, recordings of current hits, favorite disc jockeys, to name only three. So what, you ask? So each of these pursuits, indeed every activity you indulge in, has a vocabulary of its own, and one of the best ways to become truly word-conscious is to make up lists of words used in each of these activities.

Don't burden yourself with too much of the apparatus of the formal dictionaries—abbreviations, principal parts of verbs, and the like. For your purpose a simple list of interesting words and their definitions—a glossary, if you will—is all you need. Then compare your list with those your friends make up and combine them all into one master list of your very own language.

This method of increasing word awareness and thus developing an exciting new interest in language as a whole need not be limited to high-school students, of course. College campuses have long been famous as breeding grounds for colorful, vivid slang expressions, many of them common to all colleges, for instance, *Greek* for a member of a fraternity or sorority, but others unique to particular campuses. Dean Kenneth Wilson of the University of Connecticut tells me, for instance, that the verb *to hawk* has a meaning at Connecticut very different from any listed in the dictionaries. It doesn't mean to peddle one's wares by street cries, nor does it mean to clear your throat —the two senses listed in the orthodox lexicons. No, up at the University of Connecticut a student who is *hawking* is indulging himself in the most traditional occupation of male undergraduates—looking at pretty girls.

The expressions of collegians today, of course, are a far cry from the innocent jests of the years when the junior prom was one of the chief events of the academic social year—ranking with the Homecoming Game and Frat Rush Week. Gone with the *bobby-soxers, smoothies, skinheads* and *hepchicks* are the *greasy grinds, BMOC's* and the *barbs* or *barbarians*, as non-affiliated students used to be called in pre-SDS times.

Today the language of the campus seems to run more to terms like *confrontation, non-negotiable demands, pigs, freaking out,* and *trashing.* And, of course, *underground,* as in "*underground* press," "*underground* revolution," and "*underground* justabouteverything.*" It's a word that has rapidly lost the power it had when, in earlier periods of our history, it referred to the Underground Railroad of the Civil War period or, during World

War II, to the *"underground* Resistance fighters" of France and other German-occupied countries. Today on campus, however, *underground* merely means "anti-Establishment" and even *Establishment* has broadened greatly in meaning until now it means little more than orthodox, traditional or "square."

There are, of course, many other special vocabularies that any one of us may know. It will prove helpful to make lists of these special words and phrases, whether as part of a classroom project or as amusing, pleasant and eventually profitable word-game play with your friends.

For instance, on one occasion a fellow editor remarked to me at lunch, "You would never guess that I was once a *whistle punk,* would you?" I looked over at his quietly twinkling eyes, recalled our many years of association in various literary ventures, and replied: "No, I wouldn't. But then, I don't know what a *whistle punk* is, to begin with."

"Perhaps you can guess when I tell you that, at various other times in my youth I was a *flunky,* an *ink slinger,* a *timber beast* and a *faller*—but never a *flathead* or a *donkey doctor*."

"I do think that *timber beast* gave you away," I replied. "I never realized that you had been a lumberman."

"Just a couple of summer seasons in my youth up in the Pacific Northwest," he answered, "but the lingo of those loggers surely is worth recording. Make some notes and I'll tell you what it all adds up to. *Whistle punk,* my first job, is absolutely the lowliest position in a lumber camp. He's a kid, a punk, who blows a whistle when a tree is felled. In the movies they always have someone yelling 'Timber' or even 'Thar she blows' —but in real life they blew a whistle and the *whistle punk,* despite his low rank, saved a good many lives.

"Now the other jobs I held," he continued. "A *flunky* was a waiter at the camp dining hall. An *ink slinger,* as I'm sure you could guess, was simply a clerk who kept the daily records. The *timber beast* was a logger, *the faller* was the fellow who felled the trees, the *flathead* was a sawyer, and the *donkey doctor* was the mechanic who tended to the various machines around the camp. And just one thing more," he went on, "don't ever say *skid row* to a logger and don't ever call a logger a *lumberman*."

"Well, that last sentence seems to add up to two things more, not one," I replied. "But clarify, please."

"Glad to oblige. The correct expression is *skid road* and the first one of them was in Seattle. It was made of greased logs over which loggers used to skid logs to the mills. In time the street, as often happened in frontier communities, acquired quite a few flophouses, saloons and houses of ill-repute, and it became little better than similar places in New York, Chicago and elsewhere that you call *skid rows*. But the original and only correct name is *skid road*—and don't you forget it."

"Will do," I told him, "although you must bear in mind that, in matters of this kind, usage governs and if more people say one than the other, the preference must be for the term more widely used. But, before you explode, why would you not want to be called a *lumberman?*"

"Because I was a logger, that's why," he snorted. "A lumberman is simply a *sawdust eater* down at the *macaroni mills*—in other words, a sawyer in a sawmill."

And that's a good example of how a special language, particularly one learned in youth, can live with a man all his life. And it's a good example, too, of how colorful expressions from the jargon of an offbeat trade can add sparkle to conversation many years after the words first were learned.

Another one of my offbeat editor friends, this one a very able lexicographer who served as my most trusted assistant on the *American Heritage Dictionary*, was a musician in his younger days and numbered among his closest friends a trombone player in the band that traveled with the Ringling Brothers and Barnum & Bailey Circus. After a visit to the circus my friend wandered into my office one day with this observation: "Bet you can't tell me what an *understander* is." "Certainly," I replied. "An 'understander' is a person who comprehends something, understands it." "Wrong again," said my fellow editor, "At least, not under the big top. There an *understander* is the fellow at the base of the human pyramid, the colossus who stands under and supports all the other men."

Most of us never have a chance to get close to the world of circuses and carnivals, and this is a pity for the language spoken in the world of tan bark and sideshows is a colorful and, to the outsider, impenetrable as any part of our common tongue. The chief reason for its impenetrability, of course, is that the denizens of the world of show business regard themselves as a culture apart from the "square world" of the layman. They want to be able to converse in such a fashion that those on the "inside" will understand perfectly, while the outsiders, you and I, are blissfully unaware of what the message is. And the message is always the same: We are *marks* to be taken by the *operators* and their *shills*.

If you were to spend a summer traveling with one of these shows, here are a few of the terms you would be able to add to your very own lexicon at summer's end.

Mark or **sucker.** A member of the general public.

Grinder. The *barker, spieler* or *come-on-man,* the fellow who gives you the spiel in front of the *pitch,* or concession, to entice you into one of the many games of chance that may or may not be *gaffed,* fixed, although they usually are.

High striker. The device you hit with a heavy mallet, trying to push the marker high enough to impress your girl friend.

Kinkers. Performers in tent shows, usually the freaks, not the strippers or other participants in the girlie shows.

shill. A member of the audience who is paid to help boost the price or stakes in a game of chance. He is supplied with marked bills to pay with if he loses—which he seldom does, since his purpose is to get you to outbid him. If he wins, through some miscalculation, he is paid in marked or bogus bills.

Laying the note. A technique of giving bills a fast shuffle so that the *mark* winds up with much less money than is due him.

Stand-Up Grab Joint. Very nearly the most ethical booth at any carnival. It's simply a counter where you can grab a hamburger and a soft drink as you make the rounds. Just be sure to count your change carefully. After all, this is a carnival and you are a *mark*.

The language of the Big Top overlaps that of the carnival to some extent. The Big Top (and that, by the way, is rapidly becoming an obsolete expression, since few of the large circuses still play under canvas) has its *kinkers,* like the carnival, except that the circus *kinker* is likely to be an acrobat, rather than a freak.

The *high man* or *top mounter* is exactly the opposite of the *understander* we met earlier. He lands on top of the human pyramid.

The circus band musicians are simply *windjammers* and *lot-lice* is the circusman's disrespectful name for the townsfolk who hang around, usually underfoot, while the circus tents are being erected.

In an earlier chapter we mentioned that the generic name for the circus clown is *joey* from the great British clown Joseph Grimaldi. Actually there are three main classes of *joeys,* the *auguste,* the *grotesque* and the *character,* in ascending order of importance. The *auguste* is the average, garden variety clown, who will, as the saying goes, do anything for a laugh, pratfalls, included. His make-up is wildly painted and he wears a variety of ludicrous costumes in the course of the show. The *grotesque* lives up to his name by wearing ridiculous hats and weirdly padded-out costumes and is usually found carrying a preposterously too small or too large parasol. The top rank is held by the *character,* who portrays the eternally frustrated little man. His costume may be that of the hobo, or it may savor a bit of Charlie Chaplin's early soup-and-fish attire. Whatever he attempts fails—even to the most famous *character* bit of all, Emmet Kelly's attempt to sweep a spotlight circle from the sawdust.

A generation ago you might have heard the call "Hey, Rube" to signal that a fight had broken out between circus hands and townies. No more. Now the call is simply "Clem!" and that's circus slang for any kind of fight. Even a couple of disgruntled clowns might wind up in an offstage *clem.*

The main *guy* is not the circus owner; it's the *guy* rope or wire that supports the center pole of the big top. And a *dog-and-pony show* is not that at all. It's simply the condescending term used by circus performers who have made the big time to describe any small, rundown circus.

The *rubber man* is not a part of the sideshow or freak show. He's the fellow who wanders through the aisles selling balloons, which he calls *bladders.* And a *convict* is nothing to be worried about. That's just circus slang for the zebra.

Even the more prosaic occupations, like waiting on table in a restaurant, tending a soda bar or serving an apprenticeship in summer stock can add interesting words to your vocabulary. Let's look at a few that might wind up in your note books from the soda fountain and restaurant scene.

fountain jockey, fountain jerk, soda jerk, soda popper. That's you.

black-and-white. Chocolate soda with vanilla ice cream.

black cow. Chocolate milk shake.

brown cow. Root beer ice cream soda.

white cow. Vanilla milk shake.

side of mama. Side order of marmalade.

eighty-one. A glass of water.

eighty-eight. No more left or, in a barroom, no more service for him.

ninety-five. Watch that customer; he's trying to exit without paying.

ninety-eight. The assistant manager is watching.

ninety-nine. The manager is ditto.

draw one, hold the cow. A cup of coffee without cream.

Adam and Eve on a raft, wreck 'em. Scrambled eggs on toast.

stretch a Grade A. Send out a large glass of milk.

B, L and T, wheat down. Bacon, lettuce and tomato sandwich on wheat toast.

don't forget the shoes. Add shoestring potatoes to the order.

blue bottle or **belch water.** A serving of Bromo-Seltzer.

spla. Whipped cream topping on soda or sundae.

Show business affects the lives of all of us, in one way or another. Thirty years ago in *The American Language*, Henry L. Mencken defined it as "the stage in all its branches," by which he meant the legitimate theater, musical comedy, vaudeville and burlesque. The latter two have virtually ceased to exist by now, but other forms of popular entertainment have moved in to take up the slack. Television, which, in its endless parade of variety shows, is really little more than the electronic equivalent of old-time vaudeville, is now a recognized part of show business. So also are motion pictures, radio and, judging by their inclusion in *Variety*, the "bible of show business," night clubs and phonograph records.

Each of these areas has its own special language. A TV cameraman, for instance, may speak of *BCU's, MCU's* and *pocket shots*. The first is shorthand for *big close-up* showing nothing more than the subject's face. *MCU* is, obviously, *medium close-up*, showing the person plus some scenic background. The *pocket shot* is somewhere between the two, showing the subject from the handkerchief pocket up. That list of credits naming everyone from producer to stagehand that follows many programs is known variously as the *credit crawl* or the *play off*. And the MC who smiles wistfully at the videots in the unseen audience and goes into the routine about "We're going to have to say so long for tonight, but . . ." is delivering what, in TV trade parlance, is known as the *bye-bye*.

Most of us are unlikely to become sufficiently involved in TV to be able to compile very extensive lists of trade terms, but nearly everyone at one time or another becomes involved in the theatrical side of show business and can scarcely avoid learning some of the trade jargon. Even Richard Nixon once confessed, in your author's presence, that he and his wife had been involved in amateur theatricals in their home town of Whittier, California, "and not very successfully, either."

Here is the kind of glossary you might well be able to compile based upon your experiences in school, college or summer-theater activities, whether backstage or on stage.

ad lib. To improvise lines not in the original text of a show, either because you have *gone up in,* forgotten, your lines or to cover for a fellow actor who has forgotten his lines or, worse still, failed to make his entrance on cue.

apron. The front of the stage, especially that area in front of the curtain in the formal proscenium-arch stage.

business. Any movement or action not a part of the spoken dialogue. The director will usually suggest bits of *business* to emphasize certain lines or to delineate character.

cyc (pronounced SIKE). This is short for *cyclorama* and refers to a background hanging cloth which encloses the stage on three sides.

entrance. This originally was merely the door or opening through which an actor entered the stage. But long ago actors learned that the manner in which they came on stage could make an emphatic impression on the audience. So there gradually evolved the various techniques of "making an entrance," a term that has been taken over into non-theatrical life.

flat. This is any piece of standing scenery, usually made of canvas on wooden supports. A number of *flats* will be lashed together to make the traditional *box set,* which is fully enclosed save for the side facing the audience.

floods or **flood lights.** These are the lights, usually mounted in the front of the balcony, that illuminate the entire stage.

fly gallery or **flies.** This is the area above the stage to which the *flats* are flown between acts when a change of scenery is required.

foots. Originally this referred simply to the *footlights,* those lights at floor level that are located at the apron of the stage. Nowadays this area is also used, especially in musical-comedy performances, to conceal microphones needed to amplify the voices of cast members.

ghost. This is obsolescent or perhaps already obsolete theater slang for company treasurer. On payday cast members are wont to say, "The ghost walks today," just as servicemen say, "The eagle flies." The original *ghost,* incidentally, was the ghost of Hamlet's father. In the first act of that play, Horatio asks the ghost if he walks "because Thou hast up-hoarded in thy life extorted treasure from the womb of earth."

grid. The structural framework high above the stage that secures the lines by which flats are flown when the scenery is *struck,* dismantled.

grip. This is a stagehand. The term has also been taken over in television and motion pictures to designate a person who adjusts scenery and props. Occasionally a cameraman's assistant is also called a *grip.*

ham. This is the actor who overacts, usually an oldtimer who has learned thousands of bits of *business* but never knows when to stop using them. The original *hams* were, appropriately enough, players in blackface minstrel shows of the nineteenth century. They got the name from their use of ham fat to remove heavy black make-up.

heavy. The true *heavies* were the villains of oldfashioned melodrama, though the term is now used to refer to any actor who specializes in serious character roles.

house. Quite simply, the audience. "Paper the house" means to fill it by distributing quantities of free or cutrate tickets, called *paper.* To "dress the house" is to make the audience seem larger than it is by spreading the patrons throughout the auditorium, usually separating each pair from the next by one or two empty seats.

legit. The *legitimate theater,* as it is more properly called, is the theater devoted primarily to plays, both serious and comic. Musical comedy, vaudeville and the like are not considered part of the legitimate theater, that "fabulous invalid" whose demise is pronounced almost annually, but that some-how continues to exist.

naked run-through. This phrase has nothing whatever to do with nudity on the stage. It is simply a complete run-through of a show, without scenery, costumes or, if it is a musical, full orchestral accompaniment.

open cold. The play that *opened cold,* that is, opened in New York without a tryout run out-of-town, was once a rarity. In recent years, however, it has become commonplace, with many producers preferring to test the show on preview audi-ences in New York, thereby eliminating extra travel expenses involved in preopening tours. Some shows, notably musicals, have been known to play months of previews and then die within a week or two of their formal opening.

plot. The play itself, of course, has a plot, but when theater workers speak of *plot,* they are usually referring to the *light-ing plot* that guides the electricians, the *prop plot* for the property men or the *scene plot* that guides the stage hands. Each is, of course, the complete plan for a performance.

road. *The road* in theatrical parlance is any place outside of New York City and, as George M. Cohan used to say with the arrogance characteristic of the New York-oriented per-former, "outside New York every place is Bridgeport."

schtick. This show business term comes from the Yiddish variety halls of old—and has made a very successful transition into TV. It's a bit of business which, through careful repetition, becomes a sort of trademark of an actor, particularly a comedian. Jack Benny's violin rendition of "Love in Bloom" is one of his *schticks.* Bob Hope's rapid-fire monologue and identifying theme "Thanks for the Memory" also qualify as *schticks.* Your author has been told that his beard (see back cover) is his *schtick.* So, obviously, *schtick* is a word to be reckoned with, one that is moving beyond show business and into the common tongue.

sides. Nowadays most members of a cast are given the com-plete text of a play so that they can learn their parts in context. Until a few years ago, however, each actor's part was typed on half-sheets of paper together with the last few words of the previous actor's speech as a cue. These half-sheets were then stapled together and collectively formed that actor's *sides.* Directors could quickly gauge whether an actor was a *quick study* or a *slow study* by observing how early in rehearsals he was able to pocket his *sides* and play the role from memory.

spot. This, of course, is a spotlight. Often a considerable number are used, concealed inside the rim of the proscenium arch. There are various sizes of *spots,* depending on the area to be covered and the intensity of light desired. An electrician of my acquaintance used to say "No dame ever objected when I hit her with a bastard amber baby spot." By that he meant that no actress, especially no aging actress, ever complained when he lit her face with a baby spotlight fitted with a gelatin filter, bastard amber in hue.

strike the set. This simply means "dismantle the stage setting or scenery" whether by *skating,* sliding, the flats across stage to a storage space or *flying* them up to the *fly gallery,* which is usually midway between the stage and the *grid.*

tormenters. These are flats or curtains located on either side of the stage, just behind the proscenium, to mask spotlights and edges of the *flats* used in the scenery. Just why they are called tormenters nobody seems to know, since their chief function is to make life easier for both players and audience.

Well, those are some of the jargons, argots, idioms—call them what you will—that you could pick up in the course of activities outside your normal schooling or work. They all derive from more-or-less pleasurable pursuits and may be expected to evoke pleasant memories when reviewed years hence.

There is, however, one other activity to which we all seem to have been committed for decades past and for the Lord only knows how far into the future. That, of course, is war. For the most part, the active participants are our young men, although many dedicated young women also serve as nurses and in the various uniformed services as Wacs, Waves and so on. It is perhaps fitting that I end this chapter of *Your Heritage of Words* with an actual glossary of words and phrases sent to me by a young Sp/4 from Louisville, Kentucky, stationed in Vietnam.

It came about this way. I had written a column for the Los Angeles Times Syndicate about the slang used by our soldiers in Vietnam. My research was, of course, based entirely on reports from the front, as they appeared in the press and on radio and TV. I noted the incongruity of our code name for the Viet Cong, *Victor Charlie,* and suggested that this must certainly be the first time in the history of warfare that one side labeled the other *victor* while the war was still in progress.

As it developed, servicemen quickly shortened this to simply *charlie* and, before long, that became *chuck,* and seeking out the VC became *chuck-hunting.*

The combat infantryman, whether soldier or marine, came to be called a *grunt,* from the grunting sound made when he donned his heavy field pack.

Gook, a derogatory term used in World War II to designate any native of an occupied country, was applied to any Vietnamese or Cambodian, friend or foe. Alternate pejorative racial labels used by the military were *dink, slope* and *slant.*

A new member of any unit was, predictably, a *cherry* and the *boondocks*—an item of Marine corps slang dating back to 1898 and derived from the Philippine Tagalog word *bundok* or mountain—became simply *the boonies. Grunts* didn't mount an ambush, they *beat the boonies* or *blew the bush.* And the chief aim of every serviceman was to avoid being *greased,* killed, so that he could return to the *world,* the United States.

A few weeks after this article appeared in the Louisville Times, Sp/4 Joe Ott, a native of Louisville, wrote me from Long Binh to say that he had already been doing what this chapter encourages you to do—collect and define words and phrases used by your friends and associates.

"My list," he wrote, "contains words most of which belong exclusively to the U.S. soldier in Vietnam. I have collected them so that my family and friends will understand me when I return." Here is his list:

ammo. Ammunition.
arty. Artillery.
baby-san. Vietnamese baby, girl or young lady.
bring smoke. Destroy the enemy.
C&C. Command and control.
cayuse. A small helicopter.
charlie or **chuck.** The enemy.
commo. Communications.
dustoff. Medical evacuation by helicopter.
ghost rider or **red Indian.** In casual conversation, the code name for an officer above the rank of major.
grunt. Infantryman.
gunship. Armed helicopter.

hard hat. Main force Viet Cong soldier.

hooch. Sleeping quarters.

hump. To indulge in strenuous activity, as to "hump ammo."

log bird. Resupply helicopter.

LRP. Long-range patrol.

NDP. Night defense position.

rough puff. South Vietnamese Regional or Popular Forces soldier.

slick. Unarmed or lightly armed helicopter.

SRP. Short-range patrol.

wiblic. Water-borne logistical craft.

zap. To hit with a bullet.

"As some lifers might say," added Specialist Ott, "we set up our *NDP* where the *LRP's* had spotted the VC the day before. On a morning *SRP* we found so many *charlies* that we nearly ran out of *ammo*. But, thanks to the *log bird,* we were really able to *zap* them. We called for *arty* and *gunships,* and *ghost rider* directed reinforcements from his *C&C slick.* We didn't need a single *dustoff.*"

And there, we fear, is a rather saddening but perhaps therapeutic exercise of the kind we recommend. This young man has demonstrated a real flair for and interest in the language. When he comes back to the *world,* he should have little trouble finding a place in the world of letters.

12. A Word to Teachers

As Samuel Johnson said, "dictionaries are like watches—the worst is better than none and the best cannot be expected to go quite true." It's a judgment that applies equally to books about dictionaries—like this one. We have suggested that each reader of this book make up his own glossary or word list, based on the jargon of his or her peer group, because we know that such an exercise can be fun as well as informative.

There is literally no limit to the subjects your students may find worth exploring to collect and define words of interest to them. Every sport has its own special argot. Parke Cummings once did a dictionary more than a hundred pages in length of the words and phrases common to baseball—and many new ones have come into use since he did his pioneer work in 1950. Football, likewise, has a rich and varied jargon, with phrases like *red dog* and *tight end,* unknown just a few years ago, entering the language every year.

Girls will find a rich store of language in the field of fashion, and that subject being what it is, you can be sure that this year's glossary will seem quaintly dated in just a year or two.

But the subject areas are unbounded. The special jargons of card games, stamp-collecting, and the newly popular youth activities of political campaigning and ecological crusading—any or all of these can be fertile subjects for word lists. In the classroom this device, on any grade level, seems to me a very useful technique for stimulating interest in words and their meanings and can lead to a rewarding life-long interest in our language.

At a meeting of the National Council of Teachers of English (Washington, November 1969) this suggestion, together with several other approaches to vocabulary building was set forth in a talk titled *The Dictionary as a Tool in Vocabulary Enrichment Programs.* This was subsequently printed in the official organ of the NCTE, the *English Journal.* What follows is an abridged and edited version of that talk.

Let's address ourselves to the problem—and it's a massive one—of how to interest school and college age young people in words, the written language. We keep hearing from Marshall McLuhan and other self-styled prophets that the written word is doomed, that the "now" generation—dreadful phrase that! —is picture-minded, has been brainwashed by the tube and that, as Red Smith puts it, we have raised a generation of "videots."

Perhaps. But I find it significant that, to make a permanent lasting record of his theories about the death of the printed word, McLuhan had to resort to the medium of print: the book.

So the chief problem is to excite in our pupils curiosity about and interest in this richest of all the world's languages, English. Let us assume that our classroom on the Junior High or High School level has a set of dictionaries, so that all pupils may participate in the exercises I shall suggest. Let's assume further that, in college Freshman English Composition Courses, the students have been instructed to purchase a "college-level" dictionary.

One traditional approach to vocabulary enrichment is through tracing the histories of words as we have shown earlier in this book, notably in the chapter titled Names Make Words. Other material of a somewhat similar nature may be found in the long chapter devoted to the analysis of more than five hundred words to add color to your vocabulary. It is shown, for example, that *supercilious* quite literally comes from the Latin words "super" and "cilium," meaning with lifted eyebrow. Or that *shibboleth* comes from ancient Hebrew originally meaning "ear of corn," and that it acquired its meaning of "watchword" or "password" from its use by the Gileadites to determine whether one of the hostile Ephraimites was trying to infiltrate their lines.

Now this sort of thing is all very well, but the occasions when a young person is likely to use *supercilious* or *shibboleth* are nearly nil. Much better, it seems to me, are exercises involving words closer to the pupils' own range of interest. Instead of *supercilious,* how about *assassin*—which leads us to all sorts of intriguing byways including *thugs,* who were the worshippers of the goddess Kali, celebrated in Mike Todd's *Around the World in Eighty Days,* and who used hashish—close kin to the omnipresent marihuana—to stimulate them to their lethal tasks of waylaying, robbing and murdering innocent passersby, all in honor of their goddess?

Still a better way to involve pupils in the use of dictionaries in enlarging their own vocabularies is to encourage them to create their own dictionaries. Once you embark on such a project you will discover, I think, a degree of excitement among your pupils in dictionaries, language in general and their own language in particular that you would not have thought possible.

Last June in Washington, Dean Kenneth Wilson, chairman of the Department of English at the University of Connecticut and Dean of the Faculty of Arts and Sciences, reported on work he has done of this nature.

Urging a comparative study of existing dictionaries to determine the differences in the way they treat the various elements of the language, Wilson made the point that the dictionary properly used "could be the best reader you could possibly use. It's hard to kill a pupil's native interest in words, though some of us seem to try hard to do exactly that." But, he warned, the teacher must make clear to the pupil that, as Dr. Johnson said, "dictionaries are like watches." So, added Dean Wilson, "The dictionary as bible can do a lot of harm; the dictionary as reader can be very helpful."

In reporting on an experiment he conducted of having each member of his class work at defining a collection of some thirty items of campus slang, Wilson reported that one unexpected dividend was that the teacher learned a lot he didn't know about the environment in which he himself lives. In a similar experiment in the public High School of the relatively rural town of Storrs, Connecticut, where the University is located, the pupils put together a lexicon of the terminology of drugs and addiction, and the adults learned a lot from this exercise.

As proof that this is not an isolated instance and as an indication that this appeal works on the high-school as well as the college level, I'd like to report an experience Mrs. Morris and I had some years ago. One of our then teen-age daughters was saying goodnight to a boyfriend at the front door and her mother's ever-vigilant ears heard this holiday farewell: "A cool Yule and a frantic First." This amused us so that we reported it in our newspaper column and suggested that teen-agers around the country send in lists of words and phrases, with definitions, that were popular in their social groups.

The response was astounding. Hundreds of letters poured in from Milwaukee, from Washington, from Pittsburgh, from San Bernardino—from everywhere. Young people were so pleased that someone was taking their private language seriously that they pitched in with great enthusiasm—and an astonishing degree of literacy. For most of them it was their first effort at writing definitions, a challenging task, I can assure you. But from the thousands of letters we received we distilled an eight-page leaflet, written entirely in the words of the youngsters themselves, which was called—and the title tells you how out-of-date it now is—the "Real Gone Lexicon." Something over a hundred thousand copies were distributed during the next few years until we let it die a merciful death, since so many of the expressions were passé. But the fascinating aspect of the reader response was that it was divided fifty-fifty between the youngsters and the "establishment"—as it's now fashionable to call them—parents, ministers, nuns, youth leaders and the like.

Today, of course, many of the young people who contributed to the "Real Gone Lexicon" are themselves active in PTA groups and some of them may well be teaching English in high schools and colleges. If so, I hope they will remember the fun they had contributing to that collection and use the same technique to stimulate the interest of their pupils in dictionaries.

For the most important task of the teacher, it seems to me, is to bring to the pupil some realization of the riches that lie inside every dictionary. It's true that many—one might even say "most"—dictionaries tend to baffle the ordinary reader by using so many symbols and so much quirky shorthand that you need almost to be a dictionary editor yourself to puzzle your way through an involved entry. The exercise of making a class dictionary is an excellent device for teaching pupils the anatomy of the dictionary and the meaning of various of these signs and symbols.

There are, of course, many other tested techniques for developing pupil interest in words. Flash cards, for one. These can and should be made by the pupils themselves because this again will help to keep the word choice relevant to their day-to-day interests. On one side of a three-by-five card is written the word. On the reverse is given a simple definition of the word, its part of speech, and an example of its use in a sentence. The material in Chapter 8 is admirably suited to this use. If the teacher and pupils can collaborate on preparing the master word list, then an assignment of perhaps five words per pupil will result in meaningful dictionary research and the acquisition of at least five words per day per pupil for as long as the exercise continues. There are various ways in which these cards, once completed, may be used—and a lot depends on the composition of the class. If the pupils can be relied upon to play the game fairly quietly, the class can be divided into groups of five, whereupon they challenge each other to define each word after seeing only the side of the card with the word alone. In many, perhaps most, classroom situations, however, pandemonium would soon reign, if this plan were followed, so it might be best for the teacher to keep matters under control by gathering up all the cards, then acting as supervisor or master of ceremonies, while pupils other than the one who wrote the initial definition try to define the word and give an example of its use.

All of these devices, of course, are designed for the single purpose of making the dictionary an interesting and attractive book for young people to turn to for excitement and interest —not a drab gray tome which they will use, as they use the telephone book, only when absolutely necessary to find the spelling of a word, its pronunciation and some hint of its meaning. Any dictionary editor knows that there are vast and exciting riches of the language to be found in any competently edited dictionary. But perhaps I may be pardoned for feeling that many of my colleagues in the lexicographical vineyards have shown a seeming reluctance to expose these riches to the layman's eyes.

I hope, fellow teacher, that these suggestions may make your task a bit easier and will add to your enjoyment of *Your Heritage of Words*.

Answers to Quizzes

Quiz on Foreign Words and Phrases: 1c; 2b; 3b; 4a; 5b; **6b;** 7b; 8b; 9a; 10c.

Quiz on Terms from the Worlds of Business and Industry: 1b; 2b; 3a; 4c; 5b; 6b; 7c; 8c; 9b; 10b.

Quiz on Terms from the Worlds of Art, Literature and Music: 1b; 2c; 3b; 4c; 5a; 6a; 7a; 8b; 9b; 10b.

Quiz on Terms from the Language of World Affairs: 1c; 2b; 3b; 4c; 5b; 6b; 7c; 8a; 9c; 10b.

The A-to-Z Word Game: 1a; 2b; 3b; 4b; 5c; 6a; 7b; 8b; 9b; 10b; 11b; 12c; 13c; 14b; 15c; 16c; 17a; 18a; 19a; 20a; 21b; 22b; 23c; 24c; 25c; 26c; 27a; 28b; 29c; 30c; 31b; 32b; 33a; 34a; 35c; 36a; 37a; 38b; 39b; 40b; 41a; 42b; 43b; 44a; 45b; 46c; 47b; 48b; 49c; 50b.

The William Morris Self-Scoring Vocabulary Test: Section I: 1t; 2o; 3w; 4q; 5m; 6y; 7a; 8p; 9s; 10f; 11u; 12h; 13c; 14l; 15k; 16i; 17x; 18j; 19g; 20n; 21d; 22r; 23b; 24e; 25v. Section II: 1v; 2x; 3f; 4t; 5e; 6m; 7p; 8c; 9r; 10n; 11u; 12y; 13h; 14q; 15b; 16k; 17j; 18a; 19i; 20w; 21g; 22s; 23o; 24l; 25d. Section III: 1d; 2c; 3b; 4d; 5a; 6b; 7b; 8c; 9d; 10a; 11c; 12d; 13d; 14d; 15d; 16a; 17c; 18b; 19d; 20c; 21b; 22b; 23a; 24b; 25b; 26a; 27b; 28d; 29a; 30d; 31b; 32a; 33d; 34c; 35c; 36d; 37b; 38a; 39d; 40b; 41b; 42d; 43c; 44a; 45d; 46c; 47a; 48b; 49d; 50a.